ENGLISH RADICALS
AND REFORMERS
1760–1848

ENGLISH RADICALS AND REFORMERS 1760-1848

Edward Royle
and
James Walvin

THE UNIVERSITY PRESS OF KENTUCKY

Library of Congress Cataloging in Publication Data

Royle, Edward.
  English Radicals and Reformers, 1760–1848.

  Bibliography: p.
  Includes index.
  1. Social reformer—Great Britain. 2. Radicalism—
Great Britain. 3. England—Social conditions—
18th century. 4. England—Social conditions—
19th century. I. Walvin, James. II.
HN388.R69 1982   303.4'84   82–40179
ISBN 0–8131–1471–3   AACR2

Scholarly publisher for the Commonwealth,
serving Berea College, Centre College of Kentucky,
Eastern Kentucky University, The Filson Club,
Georgetown College, Kentucky Historical Society,
Kentucky State University, Morehead State University,
Murray State University, Northern Kentucky University,
Transylvania University, University of Kentucky,
University of Louisville, and Western Kentucky University.

Editorial and Sales Offices: Lexington, Kentucky 40506

CONTENTS

ABBREVIATIONS

ACLL	Anti-Corn Law League
Add. MSS	Department of Additional Manuscripts, British Library
APLP	Association for the Preservation of Liberty and Property against Republicans and Levellers
BAPCK	British Association for the Promotion of Co-operative Knowledge
BPU	Birmingham Political Union
CSU	Complete Suffrage Union
GNCTU	Grand National Consolidated Trades' Union
HO	Home Office Papers
LCS	London Corresponding Society
LDA	London Democratic Association
LWMA	London Working Men's Association
NCA	National Charter Association
NMW	*New Moral World*
NPFRA	National Parliamentary and Financial Reform Association
NUWC	National Union of the Working Classes
PC	Privy Council Papers
PMG	*Poor Man's Guardian*
PRO	Public Record Office
SCI	Society for Constitutional Information
T	Treasury Papers
TS	Treasury Solicitors' Papers
WPR	*Weekly Political Register*

ACKNOWLEDGEMENTS

We are grateful to the following individuals and institutions for their co-operation and for permission to use source materials in their care: Bristol Central Library (Diary of William Dyers), British Library (Dept of Additional Manuscripts; Place Collection), Chetham's Library, Manchester (Minute Book of the Association for Preserving Constitutional Order), William L Clement's Library, University of Michigan (Pitt Papers), Lt Col Lloyd-Baker (Sharp Manuscripts), Manchester Central Library (papers and tracts of the 1790s), National Secular Society (Bradlaugh Papers), Public Record Office (Home Office, Privy Council, Treasury and Treasury Solicitors' Papers), W M Roach (thesis), and York City Archives. Transcripts of Crown copyright records appear by permission of the Controller of H M Stationery Office.

INTRODUCTION

The word 'radicalism' has so many meanings that as a concept in historical analysis it is practically useless. Taken in its literal sense of going back to the roots it has strongly conservative implications — the desire to purify the present and return to a more virtuous Golden Age of the past. Alternatively it can imply returning to first principles, which might lead to a complete rejection of the past. Thus both Burke and Paine were 'radicals' of a kind, and both supported the Americans in their struggle against the government of George III. Written as 'Radical' the word gains additional meanings in the nineteenth century: a school of thought evolving from the ideas of Jeremy Bentham, the Philosophic Radicals; and a self-identified group in Parliament which, although including Benthamites, was by no means exclusive to them.

Not all radicals wanted the same things. Radicalism was more a state of mind or loose collection of ideas than a plan of action. Indeed some groups of radicals were diametrically opposed to others. The readers of the *Poor Man's Guardian* in the 1830s were very suspicious of the Philosophic Radicals. Chartists and Anti-Corn Law Leaguers, Englishmen and Irishmen were sometimes at each other's throats.

The notion of 'popular' radicalism is no clearer, for one is uncertain whether this is meant to suggest that a form of radicalism appealed to large numbers of people, or that it was advanced on behalf of large numbers of people. Who these 'people' were is also vague. Were they 'the People', whom the Whig reformers wished to enfranchise in 1832, or the masses about whom they had grave doubts?

Reform is an equally difficult concept, for it implies subjective value-judgements about which changes are reforms. Not all reformers were radicals by any means. The moral reformers of the Society for the Reformation of Manners and the Society for the Suppression of Vice, and many of those who campaigned against slavery, were opposed to radicalism in practically all its manifestations. Even such a movement for reform as Chartism has been interpreted as lacking some of the essential characteristics of what some radicals regarded as the true form of radicalism.

To impose coherence on this evidently vague topic is misleading. There is no clear picture of tributaries feeding into a main stream which can then be followed to the estuary and the sea. Rather, there is a delta, with many streams and outlets and no single or clearly defined ending. The historian, like the pilot, has to select what seems to him the best way through. His route may be different from that chosen by other navigators, but whichever way he chooses he will then begin to attribute artificial significance to his preferred route. One object of this book is to try to indicate the variety of streams of radicalism which in their several and sometimes conflicting ways contributed to the reform movement in Britain between 1760 and 1848. The way we have chosen is not original and owes something to what contemporaries understood radicalism to be. We have taken it as that set of ideas and associated organisations which sought to institute a reform of the political system in a democratic direction. At the centre of our attention are those men and women who worked for this from outside the political nation and who claimed to speak on behalf of and appeal to the bulk of their fellow countrymen. We do not offer a study of personalities, but certain familiar figures are regarded as important — Wilkes, Tooke, Cartwright, Paine, Hardy, Place, Cobbett, Hunt, Carlile, Owen, Hetherington and Lovett. To these we have added others who do not fit easily, even amongst this heterogeneous group — Wilberforce being the most outstanding.

Anyone writing since 1963 about radicalism in the late eighteenth and early nineteenth centuries has had to take account of Edward Thompson's important book, *The Making of the English Working Class*.[1] Whatever their conclusions, historians have been influenced by this work in the questions that they ask, the sorts of evidence that they use, and the range of interpretations which they have to consider. This book would not have been possible without the research conducted by Thompson and those inspired by him, though since our starting point is radicalism, not class, our perspective is somewhat different. To the work of others we have added our own specialist knowledge, without claiming the same level of expertise over the whole period.

The limitations of a short, general book on a large, complex topic are obvious. The need to compress has led to many omissions, including topics doubtless held dear by our critics. The illustrative evidence is drawn heavily from certain parts of the country – notably London, Lancashire and Yorkshire. This is justified by the weight of evidence as seen both by contemporaries and subsequent historians, but it has led to the neglect of other important parts, such as the West Country, where Bath has recently found a worthy social historian in Professor Neale.[2] Like most English historians, we have also said less than we should of Wales and Scotland.

Interpreting the detailed regional evidence gathered and presented by other historians is especially difficult. Over the central issue of the relationship between industrial protest and political radicalism there is no consensus. Without re-working all the sources it would be difficult to tell how far differing interpretations reflect the views of different historians and how far the peculiar characteristics of different localities. On the matter of Luddism in the textile districts we are in general not persuaded by Malcolm Thomis' non–political view.[3] On the other hand we have been inclined to accept Norman McCord's view that in the North East politics were not usually high among working–class priorities, without seeking to generalise from Tyneside man about the attitudes of workers in Lancashire and Yorkshire.[4] In the end, though, the historian of the 'common people' is lost for lack of evidence. That which has survived may, by its very nature, be atypical, though we cannot even be sure of that. The mood of empathy and the language of possibility become the legitimate tools of understanding, and we trust we have not abused them. Even so, we offer this book bearing in mind the cautionary words of Edmund Burke and D H Lawrence.

> Because half a dozen grasshoppers under a fern make the field ring with their importunate chink, whilst thousands of great cattle, reposed beneath the shadow of the British oak, chew the cud and are silent, pray do not imagine that those who make the noise are the only inhabitants of the field; that, of course, they are many in number; or that, after all, they are other than the little, shrivelled, meagre, hopping, though loud and troublesome, insects of the hour.
>
> (E Burke, *Reflections on the Revolution in France*, 1790)

Mrs Morel: 'Very well, then why talk about the common people?'

Paul Morel: 'Because – the difference between people isn't in their class, but in themselves. Only from the middle classes one gets ideas, and from the common people — life itself, warmth. You feel their hates and loves.'

Mrs Morel: 'It's all very well, my boy. But, then, why don't you go and talk to your father's pals?'

Paul Morel: 'But they're rather different.'

Mrs Morel: 'Not at all. They're the common people. After all, who do you mix with now — among the common people? Those that exchange ideas, like the middle classes. The rest don't interest you.'

(D H Lawrence, *Sons and Lovers,* 1913)

Chapter 1

WILKES, AMERICA AND AFTER

The 1760s have long been recognised as an important decade in the development of reform politics in Britain, but this is not to say that the movements which agitated the first few years of the reign of George III did not have roots reaching back into the earlier eighteenth century and even beyond. In an important article which has inspired much recent thinking on the subject, J H Plumb has criticised those who, following the analytical approach to parliamentary connection developed by Lewis Namier, have missed the significance of continuity in political issues beyond the narrow confines of Westminster.[1] On the one hand the world of parliamentary politics, dominated by Walpole and the Pelhams throughout most of the first two Hanoverian reigns (1714–60), was visibly shrinking; but on the other a new political nation was developing which came of age with the issues of Wilkes and America.

Since the disturbed years of violent political controversy under the later Stuart monarchs, 'the rage of party' had been tamed by an obligarchy strengthened by economic and social developments and acts of political will. The contact between the electorate and the House of Commons was reduced to a minimum. In cases of disputed borough franchises, the narrower definitions were imposed to restrict the size of the electorate. The Septennial Act (1716) extended from three to seven years the maximum duration of Parliament, and most parliaments thereafter in the eighteenth century went their full term. Such generous security of tenure made a seat in the Commons a worthwhile investment, the cost of elections rose, and contests became less frequent. Between 1715 and 1754 the population increased by 18 per cent, but the overall electorate by only 8 per cent and this growth took place mainly in the counties, which controlled less than a third of all seats. Even so there were proposals to raise the qualification for the county vote above the medieval 40 shilling freehold. As a consequence of growing wealth and population in the counties, the electorates of such places as Middlesex and Yorkshire became increasingly influential in the expression of what from the

1760s was to be known as 'public opinion'. The electorate of Yorkshire increased from 15,000 in 1715 to 23,000 in 1807. Even so,
between 1754 and 1790, twelve counties experienced no contested
elections at all, and a further fifteen experienced only one.[2]

This was the political world which the reformers wished to
change, but there was hardly agreement among them as to what they
wished to change and why. Most, from both conservative and
radical viewpoints, desired to strengthen the legislative part of the
constitution (especially the House of Commons) against the executive (the king and his ministers). Radicals who argued thus on both
sides of the Atlantic regarded themselves as 'True Whigs' in the
Commonwealthman tradition, imbued with the writings of Locke,
Harrington and Machiavelli and ideas expressed after 1688 by such
men as Robert Molesworth, Walter Moyle, John Toland and James
Tyrrell. These men gloried in the Ancient Constitution, lately undermined by Stuart absolutism and standing armies, and to be
safeguarded by a restoration of the balanced constitution as the
guardian of liberty. Such views were readily applicable in the reign
of George III by Whig politicians and apologists anxious to explain
the king's actions against them, and were enshrined in an historical
tradition by Catherine Macaulay (sister of the Wilkesite Lord Mayor
of London, John Sawbridge) whose *History of England* was published
in seven volumes between 1763 and 1783. Part of this radical critique
was appropriated in the 1720s for country gentlemen of a more
conservative frame of mind by Henry Bolingbroke who used it in
the *Craftsman* newspaper to attack the Whig oligarchy constructed
by Robert Walpole to the exclusion both of Bolingbroke Tories and
True Whigs. In this independent 'Country' view of political reform,
elections should be held more frequently (even annually), the
number of country gentlemen in the Commons should be increased
with perhaps corrupt borough seats transferred to the virtuous
counties, taxation should be kept down, the standing army should
be replaced by a volunteer militia, and Place and Pension Bills should
be carried to limit those means by which the King's ministers were
able to subvert the balance of the constitution by purchasing support
in the Commons.[3]

These ideas, held in common by Whig republicans and country
gentlemen, appealed also to the American colonists as they con-
fronted a similar experience of ministerial despotism and furnished
them with a practical ideology of reform and eventually revolution.

Throughout the seventeenth and eighteenth centuries the colonies attracted large numbers of political and religious refugees, many of whom took with them to America the radical experiences and intellectual traditions of their homelands. Many were indeed seeking in the New World the very liberties and freedoms which they were denied in the Old World. The structure and spirit of American political life, enhanced by the remarkable degree of popular literacy which developed in the northern colonies, drew on two major traditions: the intellectual origins of American radicalism are to be found generally in classical political theory, but more immediately in that rich outpouring of English radical writing which had flowed from the mid-seventeenth century. Few thinkers were more influential than Thomas Hobbes and John Locke, together with writers in the Commonwealthman tradition, as the Americans turned their attention to the government and ordering of colonial political life. In this respect colonial political issues were part of a much wider debate on both sides of the Atlantic.[4]

These same republican ideas also had some currency on mainland Europe, where John Toland in particular forged an intellectual link between the ideas of seventeenth-century English Commonwealthmen and some of the more radical thinking of the Continental Enlightenment. Much of that revolutionary French philosophy which afflicted Britain in the later eighteenth century was itself of British origin.[5]

A further connection between the earlier and later traditions of English radicalism is embodied in the history of religious Dissent. The heirs to the major Commonwealth sects, excluded from political life after 1661, had little political or religious significance for much of the following century, but from the 1760s their leading intellectuals again contributed to the ferment of radical ideas. Herbert Butterfield has sensitively described these Dissenters as

A crop of controversialists and publicists who represented the world of the disinherited — the men who had never entered into the great tradition or possessed a share in it — [who] formed a kind of undergrowth, an underworld, vividly alive and too often overlooked by students of the more formal literature or the more academic thought of the period. These men represented common sense and took short cuts to truth, assisted by influences that either came from the French *philosophes* or are traceable to the same origin. And the significance of the breach that they made in English thought and tradition in the eighteenth century was clearest of all when these people turned to questions of politics.[6]

Teachers in and products of Dissenting Academies, they personified the rejection of the tradition of landed oligarchy in the Augustan age. From among their number came Richard Price, James Burgh and Joseph Priestley, whose writings were to reshape the radical debate in England and America in the 1770s and 1780s. The old cry of 'Civil and Religious Liberty' was to come to mean far more than merely the repeal of the Test and Corporation Acts.

Practical opposition to governments was not new in the 1760s. London in particular had long symbolised and led the attack on oligarchy, from 1725 when Walpole had proposed to remodel and restrict the City Constitution, through the Excise Crisis of 1733 when ferocious opposition forced Walpole to abandon an unpopular policy, through to the Patriot opposition to his foreign policy in 1739 to 1742 which eventually brought the great man's downfall. What was new from the 1750's, however, was the transmutation of London opinion as an adjunct of parliamentary opposition into an expression of opinion which was in itself an independent opposition beyond the walls of parliament. Architect of this new development was William Beckford, a wealthy Jamaican slave–owner who made the City of London the basis of his political power from 1754 until his death in 1770. As MP for the City during these years, and Lord Mayor in 1762–3 and 1769–70, he not only led London opposition to the Peace of Paris which concluded the successful Seven Years' War but also united in his views the various critiques of the political system. As early as 1761 he was criticising rotten boroughs and supporting traditional 'country' ideas on Place and Pension Bills, but in 1770 he declared himself more radically for 'a more equal representation of the people'. With James Townsend (Lord Mayor, 1772-3) and John Sawbridge (Lord Mayor, 1775-6) he built up in the City a powerful force for political change, willing to work both with oppositionist politicians such as the Rockinghamites and Chathamites, and also with that disreputable champion of popular feeling, John Wilkes.[7]

The methods used by the Beckford group were not new but were exploited by them to a new degree. Important social developments in the eighteenth century were facilitating the growth of public opinion, and to this they appealed. The expansion and quickening of communications — turnpike roads, the postal service, newspapers — was fostering a new interest in politics beyond the narrow oligarchy at Westminster. Coffee houses and discussion clubs were multiplying in London and in increasingly affluent provincial towns. There were 550 coffee houses in London alone by 1740. The *Norwich Gazette* was reporting London opposition to Walpole's policy in 1741; Birmingham acquired its first local paper, *Aris' Birmingham Gazette*, the same year; and by 1760 there were some forty provincial newspapers in existence. John Freeth's *Leicester Arms* in Birmingham claimed in 1772 to have files of all the London papers for the previous thirty-seven years, and was receiving personal reports of parliamentary proceedings. The source of these reports was probably John Almon, a friend of Beckford and of Wilkes, who ran the *London Evening Post*. But it was Wilkes himself who displayed the greatest ability in exploiting this burgeoning press, expanding public opinion, and mounting opposition to the conduct and influence of the king's government in the 1760s. [8]

John Wilkes, MP for Aylesbury since 1757, was associated in the last Parliament of George II's reign with the Temple group in the Commons, and was thus a supporter of William Pitt. He does not himself appear to have been overburdened with moral or political scruples, yet he had the ability to seize upon and develop other men's principles in the service of his own needs and ambitions. Other men were in their turn prepared to exploit the extraordinary talents of Wilkes. In 1762, when almost bankrupt, he launched himself against the young George III's favourite, the Earl of Bute, whose paper, *The Briton*, put forward policies anathema to Pitt and Temple. In October 1761 these latter had demanded war with Spain but, lacking support from other ministers, had resigned and moved into opposition. Though war came nevertheless, Bute was anxious to secure a peace with all countries, and it was this policy which both Wilkes and the City of London denounced. In an anti-Bute paper of his own called the *North Briton* Wilkes exploited every opportunity to embarrass the king's intrusive Scottish minister. In March 1763 he whipped up opposition to the Cider Tax in a manner reminiscent of that employed by Bolingbroke in the Excise Crisis of 1733. Then came the Peace of Paris, signed on 22 March and lauded in the king's speech proroguing Parliament on 19 April.

Incensed, Wilkes denounced the peace and the speech in *North*

Briton no 45 (23 April 1763). Within three days the government, now led by George Grenville, issued a general warrant for the arrest of the 'authors, printers and publishers' of no 45. In all forty-eight people, including Wilkes, were arrested on this one warrant. Wilkes immediately challenged the legality of this device, portraying it as an instrument of arbitrary government. This was something of an exaggeration, but Wilkes was fortunate enough to appear before Chief Justice Pratt, a political ally of Temple, who released Wilkes and then ruled the illegality of general warrants. Though the government was supported in the Commons, the margin was only fourteen votes, and when the public hangman tried to burn the offending issue of the *North Briton* the London mob expressed its feelings by burning a jackboot and a petticoat, symbolising Bute and the Dowager Princess of Wales respectively. But Wilkes' victory was short-lived. Whilst searching his premises under the general warrant, the government's agents discovered a privately printed copy of an obscene parody on Pope's *Essay on Man* — the *Essay on Woman*. Hopelessly wrong-footed and faced with a trial before a political opponent, Lord Mansfield, Wilkes felt that discretion was the better part of valour. He departed for France, was expelled from the Commons, and outlawed.

This was not the end of Wilkes. With debts pressing hard on him in Paris, he returned to London in 1768 to seek election to the Commons and with it the protection of parliamentary privilege. The electors of London put him bottom of the poll, but in Middlesex, a largely urbanised county with many London and Westminster forty shilling freeholders having the county vote, he came head of the poll at the end of March 1768. When the new parliamentary session began in May, however, the Commons excluded him as an outlaw, and though the disqualification was quashed on a technicality he was still fined a thousand pounds and imprisoned for twenty-two months on the obscene libel charge. Whilst in prison he exploited the Middlesex election to keep his name before the public. In three successive by-elections he was returned to Parliament by the Middlesex electorate; on the third occasion in April 1769 the House of Commons declared his opponent duly elected instead. Wilkes could once more, as in 1763, pose as the victim of ministerial despotism (though his exclusion was an act of the whole Commons) and as a champion of the rights of the electorate. Barred from the House, Wilkes meanwhile built himself an alternative political career in the

City, becoming an Alderman in 1770. As a magistrate he used his power to give protection to the printers of press reports of parliamentary proceedings, hitherto regarded as a private matter. Wilkes once more had found an important issue of principle, for a knowledge of what was said in Parliament was essential to the development of a well-informed and co-ordinated opposition based on public opinion.[9]

Whether Wilkes can be regarded as a serious champion of liberty is open to doubt. His actions bear much of the stamp of the opportunist and political cynic. Yet on occasions he knew what to say to gladden the hearts of reformers, and he appreciated that a man who could never hope to win the favour of the king could always make a virtue of the necessity of opposition. At his trial for the *North Briton* libel in 1763 he declared with an eye on the public gallery:

> The liberty of all peers and gentlemen — and (what touches me most sensibly) that of all the middling and inferior set of people who stand most in need of protection — is, in my case, this day to be finally decided upon.[10]

After his successful return to Parliament in 1774, he devoted his first and last speech on parliamentary reform to a radical statement of the view developed by Beckford and expounded by James Burgh in his *Political Disquisitions* (1774–5), calling for manhood suffrage. This undoubtedly endeared him to many who found the man personally distasteful.

Wilkes drew his support from many different types of people, not only artisans, small shopkeepers and 'the mob', but also new men in business, banking and commerce, scattered across the country as well as in London, alarmed that the sound conduct of the nation's affairs was being endangered by political faction. The fragile system of public credit demanded a government responsive to the needs of new interest groups in England and America alike. Wilkes, the outsider who so potently challenged old entrenched interests and factional Court politics, appeared to speak to their needs.[11] In 1768 reformers distributed his publications, argued his case throughout the country and helped create a national support upon which his subsequent activities were to be built. Repeatedly elected to Parliament, wildly supported by mob activity, by friends across the nation and in the American colonies, he came to personify the wider struggle for liberty: the catchphrase 'Wilkes and Liberty' was echoed in all kinds of (often bizarre) political situations and the number '45' acquired a talismanic quality. And though Wilkes himself did not look beyond the bounds of Middlesex, there evolved around his person a comprehensive demand in the country and in the City for real political change. Among men of substance who lacked corresponding political power Wilkes found ready support, with John Horne (later Horne Tooke), John Sawbridge, James Townsend and their friends founding in February 1769 the Society of the Supporters of the Bill of Rights. Though formed with the immediate purpose of settling Wilkes' debts, the Society was also a genuinely radical body devoted to ideas of political change beyond the personal concerns of John Wilkes himself.[12]

By the end of the 1760s this genius at propaganda had become the cause and occasion for a new political phenomenon: a movement which offered a critique of an apparently unrepresentative government and an arbitrary political system, and which demanded a defence of the right of the people to choose their own political spokesmen. The Wilkes movement asserted the belief that political power should emanate from below and not percolate down from above. And the political significance of Wilkes was swiftly appreciated by the American colonists who, at the same time, were beginning to feel themselves victims of what they considered to be the same arbitrary hand of British government. Whatever one thinks about Wilkes' subsequent political career (he appears from 1776 onwards to have espoused an increasingly conservative view), his contribution to radicalism was formidable. He helped to bring king, ministry and the structure of government into disrepute; he was the figurehead for a truly national movement of political dissent (with strong support from America) and he helped to secure the right to publish (and hence scrutinise) parliamentary affairs. These were all major achievements, whatever reservations remain about his own lack of radical views. Indeed it seems hard to deny that this unprincipled maverick was, for all that, the start of a new phase in the history of radicalism in Britain. The importance of the Wilkes years was, in the words of John Brewer, that there was 'planted the seeds of a political sensibility that was to flower in the 1780s and the 1790s'.[13]

What alarmed the government throughout the Wilkes episode was the array of social forces surging around the banners which proclaimed 'Wilkes and Liberty'. While the new men of economic substance remain the best known and most articulate, there were also ranks of poorer types — the 'middling and inferior sorts' throughout the country, London apprentices, artisans and even the wilder fringes of the London mob supporting Wilkes in their own raucous fashion. These middle-class and plebeian groups were encouraged in their support by financial and industrial hardships in the post-war years (with high food prices, slumps in employment and food shortages). But it was the political unity of these diverse groups which gave such cause for governmental alarm. Pitched in unrelenting opposition to Wilkes was the king himself, with the loyal support of various senior ministers. Though support for Wilkes in the Lords and Commons fluctuated from issue to issue, and while many, including Burke, supported his causes but refused to help the man, there was a consistency of support in the mercantile community, more especially among the freemen of London and Middlesex. And there were always 'the lower orders of people' variously described as the 'dirty people' and a 'most blackguard set of shabby fellows' on hand for the more turbulent public displays of support for their hero. Such a broad band of support in a society which was changing, notably under the pressure of population growth, was an alarming phenomenon for men of authority and was to be repeated, though on a different scale, in the early years of the 1790s. Yet this demographic and economic context will only partly explain the sharpness of Wilkesite support, for many of the complaints were, like those of the Americans, against *specific* acts of the new king's government. In the words of George Rudé — it was small wonder that 'among those people alarmed at the whole trend of events since the accession of George III, there should be many to whom Wilkes, who had been persecuted more relentlessly than any other by the new administration and returned blow for blow and insolence for insolence, might appear as an object of sympathy, respect, or even of veneration'.[14]

Perhaps the most lasting and effective political lesson of the Wilkes saga was the use of the petition to Parliament to express specific grievances (in this case, protests against parliament's rejection of Wilkes as MP). To organise support, express opposition, and draft a petition Wilkesites were forced to create a political machinery, the structure of which was to be reflected in radical politics through to the end of Chartism. Best organised by the Supporters of the Bill of

Rights, this creation of a machinery of extra-parliamentary opinion was a new factor in British politics (one moreover which some regarded as unconstitutional). Local political groups, directing their opinion to Parliament through petitions presented by sympathetic MPs, was a Wilkesite device bequeathed to a wide range of subsequent reforming movements.[15]

Although it is easy to see that the tactics of the Wilkes movement were to prove important in later radical history, it is much more difficult to place Wilkes in the wider history of English radicalism. This is, in part, because it is very difficult to define the political principles of the Wilkes movement, apart of course from its resistance to royally-inspired government interference. In a sense, it was a negative movement more certain about the issues it opposed than those it supported. Wilkesites frequently mouthed general support for the constitution and the ancient liberties of the English freeman, but these were principles with which no active politician, from the king downwards, could openly disagree. Moreover it is striking that their belief in the ultimate perfection of the British constitution was shared by the colonists in America. Even the Stamp Act Congress was satisfied to live under 'the most perfect form of government'. Another man declared in 1775 that 'The constitution of England is without doubt the most perfect form of government that ever was devised by human wisdom'. Even the American revolutionary, John Adams, thought it a 'Stupendous fabric of human invention'.[16] Throughout the four decades between the Peace of Paris and the end of the century Englishmen and Americans seemed to be dazzled by the glories of the constitution. But as the century advanced and the imperfections in political life and, more notably, representation became ever more noticeable, a more critical voice came to be heard, (particularly among those outside the political pale). So serious did political turmoil become, especially in the years of the American and then the Revolutionary wars, that growing numbers of men asked the question: what was wrong with this much-vaunted political system which allowed such débâcles to arise?

Among the most assertive of Wilkes' supporters had been the Americans. And just as Wilkes spoke for those Englishmen who felt oppressed by a confused yet intolerable government, so too did many Americans feel the encroachments of British government after 1763. The British insensitivity towards American fears was compounded by colonial suspicions which were, in their turn, inflated by news of the conflicts between Wilkes and the government. Yet it could be argued that the British government was not utterly unreasonable in expecting the colonists to pay more towards the onerous task of financing their expensive frontier society. The war had after all left the British with a crippling national debt of £140 million, making it imperative that a more equitable way be found of financing the colonies.[17] The British government therefore looked towards the less heavily taxed Americans for a fairer contribution. Their first step to this end was the Sugar Act of 1764, a form of taxation which was effectively implemented and deeply resented throughout the colonies. A year later there followed the Stamp Act which, unlike the Sugar Act, was a marked innovation and a clear tax upon the colonists from Whitehall. Constitutionally sound and fiscally moderate, the Stamp Act was violently opposed in the colonies and proved politically disastrous. Along the Atlantic seaboard the cry went up 'No taxation without representation', (though this could as easily have come from the inhabitants of Manchester). At a stroke the government had raised the thorny issue of the nature of representation itself. The ensuing arguments about virtual representation offered by supporters of the government unwittingly played into their opponents' hands and ultimately expanded the argument. As James Otis said:

> To what purpose is it to ring everlasting changes to colonists on the case of Manchester, Birmingham and Sheffield, who return no members? If these now considerable places are not represented they ought to be.[18]

All this took place at a time when Wilkes had already focused sympathetic attention on the apparently autocratic activities of the government. Although in both cases the British government backed down — revising the Stamp Act and ultimately admitting Wilkes to the Commons — irreparable damage had been done. Both in London and in the colonies there were substantial groups of men, prosperous, articulate and politically alert, and able to call up even wider groups of non-propertied political support, who looked upon the British government with the deepest suspicion. Not surprisingly, American critics warmed to Wilkes for he seemed to stand firm at the very centre of London life, and against the men and attitudes which, they felt, threatened their own colonial freedoms.[19]

The Assembly of South Carolina sent £1500 for Wilkes' cause; and friends in Boston asserted that 'the fate of Wilkes and America must stand or fall together'. The *New York Journal* reported in 1769 that 'All Mr Wilkes's friends are friends of America. Some of them talk of seeking a shelter from arbitrary power in those peaceful deserts'. On Wilkes' release from gaol in 1770, a toast was drunk in Boston to the 'illustrious martyr to Liberty'. Wilkes for his part was no less effusive in praising the colonial case and his words were seized upon and repeated time and again by Americans: 'I hold Magna Carta to be in full force in America as in Europe' — a comment which, in retrospect, was to be of enormous significance when relations deteriorated between London and the colonies. Much of what Wilkes said about America was, of course, like the rest of his political commentary, designed more for effect than accuracy. North America, he claimed, was 'a territory containing near four hundred and fifty thousand inhabitants, which had never hitherto produced a single Jacobite'.[20] Yet this hyperbole, repeated and applauded throughout the colonies and in British radical circles, was effective in rallying support from the Americans against king and government long before the drift towards separation had become noticeable. And this support, which found strength and succour in Wilkes' agitation, was to be an irritant to the government throughout the ensuing débâcle with America.

American pleasure at the repeal of the Stamp Act was short-lived, for subsequent British governments remained intent on re-asserting their political and fiscal grip on the colonies which, for their part, had become accustomed to leniency and self-regulation in the conduct of their daily lives. In the colonies a greater sense of unity had emerged; to combat British intrusions, political leadership had fallen into the radical hands of the prominent men of Massachusetts and Virginia. Equally important, however, in a society which was more literate and educationally sophisticated than any in Europe, was the debate about rights which had begun and which could not be silenced. In 1767 Americans found further bitter cause for complaint in the crass legislation of Charles Townshend which both taxed the colonies and imposed on them the cost of the local military. Moreover Townshend's 1767 Revenue Act in seeking to make colonial govenors independent of their assemblies smacked, to those American radicals steeped in the constitutional history of the seventeenth century, of a Stuart-like denial of legislative rights. There followed an American resistance led by Massachusetts which rapidly brought all administration to a standstill. British authority slumped in proportion to the rise of American self-confidence and independence, though British concessions — dismissed by radical Americans — helped to restore trade in the colonies.

In a number of colonies, particularly in the south, the action of governors, under instructions from home, continued to cause friction and did nothing to dispel the by now widespread belief that the British were intent on restricting American liberties. The 'Boston Massacre' of 1770 provided the occasion for the sharpening of the American belief in encroaching British autocracy and it was skilfully exploited by Samuel Adams. Perceptibly, the men from Massachusetts re-asserted a new kind of colonial rights, making compromise with the agents of Royal government more difficult at a time when the British government was quite unaware of the true strength and depth of colonial feeling. The political distance was widened by the infamous (and, again, politically insensitive) Tea Act of 1773 which triggered off further widespread and highly successful American resistance. By now, however, America's friends had quit the British government which, under the more hostile control of Lord North and a resistant king, was determined not to bow or back down before American truculence. The consequent 'Coercive Acts' of 1774 guaranteed not (as desired) effective implementation of British rule but an irreparable break between the two sides and the inevitable drift to war between 1774–6.

America's friends in London spoke up. Burke vainly but valiantly urged the government to 'revert to your old principles — seek peace and ensue it — leave America, if she has taxable matter in her, to tax herself . . . Do not burden them by taxes; you were not used to from the beginning. Let this be your reason for not taxing.'[21] Pitt, now Lord Chatham, was even more aggressive in the Lords, declaring *'that this country had no right under heaven to tax America. It is contrary to all the principles of justice and civil policy'.*[22] Those men who had rallied to Wilkes now rallied to the side of the colonists. London's Common Council declared the Coercive Acts 'not only contrary to many of the fundamental Principles of the *English Constitution*, and most essential Rights of the Subject but also apparently inconsistent with natural justice and Equity —'.[23] And as war drifted closer, London's radical voice supported the American case with ever clearer suggestions that the fault lay with the monarch and his advisers. With Wilkes as Lord Mayor, London's Livery, their natural radicalism played upon by colonial agents, petitioned the king for conciliation with America — but in the most insolent of terms, comparing 1775 to 1688 and the king with James II.[24] There is strong evidence however, London's position notwithstanding, that public (i.e., political) opinion at large was generally behind the government's hard line against the colonies in 1775-6.[25]

Between 1775 and 1776, British authority in colonial America disintegrated and was replaced by *ad hoc* local government. On 4 July 1776 the Declaration of Independence, drafted by Jefferson, established principles of government which were to become not merely the cornerstone of the Republic but the exemplar for modern democracy, though modelled on seventeenth century ideas. The belief that 'all men are created equal' and 'that they are endowed by their Creator with certain inalienable rights' was to establish a totally new concept in the world of politics and was to have the most profound effects not merely on America but throughout Europe before the end of the century. The war which followed was by no means an inevitable American victory, but the British side was characterised by confusion and ineptitude, their task made considerably more difficult by the entry of France in support of America. Those men sympathetic to the Americans before 1776, but afraid to speak out in wartime, found events going their way and gained political credit from the confused conduct of the war. And just as Americans had gone back to the first principles of government, so too did many Englishmen (often friends of the colonists) seek to find in the turmoil of the years 1776–83 some theoretical and political solution to the confusion which had descended on British politics.

It was perhaps fitting that in March 1776 it was Wilkes who first laid before Parliament serious proposals to reform representation. They were, predictably, dismissed with contempt.[26] The drive to reform Parliament came however not from within Parliament but from outside, and it took the form of political pamphleteering. Moreover reform seemed imperative in the light of events in America. In 1776 in his tract *Take Your Choice* Major Cartwright called for annual Parliaments and equal representation, though he considered both these demands not so much innovations as a return to the traditional constitution. Nor was it mere accident that those men now openly advocating a more representative form of government were prominent supporters of the Americans; it seemed all too clear that the contagion of American dissent had spread to Britain. In some respects there was nothing new in demanding a reform of representation. There had been, after all, a wealth of publications directing themselves to the need for reform. And in many of these books and tracts, notably by Cartwright, John Jebb, Richard Price, Joseph Priestley, John Horne Tooke and Thomas Brand Hollis, the influence of American ideas was clear and admitted.[27] But apart from the massive nationwide Wilkes agitation, this political debate had been conducted very much at the level of the printed word; a sort of intellectual exchange of ideas among like-minded, educated men. What was needed was the ability and organisation to translate reforming ideas into practical solutions. The question remained: how were the necessary reforms to be brought about?

A number of radical publicists had suggested means of lifting the arguments for reform to a practical level. On the eve of the American war James Burgh suggested (in his *Political Disquisitions*) the calling of a national association of men of property to test opinion, petition and press for reform. And it was these ideas which were to pass into the mainstream of subsequent radical ideas and agitation and be expressed time and again by radical proponents, notably Cartwright, Wyvill and Jebb.[28] After Burgh, British radicals needed never be at a loss (unless legally debarred) for a method of co-ordinating and expressing their radical views. Cartwright emblazoned the notion in bold letters in demanding a GRAND NATIONAL ASSOCIATION FOR RESTORING THE CONSTITUTION.[29]

It was however the American war which transformed British domestic politics. Indeed it is quite impossible to consider the evolution of British radicalism in these years independently of events in America. It was as if America had cast a shadow across British politics. The American Declaration of Independence (and the events preceding it), the outbreak of war, and the gradual realisation that the British had been sucked into a conflict they could not afford, control or win, produced the most profound political repercussions in Britain. America once more proved decisive. The Americans, as John Brewer has written, 'not only strengthened the case for reform, they acted as an ideological midwife, bringing into the political world a qualitatively different sort of reform'.[30]

The entry of France on the American side in 1778 multiplied British problems and expenses. So too did opposition to the war, particularly when it became apparent that the conduct of the war was incompetent and bungled. Politicians who had opposed the war in principle now found allies among men who objected to its detail and conduct.

The war highlighted defects long apparent in the British political system. The widespread deployment by ministers of patronage and pensions was undeniably costly. Furthermore, by giving the government a strong guiding hand within Parliament it blurred that distinction between the legislature and the executive which was held to be the hallmark of sound constitutional practice. The Americans were to resolve this constitutional problem by removing the executive from the legislature. Such a revolutionary step was not possible within Britain, though the ineptitude of the government during the American war, coming on top of suspicions about George III harboured by Whig politicians out of office, resulted in a renewed cry for 'economical reform' at the close of the 1770s. As the situation in America deteriorated the demand grew for a purging of placemen and pensioners, and a reduction in the cost of government. The British political system had been exposed as both costly and inefficient. But once the call was taken up for a reform of the means by which the king's ministers exerted their political power, it was only a short step to the more radical insistence on a reform of the very basis of that power. Whigs like Lord Rockingham and his secretary, Edmund Burke, pressed for economical reform, but the movement they started was soon transformed into a nationwide campaign on a scale and with a vigour which few could have predicted.

In 1779 discontented country gentlemen from Rockingham's own county of Yorkshire despatched a petition calling for economical reform. By August 1780, this 'Yorkshire Association' was able to secure 5800 names to its petition.[31] Led by Christopher Wyvill, the Association became not merely a vehicle demanding wide-ranging reform, but also the centre of a national, county-based movement, as gentlemen throughout the counties, inspired by the Yorkshire example, took up the cry for economical reform. What is significant about this movement is not that it eventually enjoyed a measure of success when Rockingham headed a brief Whig ministry in 1782 (much against the king's will), but that through the demand for economical reform the more radical demand for political reform became established even within Parliament itself. In the correspondence which began to flow in 1780 between the various County Associations the idea of parliamentary reform was incorporated into the debate, and in the spring of 1780, when delegates from the various counties met in London, they agreed to press for parliamentary as well as economical reform.[32] Political reform now became a live issue, largely stimulated by the extra-parliamentary pressure of Wyvill's Association movement.

Wyvill was, however, in a minority among the members of the Associations in his desire to secure a moderate reform of Parliament and a change in representation. Many more were concerned simply to reduce the cost and inefficiency of government. Consequently the usefulness of the Associations to political reformers was limited, and many men who had earlier been involved in the cause of parliamentary reform now felt the need to shift to a different and specifically political level. The outcome was the establishment in April 1780 of the Society for Constitutional Information (SCI), a body which was to prove enormously influential both in advancing the arguments for parliamentary reform and in laying the groundwork for radical politics in subsequent decades. By means of radical tracts, freely distributed, the SCI hoped to revive in 'the COMMONALTY AT LARGE a knowledge of their lost rights'. The Society set out to distribute this information 'throughout the realm, to circulate it through every village and hamlet and even to introduce it into the humble dwelling of the cottager'.[33] This lowering of political sights and the aiming of propaganda at a lower political constituency had of course been characteristic of the earlier Wilkes movement. But the SCI's ambition represented a marked shift in English radical politics even though the Society's own members were men of property and education. Led by Cartwright, Jebb and Capel Lofft, the SCI could boast among its founding members, fourteen MPs, four aldermen, seven doctors, and fourteen peers and knights.[34] Ideologically the SCI was as moderate and reformist as its membership was respectable, rooting its faith in the constitution 'handed down to us from a long succession of ages from our Saxon and British ancestors'.[35] Time and again the Society sought to show that its proposals for parliamentary reform involved little more than correcting newly-acquired imperfections in the British constitution. Occasionally however the Society struck a note which must have seemed, to outsiders at least, more radical than intended:

> Since the *all* of one man is as dear to him as the all of another, the *poor* man has an Equal Right, but more need, to have a Representation in Parliament than a rich one.[36]

Most remarkable of all the SCI's features was its industry and vigour in bombarding the country with free or cheap radical literature. Within three years the Society had published more than 88,000 copies of thirty-three different titles, some of which proved immensely popular; Cartwright's *Declaration of Rights*, for example, ran to five editions.[37] Moreover, they were able to reach an audience throughout the country thanks to their national network of provincial members, friends and contacts. By the end of the American war, the SCI had members in twenty-seven towns outside London and their material was given wide publicity in the provincial press.[38]

SCI members however met in London, debating the political issues which lay at the heart of their publications. From the first, the Society remained a small, exclusive body not concerned to increase its membership. Indeed by 1783 there were only 130 members on the Society's books and their weekly meetings were sparsely-attended. Yet their work was more influential than their numbers might suggest. However, despite the Society's efforts, the immediate prospects for reform looked bleak; change after all could only materialise if and when Parliament was persuaded to implement it. Within Parliament, Wyvill's friends concentrated increasingly on overthrowing the unpopular Lord North. His successor, Rockingham, favoured economical and not parliamentary reform. The greatest hope within Parliament in 1782 was the young William Pitt — a friend of many reformers — who was, at once, perhaps the only hope both for a more stable political system and for changing it. Though Pitt thought the SCI's proposals for reform too extreme, he promised Wyvill that he would press for reform, a promise made all the more exciting by Pitt's elevation to senior office in 1783. In December 1784 Wyvill told the SCI that Pitt had promised

> to bring up the Question of a Parliamentary Reform as early in the next session as possible . . . he will support his proposition to the utmost of his strengths and exert his whole power and credit as a man and as a Minister honestly and boldly, to carry such meliorated system of representation as may place the constitution on a footing of permanent security.[39]

Looking back there seems to have been little chance of implementing such promises, for both the king and a majority of Pitt's ministers were opposed to any such reforms. So too was a majority in Parliament. But it is interesting to remember that Pitt, the young parliamentary torch bearer of the reforming cause in the years 1784–5, was the man who, a decade later, was to be responsible for the vigorous and punitive repression of men and organisations seeking a radical reform of Parliament.

Pitt's role in the 1780s was not, however, totally negative. Indeed his greatest achievement was in creating the political stability so lacking during and immediately after the American war and imposing upon a divided and generally truculent Parliament the firm hand of the king's government. But Pitt's securing of stable government was at a price — most notably the failure of the chief minister to implement his own ideas for parliamentary reform. Equally, it seemed to many, particularly those reformers who attached their loyalties to Fox, that Pitt was merely the puppet of a king who cared nothing for constitutional government and who was working, through Pitt, to undermine the power of the Commons. Those reformers following Wyvill, however, supported Pitt and worked hard in 1784 to secure for him an electoral victory.

In 1785, when Wyvill's county supporters in Yorkshire petitioned Pitt for reform, they found that their support in other parts of the country had declined. Nonetheless, with Wyvill's help Pitt proposed a limited measure for abolishing a number of rotten boroughs, yet even this gesture was too strong for the Commons who rejected it.[40] This defeat proved a body blow. Pitt was never again to stake his ministerial career on the prospect of reform, while the defeat reduced even further the support for reform in the country at large. The Association movement collapsed, and the SCI slid into inertia and inactivity. The cause of parliamentary reform languished, paradoxically, under the government of the one chief minister who above all others had seemed to herald the brightest prospects in living memory for government-backed reform. Those men of sensibility who sought a refinement in the conduct of British society and politics did not despair, however. Indeed it is striking that at the very time the cause of parliamentary reform seemed lost, there was born a movement for reform which was, in many respects, to prove most effective and was to establish the pattern for subsequent radical agitation. In 1787 the Society for the Abolition of the Slave Trade was founded and in the next twenty years its progress, tactics and ultimate success were to be a striking example for those men who wished to transform an established political institution by dint of extra-parliamentary activity.

Chapter 2

EARLY PROGRESS 1783-91

A number of prominent members of the SCI were opponents of the slave trade, none more so than Granville Sharp, the man who in many respects initiated the movement which culminated in 1807 in abolition. But when the campaign formally began in the 1780s to oppose the trade in Africans it must have seemed an even more daunting task than the reform of Parliament. For a century and a half, the British slave trade had gone relatively unquestioned. Buttressed by Navigation Acts, colonial legislation and English Common Law, the buying and selling of humans had wrought the most profound effects on both sides of the Atlantic. Quite apart from the human and social dislocation in Africa itself, the European slave trade had enabled the settlement and expansion of vast areas of the tropical Americas, while generating abundant trade and commerce for the metropolitan nations. In Britain, the ports of London, Bristol, Glasgow and Liverpool had particularly benefited from slave trading while in the capital there had developed a significant black population – the human flotsam and jetsam of the Atlantic slave trade. Blacks were a common sight on the streets of mid-eighteenth-century London, as contemporary cartoons and caricatures testify. No one living there could long remain in ignorance of the human results of the trade.

Sharp first encountered the problems of slavery when helping a distressed London black, Jonathan Strong. In 1765, having helped him recover from a severe beating administered by his master, Sharp was outraged to discover that Strong was about to be sent back to slavery in the Caribbean. Sharp thus set out both to secure Strong's freedom and, more important, to establish, through detailed legal and historical research, the illegality of slavery in England.[1] His subsequent publications, legal defence of aggrieved blacks, and promotion of anti-slavery cases in English courts (culminating in the important but generally misunderstood Somerset case of 1772) succeeded in focusing political and social attention both on the issue of English slavery, and on the wider question of slavery in the colonies.

Despite his work, outrages continued. In March 1783 he recorded in his diary, 'Gustavus Vassa, a Negro called on me with an account of 130 Negroes being thrown alive into the sea from on board an English Slave Ship'.[2] The subsequent horrific story of slaves being deliberately drowned when their slaver, the *Zong*, was running short of water, eventually found its way before an English court, but only as a contested insurance case concerning the loss of the dead slaves. The Lord Chief Justice asserted 'they had no doubt (though it shocks one very much) that the case of the slaves was the same as if horses had been thrown overboard'.[3] With such vivid examples available Sharp had no difficulty in bringing forth the horrors of the slave trade. Here was an obvious and glaring issue for men of sensibility to concern themselves with.

It was, however, America which lifted the problem of slavery to a qualitatively different level. Slavery was a commonplace institution in the American colonies (though not as significant as it was to become in the nineteenth century) and came under attack from those Americans who felt that the concept of bondage was strikingly at variance with the claims to freedom so widely and assertively espoused by the colonists. Led by Quakers and other Americans steeped in European and Scottish Enlightenment writings, opposition to slavery was widely disseminated by a growing body of American anti-slavery literature. Like other forms of radical American literature, anti-slavery tracts found their way to Britain. Similarly, American abolitionists corresponded with like-minded friends in London, most notably with Sharp. Not all revolutionaries in America were abolitionists, however, but there is some significance in the fact that the centre of American anti-slavery was Philadelphia, the epicentre of American revolutionary sentiment. The trans-Atlantic correspondence, so much in evidence in the Wilkesite and revolutionary years, was equally important and noticeable in the early campaign against the slave trade. American Quakers and other provided their British colleagues with regular offerings from the American presses; American visitors to London often traded ideas and publications with English sympathisers, notably with the omnipresent and energetic Sharp. And to prove the illegality of slavery in England, Sharp turned to that body of Enlightenment, scriptural and legal literature, which was soon to become the battleground of the anti-slavery contest.

With the publication in 1769 of Sharp's *A Representation of the*

Injustice and Dangerous Tendancy of Tolerating Slavery in England, the
author not merely documented the illegality of English slavery, but
clearly illustrated the degree to which the English were enmeshed in
the wider slaving phenomenon. Sharp was not alone in his campaign. Others found slavery repugnant, notably the growing
Methodist community whose leader, John Wesley, had seen slavery
in practice in Georgia and who openly castigated it in his *Thoughts
upon Slavery* (1774). So far, however, the objections to black slavery
had come from small, albeit articulate, groups. But the ending of the
American war in 1783 heralded a new upsurge in the fortunes of the
pioneering abolitionists.

Peace had two major effects on the problem. First, American
independence removed from London's political scene the American
planters who previously had promoted their slaving interests in
co-operation with their Caribbean colleagues. Henceforth, the West
Indians were left to fend for themselves — an increasingly difficult
and isolated task. Secondly the peace of 1783 brought on to the
streets of London large numbers of former slaves who had fought on
the losing British side in America. At the very time the *Zong* case was
making such news in London, London's black community, already
substantial, was swollen by these (generally distressed) blacks from
America. Black beggars and discharged black sailors swelled the
ranks of London's poor. By the spring of 1786 it was reported that a
'great number of Blacks and People of Colour, many of them
Refugees from America and others who have by land or sea been in
His Majesty's service, were from the severity of the season in great
distress'.[4] The traditional charitable efforts for the poor proved quite
inadequate: Sharp alone had 400 'pensioners' and 'orphans' to care
for.[5] Clearly a more organised basis was needed for black relief, and
in 1783 Sharp drafted proposals for resettling London's blacks in
Africa. His ambition was to create a perfect society, shaped by
Enlightenment ideals, which would both relieve black distress and
demonstrate to the world the full social potential of free blacks.[6] It
was not until 1786, however, that effective relief for the black poor
was implemented through a committee of sympathetic men headed
by Jonas Hanway. Raising £800 by newspaper appeal, the committee dispensed aid at two London taverns and opened a special hos-
pital in Warren Street.[7] Yet even with government assistance these
efforts remained inadequate to the task, and in May 1786 the idea of
repatriation to Africa was widely mooted. Thus from the determi-

nation to solve the problems of London's poor blacks there emerged the Sierra Leone scheme of 1786-7.

In its turn this scheme generated great expense, bitter political argument and, most important, disaster for the early black settlers.[8] Of 459 who finally left London in February 1787, by October 1788 only 130 remained alive in Sierra Leone. Not surprisingly those blacks who were initially doubtful of the scheme and stayed in London felt that their fears had been justified. Whatever the horrors of the scheme, it had the indirect effect of keeping the problem of slavery firmly in the public eye. Thus at the very time when parliamentary reform was at a low ebb, the problems of slavery were slowly being transmuted from the political and intellectual concern of a small band of educated men into an important national issue about which growing numbers of people came to express strong opinions.

Such a political transition is difficult to trace with precision but it clearly took place in the years 1785-7. In that time the man who was perhaps *the* most important single person in the evolution of abolitionist sentiment, Thomas Clarkson, was himself converted to abolition when writing his Cambridge prize-winning essay 'Is it right to make slaves of others against their will?'[9] With the zeal of a convert, Clarkson plunged into the small London world of abolitionists, translating his essay into English (from Latin). He then began to accumulate a research dossier on the slave trade by visiting slaving ships in English ports. And in May 1787 the Committee for the Abolition of the Slave Trade was founded, composed largely of Quakers, but including Sharp, Wilberforce and Clarkson; their collective aim being to procure 'such information and evidence, and for publishing the same, as might tend to the abolition of the trade'.[10] Clarkson was despatched on a fact-finding and, later, lecture tour while the London Committee began to disseminate their publications across the country. At the same time, their arguments were skilfully displayed in the Commons by Wilberforce. Their impact was immediate and startling, and their success can be gauged by the fact that in 1787 'the question of abolition had never been moved in either legislative body: but in 1792, the House of Commons had voted overwhelmingly for the gradual abolition of the slave trade'.[11] In 1807 — a mere twenty years after the campaign began — the slave trade was abolished.

The speed with which abolitionism spread in the late 1780s was partly due to the number of sympathisers throughout the country who, earlier in the decade, had stepped forward to support reform. These men now rekindled their old radical enthusiasm, joined with local friends, and began to press for abolition. The case of Manchester is instructive. In 1787 two members of the SCI, Thomas Walker and Thomas Cooper (the former an ex-pupil of James Burgh) and Thomas Bayley had, even before Clarkson's arrival in Manchester, been active for abolition. Indeed, when he lectured in the town, Clarkson was pleased to find 'the spirit which was then beginning to show itself among the people of Manchester and of other places, on the subject of the slave trade'. It is perhaps not so surprising that this embryonic industrial town should have been so prominent for it was the home of the Manchester Literary and Philosophical Society, a body of enlightened character which attracted to it men of reformist feelings steeped in Scottish and European rationalist thought and science. Walker and his abolitionist friends suggested the raising of an abolitionist petition in the tradition of earlier agitations (they had recently been successful in petitioning against a locally unpopular Fustian Tax). Advertised locally (and in the press in other cities) the Manchester abolition petition was hugely successful, attracting 10,639 names. The idea was swiftly adopted nationally and by May 1788 similar petitions flowed into Parliament.[12]

The Manchester abolition society wrote to all major towns, through the newspapers, urging them to petition for abolition. And the Manchester abolition resolutions were advertised in the hope that others would follow the example. This Manchester initiative proved seminal. A London paper, *The World*, praised the 'late interference of the town of Manchester'.[13] Other towns swiftly followed, often encouraged by the arrival of Clarkson whose lectures took him throughout the country, meeting the converted, informing the ignorant and persuading the uncommitted. Town after town fell to the cause. In Birmingham the local abolition society (with Dr Priestley prominent) claimed that local people who had 'the commercial interest of the kingdom very deeply at heart' none the less opposed 'any commerce which always originates in violence and often terminates in cruelty'.[14]

Dissenters were frequently at the front of this initial abolitionist push, partly because they had opposed it earlier but also because they had determined to secure their own political rights by campaigning against the Test and Corporation Acts. Furthermore, sermons against the slave trade became a common feature of church services. Much of the abolitionist sentiment was stirred up by literature from the Abolition Society who published a vast number of tracts and bought space in newspapers. Thousands of tracts spilled from the presses (costing the Society more than £1000 in the summer of 1788), and these publications often persuaded others to take up the pen against the slave trade.[15] Crude pamphleteering, sophisticated verse, religiously-motivated attacks — these and many more swelled the growing body of literature which directed the attention of the reading public to the iniquities of the trade. As a propaganda campaign, the attack on the slave trade in 1787-8 was successful beyond the hopes of the small band of pioneers behind it. Abolitionist literature grew at compound interest, and the initially small band of provincial correspondents of the Abolition Society gathered to themselves ever more local supporters and organisations. There was quite simply an explosion of abolition sentiment which was both trenchant and vociferous, and whose national appeal surprised its organisers. Moreover the new members recruited to the Abolition Society had, by and large, already stated their support for reform at a wider level.[16] It was as if the old fervour for radical change, dormant by the mid-1780s, had been rekindled and transformed into abolitionism.

The most immediate result of this growing sentiment for abolition was an increase in petitions calling for an end to the trade.[17] Contempories were surprised by the suddenness of this feeling. The *Annual Register* reported that the slave trade

> does not appear, till of late years, to have been considered with that great attention, which a practice so abhorrent in its nature to mild principles of modern policy and manners might have been expected to excite.

Now, however, the cause had been 'taken up with great zeal and earnestness by various descriptions of people'.[18] Few doubted the effectiveness of these efforts, or the fact that abolitionism had become a major popular sentiment. By July 1790 the Abolition Society felt that the public was convinced 'that there is something both in the principle and conduct of this trade fundamentally wrong'.[19]

From an early date objections to the trade were not merely sectional or religious, but were rooted in a fundamental rejection of the economics of the trade and a denunciation of its inherent injustices. The City of York for instance felt that the trade was 'wholly inconsistent with the dictates of Morality and true Religion' but also asserted that 'the profits from this disgraceful Traffic bear no proportion to the injuries it is attended with not only to the Public in general but to the West India planters in particular and that it is inconsistent with true Policy as it is with virtue and Religion'.[20]

Expressing these and similar sentiments, petitions to the Commons had by May 1788 surpassed one hundred including one from Bristol, heart of the slave trading country, which 'was signed by a great number'.[21] Clarkson remarked that 'It was obvious from the great number of petitions, which had been presented concerning it, how much it had engaged the public attention, and consequently how much it deserved the serious notice of that house'.[22] When in May 1788 the Commons debated the slave trade it did so in a transformed political atmosphere. Extraordinary public interest had been revealed in the issue and enormous pressure brought to bear on Parliament. Simultaneously, Parliament and government had been carefully prepared, not least by Wilberforce's influence over Pitt. The First Minister himself had recorded in December 1787 'the more I reflect upon it, the more anxious and impatient I am that the business should be brought as speedily as possible to a point'.[23] Though personally keen on abolition, he was unable to stake his government or career on the measure; he was in fact concerned to air the issue of the slave trade and to refer it to an investigating committee. Wilberforce however was thinking along bolder lines. There is, he wrote, '*no doubt of our success*'.[24]

Initially the cause seemed to face delay, for Pitt and Wilberforce agreed to institute a committee of the Privy Council to investigate the slave trade. Regarded by some as merely a delaying tactic, this investigation proved of crucial importance for it became a forum for the abolitionist arguments and, perhaps even more important, the occasion for the most detailed researches to date about the stark facts of the trade. An unprecedented stream of information about the trade flowed into the committee from both sides, in its turn helping to spread even further political and public awareness of, and interest in, the politics and morality of the slave trade.

Pitt was invaluable in steering the abolitionist case through the committee, and in May 1788 proposed a Commons resolution that the House should, in the coming session, consider the slave trade. In the debate speakers took it as axiomatic that the piles of petitions before them represented a genuinely popular feeling. Pitt said of the trade that it was

> a subject which, it was evident from the great number and variety of petitions presented to that House respecting it, had engaged the public attention to a very considerable extent, and consequently deserved the most serious notice of that House.[25]

Burke made the point even more forcefully: 'If that House neglected the petitions from its constituents, that House must be abolished, and the privy council substituted in its stead'.[26]

Even in the Lords, the centre of support for the slave trade, few doubted the accurate reflection of opinion in the petitions. It was 'a matter of public notoriety [said Lord Carlisle] that the question of the Slave Trade had engrossed the attention of every part of the kingdom for above these twelve months'.[27] And the first political gain came with the passage of Dolben's Act, a private member's Bill designed to restrict the worst overcrowding on British slavers. Pitt's support was crucial and the Bill overcame opposition, notably in the Lords, only by Pitt's threats to break up the government.[28]

In the summer of 1788 abolitionists realised that a major effort was needed to prepare for the forthcoming parliamentary session. Clarkson once again set out to muster support, while the lobbying of MPs continued apace. And the abolitionist cause was helped, in April 1789, by the publication of the committee's report on the slave trade, providing the cause with an abundance of empirical and statistical data useful to their arguments. Even Pitt thought that the report's evidence was 'irresistible' and would push parliamentary opinion towards abolition.[29] On 12 May 1789, Wilberforce accordingly moved twelve resolutions intended to show that 'no . . . inconvenience would result from discontinuing the further importations of African slaves'.[30] The outcome however was most disappointing, the Commons deciding to hear further evidence from the Bar of the House. Thanks to successful delaying tactics by the slave trade lobby it was to be April 1791 before it was again possible to put an abolitionist motion before the Commons.[31]

In the intervening year, abolitionists struggled to keep up their political momentum, and though lobbying in London continued it proved difficult to maintain interest in the provinces. When in April 1791 the motion for abolition was put to the test it failed in the

Commons by 88 to 163 votes.[32] It was none the less a considerable achievement for a body which, a mere four years before, had set out to challenge so powerfully entrenched and unquestioned an institution as the slave trade. Moreover, with the issue so firmly lodged in Parliament — pushed there by successive waves of petitions, carefully manipulated lobbying and astute propaganda — abolition had secured a firm parliamentary base. Thereafter Wilberforce and the Abolition Society could concentrate on the detailed though crucial task of picking off and winning over the waverers and opponents within Parliament itself. And it was unclear just how that process could henceforth be assisted by *extra*-parliamentary efforts, rather than internal lobbying and dealing.

Abolition of the slave trade was not of course the sole object which attracted the attention of men of reforming persuasions between 1788-91. In November 1788 throughout the country, for instance, considerable effort was invested in the celebrations of the 1688 Revolution. Often too the November gatherings became the occasion for political statements of reforming intent. In Leicester the centenary dinner resolved 'that this town is improperly represented in Parliament'.[33] The London-based Revolution Society, which claimed to have met annually since 1688, was even more forthright in its views, resolving in 1788 'That all civil and political authority is derived from the people', and 'That the right of private judgment, liberty of conscience, trial by jury, the freedom of the press and freedom of election ought ever to be held sacred and inviolable'.[34] Moreover it is clear from the Society's correspondence with like-minded societies in other parts of the country that the old cause of parliamentary reform was not dead.[35] Yet in comparison with the buoyant days of 1780-3 it was in a sorry state of decline and relative inactivity. Parliamentary reform as a major political issue was, on the eve of the French Revolution, overshadowed by the campaign against the slave trade, though even that campaign was in a faltering mood. But among men of reforming sympathies the centenary of 1688 provided a rare moment of encouragement and an occasion to celebrate the historical symbol of their political faith and to re-assert their continuing commitment to the need to effect parliamentary reform. But by any standards it was a pale reflection of their old reforming strengths, and fell far short of the efforts they would need if they were ever to persuade Parliament of the virtues of reform. Even the SCI, alive throughout the 1780s, was hardly noticeable in

1788-9, and indeed its internal affairs were as characterised by abolitionism as they were by reform. Its members clearly doubted the prospects for reform, as Major Cartwright confided to his wife:

> In the Constitutional Society we are also at work. The great objects of that institution are a severer trial of patience; but where truth and rights of nature are the foundation, public reform and public happiness the objects of pursuit, there are motives enough for perseverance under any discouragement. Should the West India slaves, who but the other day had not the slightest prospect of such an event, find themselves emancipated, who shall say that there is no hope of our constitutional rights and liberties being restored?[36]

Cartwright still believed that the best hope for reform lay with Pitt, but it was already clear that because of the political constraints of holding together his diffuse government and his single-minded determination to maintain the king's government at almost any cost, any hope of government-sponsored reform or abolition was in vain and ill-founded. Moreover events in France were soon to transform the political situation so completely that even Pitt's personal (as opposed to his official) support for reform and abolition was soon to wither in the changed political atmosphere.

The British were slow to respond to events in France in 1788-9, though the local press gave France ample coverage in those turbulent months.[37] Few shared Burke's immediate and deep-seated hostility, a response which made him an isolated political figure apparently incapable of sensing the true nature of contemporary politics. Events were to show how prescient he had been. Pitt thought that the French upheavals 'must sooner or later terminate in general harmony and regular order'.[38] Indeed in the light of the recent celebration of 1688, many felt that France was passing through her own Glorious Revolution from which she would swiftly emerge, chastened and more in keeping with Britain.

More common than Burke's brooding pessimism about France was that excited and somewhat politically unrealistic enthusiasm (most popularly associated with the early Romantics) expressed by a wide circle of reforming Whigs and Dissenters. These were often the same men recently active in metropolitan and provincial societies for abolition and to celebrate 1688. Moreover the early French revolutionaries frequently replied to English congratulations in terms which tended to confirm this view. Reformers from Lille told the London Revolution Society, 'if we had not been encouraged by your example [of 1688] and enlightened by your experience, we might have been unable to break those chains'.[39] From the early days of the revolution political clubs and societies had sprung up (throughout France) and had come to exercise a great influence over the course of events. Late in November 1789 many of these French organisations were delighted to hear from sympathisers in London, grouped under the name the Revolution Society. On 4 November 1789 that Society held its annual dinner where Dr Price, doyen of the Dissenting reformers, moved a resolution of support for the changes in France:

> The Society for commemorating the Revolution in Great Britain, disclaiming National partialities and rejoicing in every triumph of Liberty and Justice over Arbitrary power, offer to the National Assembly of France their congratulations on the Revolution in that country and on the prospect it gives to the first two Kingdoms in the World of a common participation in the blessings of Civil and Religious Liberty.[40]

Passed to the Duc de Rochefoucauld, this resolution was presented to the National Assembly on 25 November; enthusiastic replies swiftly sped back to London from the Assembly and provincial societies. The Assembly claimed to see in the Society's address 'the dawn of a glorious day, in which two nations . . . shall contract an intimate union, founded on the similarities of their opinions and the common enthusiasm for liberty'.[41] Within the year no fewer seventy-seven French societies, most affiliated to the Jacobin society, had replied to the Revolution Society.[42] Thus this small, obscure and politically insignificant London Society became more widely known in France than in Britain and came to be viewed as the spokesman for English reform. In fact the Revolution Society was little more than an annual reunion for those with fond memories of 1688. Despite its unshakably English roots, its opponents were later to think that it had been guided by events in France. For their part the French even thought of the Society as the *French* Revolution Society.[43] Yet even when the Society suggested the people should 'establish societies throughout the kingdom upon Revolution Principles, to maintain a correspondence with each other and to form that grand concentrated Union of true Friends of Public Liberty',[44] it was doing no more than to suggest the pattern already established by the Association and anti-slave trade movements.

In the progress of English reform, perhaps most important of all was the campaign in the winter of 1789-90 for the repeal of the Test and Corporation Acts — a drive to remove the political disabilities of Dissenters. Dissenting agitation centred on Dr Price's academy in Hackney, with powerful allies in Birmingham (led by Dr Priestley), Manchester and Warrington. Many of their opponents feared that more than mere religion was involved and resisted the possible transfer of local authority into the hands of Dissenters, and in the partisan literature which accompanied the parliamentary campaigns for repeal between 1787-90 party political opinion began to harden on both sides. Events in France encouraged the Dissenters and bolstered their opponents' resistance. Burke's change of heart is instructive. In 1787 and 1789 he was undecided about repealing the Test and Corporation Acts. In March 1790 however, having heard Fox link repeal with the issue of the French Revolution, Burke took sides. Repeal was wrong, he argued, because circumstances had changed; Fox and the Dissenters had become too influenced by the prevailing discussion about political rights. Burke's conversion is important for his thoughts about Test and Corporation began to shape his wider political views which erupted the following year in his epic publication, *Reflections on the Revolution in France*.[45]

Parliament's rejection of repeal highlighted the reformers' disillusionment with Parliament, and sharpened their awareness of French 'progress'. There then followed the formation of a number of provincial societies committed to even wider political reform, led by men who had been weaned on SCI literature and had been active in the campaigns against the slave trade and the Test and Corporation Acts.[46] To counter these new reform societies, the first 'Church and King' clubs were established to organise local support for the political *status quo*. Thus evolved a basic polarisation of opinion and organisation, of reformers versus loyalists, which was to characterise the ensuing decade. And though much of this divide seems at first sight to have been influenced by events in France it was in fact a result of specifically local English factors.

This divide was hardened late in 1790 by the publication of Burke's *Reflections*. Burke had begun to write on the Revolution in October 1789, spurred on in the following month by the Revolution Society's enthusiasm for France and particularly by Dr Price's sermon *On the Love of Country*.[47] Burke fumed at the English sympathy for the Revolution and was stung even further by his erstwhile friend Thomas Paine who enthusiastically but unwittingly wrote to Burke from Paris announcing that 'The Revolution in France is certainly the Forerunner to other revolutions in Europe'.[48] Having read or heard of support for the revolution from Price, Fox and, apparently, Pitt, Burke in February 1790 publicly came out against it.[49] And in the course of that year the public was kept informed that he was writing a book about France (though all the while the author became an increasingly isolated and discredited figure).[50]

In November 1790 *Reflections* was published to a lukewarm reception. Its content is largely inexplicable without reference to domestic politics and particularly to the conduct of Dr Price and the Revolution Society. According to Burke, the Society had 'the manifest design of connecting the affairs of France with those of England, by drawing us into an imitation of the conduct of the National Assembly'.[51] Within the year, however, as the revolution began to disintegrate, alarm among the English propertied classes was to bestow on the *Reflections* (a volatile tract-for-the-moment) a prophetic quality which elevated the author to the rank of ideologue of the English counter-revolution.

Despite Burke's anger — and despite the apparent stimulus from France — English reform was in a parlous state in 1790. Though the SCI and Revolution Society agreed to meet to discuss reform,[52] neither was very active. The SCI met regularly, though with poor attendance and meagre income.[53] The prospects for reform seemed as bleak as ever with perhaps only the abolitionists' limited success as a small crumb of comfort. But all this was to change early in 1791 — and it changed largely because of the work of one man, Thomas Paine.

Paine, the Englishman whose writings had so helped the Americans in their struggle against the British, had returned to England in 1787 (and was elected to the SCI).[54] In France at the beginning of the Revolution, he was shocked to discover Burke's hostility to France.[55] Goaded by the *Reflections*, Paine immediately set about composing a riposte. After three months' hard work, in February 1791 he published the first part of the *Rights of Man*. Though only one of thirty-eight replies to Burke, Paine's was by far the most influential, for it fused the hitherto intellectual and rather abstract debate about the Revolution on to a new kind of practical politics. In the wake of Paine's book there emerged a style of radicalism which was to transform the face of English politics and create political turmoil lower down the social scale.

Paine's direct vernacular writing, his simple populist message, denouncing Burke's idea of society as an association between past and present generations, aroused political and popular feeling as nothing else since the days of Wilkes. Overnight Paine became the disciple and exponent of traditional English rights threatened by arbitrary and corrupt authority — rights so recently secured in a different setting by the Americans. In 1790 English radicalism was in abeyance; after the publication of the first part of the *Rights of Man* it was shaken back into activity and was not to be checked until the full panoply of state power drove it underground. People began to take sides for or against Paine. The SCI, for instance, now found that its advertisements would not be accepted in six out of twelve news-papers, though it had advertised in them for the past eleven years.[56] The Society decided to seek a correspondence with 'all correspond-ing constitutional societies in England, Scotland and France'.[57]

Paine meanwhile slipped back to France where he became dan-gerously enmeshed in revolutionary politics. Won over to Robes-pierre, Paine became an early spokesman for republicanism at the very time the Royal family fled to Varennes.[58] Leaving behind a powerful plea for a republic, Paine returned to London in July 1791 to celebrate, with his English friends in the Revolution Society, the second anniversary of the fall of the Bastille.

In preparation for that day, political feeling began to run high throughout the country. Local men of authority and the Home Office were afraid that the anniversary dinners would lead to public disturbances. In the heart of Norfolk the Rev. James Woodforde recorded in his diary:

> I hope this Day will be attended with no bad Consequences, this being the Day the French Revolution first took place and many Meetings advertised to be held this Day in London, Norwich etc. throughout this Kingdom to commemorate the above Revo-lution.[59]

Paine wisely decided not to join the 1000 London supporters.[60] In Manchester, Thomas Walker's Constitutional Club (established by Walker among friends already active in the abolitionist and Test and Corporation campaigns) organised a similar dinner. The local Church and King club was provocative, but Walker's position as

Borough Reeve ensured that the celebrations passed off peacefully. The same was not true of Birmingham where the Priestley riots, occasioned by the 14 July dinner, ravaged the town and drove the distinguished Dr Priestley to the more congenial climate of the USA. Throughout the country schisms between reformers and loyalists surfaced in July 1791 and in many places erupted into violent enmity. Without exception, however, the threats or reality of violence came from the loyalists. At worst, the radicals were guilty of naïve unawareness of the rapidly changing political climate in which they met to celebrate the fall of the Bastille.

Letters from around the country informed the Home Office of the potential dangers. There were, it is true, peaceful dinners in Dublin, Belfast, Edinburgh, Glasgow, Liverpool, and narrowly, in Manchester. Other spots were less quiet. In Norwich, the Whig reformer Dr Parr withstood a three-day attack on his home and library.[61] In Sheffield a local magistrate, a former Association man, was attacked, an insult which drove him from the radical camp.[62] The events of July 1791 were dicated largely by the peculiarities of *local* circumstances. But it is impossible to ignore the tensions created by support for or opposition to the French Revolution. After all, the meetings which convened on 14 July were called to celebrate events in France. Many of the toasts at the ill-fated Birmingham dinner, for instance, were concerned with France. The French for their part sympathised with Dr Priestley and, later, even invited him to sit in the Convention.[63] Dr Priestley and Dr Parr were attacked, Walker was threatened, not merely for being reformers but also for supporting the French Revolution (and at a time when the French monarchy was in jeopardy).

Contemporaries were in no doubt that the shadow of revolutionary France was largely responsible for the bitterness of political divisions in the summer of 1791. From Manchester, Thomas Butterworth Bayley, a former reformer and Wilkesite, and soon to become a staunch supporter of anti-reform, told the Home Office that,

> the Example of Birmingham, and an unhappy Party Spirit about the Revolution in France, heightened by the meetings of the 14th last has added to the general ill-humour and may be a pretext for mischief and Outrage.[64]

In response, the Home Office asked local authorities to examine their state of preparedness against unrest: in reply some asked for troops.[65] There was no doubt by late July 1791 that English society had become severely divided and while the radicals had a political creed which was rootedly and unshakably English, they had assembled on the anniversary of the fall of the Bastille. Inspired by France, revitalised by Paine, supporters of reform found themselves more organised, more coherent than ever before. But they also found that their inspiration and ideals had, in July 1791, stimulated an equally powerful resistance among men who sought to defend the *status quo*. From this heady political atmosphere there was soon to emerge a new kind of radical politics.

Chapter 3

THE RISE OF POPULAR RADICALISM, 1791-3

After the tension of July 1791, political animosities were dangerously inflamed in towns throughout the country. Moreover these divisions took on a particularly local form for, though there was an overall pattern, it was the distinctive structure, history and personalities of each locality which determined the nature of British politics. Around those men who had met to celebrate on 14 July there developed local reforming societies. Perhaps the most influential was the Manchester Constitutional Society founded by 'several merchants and manufacturers in Manchester, together with some members of the learned professions' to counteract a local Church and King society (founded in March 1790) and clearly modelled on the SCI, to which a number of its members belonged. The society argued:

> That the happiness of the people governed ought to be the sole end and aim of all civil government [and] . . .
> That no Law or Statute can be fairly made, which is not enacted by and with the consent of a majority of the people.[1]

By August 1791 Manchester newspapers refused to accept radical advertisements and the reformers therefore resolved to found their own newspaper which, in the words of Thomas Cooper, 'will *at first* be gently but always decidedly democratic'.[2] And, as if to confirm their opponents' worst forebodings, the Manchester radicals published Paine's latest address in November; Thomas Walker even chaired a London meeting for him.

Similar reforming societies were evolving at much the same time. In June 1791 Dr Priestley had helped to establish the Warwickshire Constitutional Society (similar in philosophy to the Manchester group), and issuing markedly radical pronouncements. It declared that 'the people at large are the only Judges in what manner their own interest is to be promoted; that they have the sole right of making laws'. Perhaps even more trenchant was their claim that when abuses are introduced into any Government, the people who are aggrieved by them ought to inquire into their Source and apply whatever remedy shall appear to them adequate to the purpose whether by making new laws, repealing old Ones or removing the Persons who administer them.[3]

The devastating Priestley riots put an end to this development. Elsewhere, however, there was more hope.

In Cambridge a Constitutional Society, originally founded by Dissenters in 1780, was revived in 1791, declaring that 'Every individual of mankind is born with a natural right to life, liberty and property'. Not surprisingly, the man at the head of the Cambridge society, John Audley, was also in the SCI. Close by in St Neots, yet another SCI man founded still another local society. Clearly, the SCI was enormously influential − by proxy − in this blossoming of provincial reform societies in the summer of 1791. But within its own ranks, there was a rumbling of discontent about its apparent shift towards a more radical stance.[4]

The major shift in radical politics in 1791 came in Sheffield, an industrial city where artisan cutlery trades had for some time past been in dispute with local masters. Backed by combinations and supported by an excellent radical (and abolitionist) newspaper, the *Sheffield Register*, the artisans of Sheffield had built up a reputation for fierce independence and collective mentality. Long before the French Revolution and Paine gave social divides a new vocabulary, class antagonism was sharp in Sheffield and was made worse in July by a 'Church and King' attack on the home of a local magistrate.[5] In December 1791 local artisans crossed the threshold from traditional economic grievances to a more fundamental political critique:

> Five or six Mechanics who, by their meeting at some of their houses, and conversing about the enormous high Price of Provisions etc. − the gross Abuses this Nation labours under from the unbounded Authority of the Monopolisers of all Ranks, from the King to the Peasant . . . together with the Mock Representation of the People . . . concluded that nothing but Darkness and Ignorance in the People could suffer the natural Rights of every Freeman to be thus violated; and this excited them to invite and visit their Neighbours, whence a small Society of Twenty or Thirty commenced.[6]

These founding fathers of local radicalism were persuaded of the need to gather for reform by having read the first part of Paine's *Rights of Man* and 'naturally considering the Force and Weight of argument therein contained'.[7]

In December 1791 these Sheffield artisans published the first address of their Constitutional Society which, like Manchester, Warwickshire and others before them was reformist, yet reverential towards the constitution, wanting 'a speedy Reformation, and an equal Representation in the House of Commons'. There was little here to offend even the Associators of 1780 − except perhaps the social composition of the activists who, with the exception of a Quaker physician, described themselves as 'the lowest class of manufacturers . . . the inferior sort of manufacturers and workers . . . the least respectable part of the people'. The growth of their organisation was staggering. From the original handful it leapt to 200 within a month, 600 in the second month and to 2000 by March 1792. By the summer of that year the Home Office was told that 'about 2500 are enrolled in the principal society'.[8] To cope with this dramatic upsurge in membership the society formed divisions, or 'tythings' of ten which sent delegates to meetings along a delegated chain. Meeting fortnightly in taverns across Sheffield, one of their major decisions was to publish a cheap edition of the *Rights of Man*. They wrote to the SCI for advice and in reply Horne Tooke spoke of another society 'similar to your own in Sheffield' recently formed in London.[9] A few days later the Sheffield men received a direct letter from the society which was to transform and then dominate the next phase of English radicalism − the London Corresponding Society (LCS).

London was in every respect utterly different from any other urban area in Britain. Enormous, growing, the magnet for generations of hopeless and depressed peoples from around the British Isles, London's population (of about 750,000) was both varied and unstable. Indeed, as recently as 1780 the Gordon Riots had demonstrated both the turbulence of the people and the fragility of metropolitan control; the nightmare of a reprise of 1780 haunted the propertied orders as they looked nervously at France − and at the LCS − in the coming years. Poverty and distress were commonplace features of London life, but even the acute distress of 1791-2 (notably in Spitalfields) can hardly provide a sufficient explanation of the subsequent radical upsurge. As in Sheffield, late in 1791 a small group of London artisans drafted regulations for a new radical society. Thomas Hardy, a Scottish shoemaker who had educated himself in the 1780s by reading the tracts 'published gratis by the Society for Constitutional Information' showed their draft to Tooke, secretary of the SCI. Tooke corrected them in his own hand (thus laying foundations for the later myth that he founded the LCS). Using these rules as a basis, a group of friends met with Hardy on 20 January 1792 over cheese and porter and unconsciously imitated their counterparts in Sheffield 'with conversation on the hardship of the times and the dearness of the necessaries of life'. Discussing parliamentary reform, 'an important subject to be deliberated upon and dealt with by such a class of men', eight of these nine men formed the LCS to press for parliamentary reform. With eight pennies in the kitty, their campaign was launched.[10]

Word of the society spread rapidly, and so did membership. The original eight doubled at the second meeting, trebled at the third and by April 1792 hovered near the 100 mark. When in that month they began publicly to advertise their existence, the LCS faced similar problems to their Sheffield colleagues, namely how best to cope with a massive influx of members. The London society sensibly decided to model itself 'in imitation of the societies in and about Sheffield'. Taking the 'division' as the basic unit (with 16-45 members) delegates passed from a division to a weekly meeting from which other delegates went to a small executive committee. Membership was unlimited, and cost one penny, a price which made it accessible to most. Members and sympathisers poured in in unusual numbers to the taverns where they held their meetings, and in October-November 1792 divisions spawned new groups in abundance. By the end of the year about twenty-nine divisions were strung across the capital, though the bulk were concentrated in Spitalfields, with a total membership of around 800-1000. Hardy, overawed by the response, thought that 300-400 new men joined each week until November, though in such crowded scenes it was impossible to calculate accurately.[11] And it is also clear that large numbers of interested but unaffiliated artisans flocked to the meetings, helping to fill the smokey rooms to bursting point. But there was no doubt at all at the astonishment (and alarm) registered by contemporaries when they described the evolution and progress of the LCS in 1792. Their opponents were quite horrified to see the people enter politics in such numbers.

Two features impressed the LCS's opponents: the Society's size and its social composition. Impoverished artisans and working men — like Hardy himself — traditionally beyond the pale of politics, entered the LCS. And the sight of 'tradesmen, mechanics and shop-keepers' proved too much even for some of the older reformers.[12] All were agreed that the Society consisted of 'inferior people' who were variously described as 'the very lowest tradesmen', 'extremely low' and 'all inferior people'. The LCS took pride in the fact that it was 'almost entirely composed of that laborious and much neglected part of the community'.[13] Yet beneath this apparently uniform social surface LCS membership reflected the varied and colourful social gradations which marked off working men in London's various trades and districts. Skilled craftsmen and journeymen from the trades rubbed shoulders with small-scale employers (themselves, of course, working men) and with the human beasts of burden, the porters and ballast men of the riverside communities. Shoemakers, watchmakers, weavers, shopkeepers and publicans found them-selves in political harmony with their skilled or labouring neigh-bours throughout the capital. Naturally, certain divisions reflected local peculiarities. Some divisions were dominated by Irishmen, others by Scots.[14] No one division was typical, though some did provide a reasonable cross-section of the Society's members. Divi-sion 30, meeting at the West End home of Thomas Spence, num-bered among its thirty-four members four shoemakers, three linen drapers, two tailors, a bookseller, carpenter, a painter-glazier, a lace and fringe maker, a staymaker, a rag-dealer, a mercer and an accountant.[15] There was clearly a wide range of men and of occupa-tions affected by the sharp rise in prices and decline in real wages in the second half of 1792 and who turned to the LCS for redress and organisation. In the process the LCS began to speak with a collective voice for London's distressed artisans and, more generally, for the dispossessed throughout the nation.

Despite the humble origins of most LCS members many of its more prominent and best remembered members were of a higher social station. Maurice Margarot, chairman from 1792, was a flam-boyant lawyer with a privileged and international background. Similarly Joseph Gerrald, educated by Dr Parr, was a barrister with experience in the West Indies and America, and both were quite unlike the humble, self-educated Hardy, or indeed most of the LCS rank and file. But all were united in the need to reform Parliament, though in this they merely followed the demands of the Associators and the SCI. The LCS, however, presented a much more dishevelled appearance and a coarser voice to a generally hostile world.

For ideology they had available the political diet of Paine's first part and, like Paine, the LCS returned time and again to the idea that every civil right was gained by the exchange of a natural right. The LCS asserted its philosophy in its first public address of 2 April 1792. On entering society, they claimed, man

> gave up certain of his rights in order to secure the possession of the remainder and voluntarily yielded up only as much as was necessary for the general good — so that he may not barter away the liberties or his posterity, nor desert the common cause by lamely and supinely suffering to be purloined from the people of whom he makes a part, their natural and unalienable Rights of Resistance to Oppression and of sharing in the government of their country — without full and uninterrupted exercise of which rights, no man can with truth call himself and his country free.[16]

This insistence that no man could be bound by his forebears and that everyone had the right to resist oppression was distinctly Paineite. But in 1792 it was events in France which gave such an ominous ring to the LCS's words.

By the summer of 1792 the Society's regular pronouncements and spies' reports had made the LCS well known to the government. But to the government's mind what made the LCS appear even more sinister was the way the Society had become the centre of a web of radical contacts, both in the capital and throughout the country, helped initially by the SCI (though the older Society never supported the more radical Society's demands for annual Parliaments and universal suffrage). From the Southwark Friends of the People — similar in almost every respect to the LCS — the LCS acquired the one man, John Thelwall, who above all others came to personify the societies. By 1794 Thelwall was regarded by friend and foe alike as *the* spokesman for English radicalism, his lectures (later published) attracting vast crowds wherever he spoke, advancing radical argument while castigating an increasingly oppressive government. Thelwall did for radicalism what Thomas Clarkson did for abolitionism, by advancing its claims through an exhausting commitment to public lectures.

There were other London Societies which were secretly scrutinised by the government in 1792, yet by the end of the year only one, the LCS, appealed to a major constituency among the dispossessed. And to compound the fears of their opponents, the LCS seemed to speak for thousands of like-minded men throughout the country. But what gave impetus to the radical upsurge in 1792 was not so much the LCS as the publication of Paine's second part of the *Rights of Man*.

Since 1791 Paine had, in the eyes of a hostile press, become scribe and prophet of an English revolution and throughout the second half of that year he worked on a sequel to his part one. On 17 February 1792, part two was published, rapidly appearing in cheap and edited versions throughout the country. Continuing his attack on the constitution, Paine criticised the most hallowed of constitutional landmarks, including the Bill of Rights and Magna Carta. But, more significantly perhaps, he embarked on a critique of monarchy and its cost. At a time when the French monarchy was on the edge of destruction (and the author a well-known supporter of republicanism in France and America), the second part of the *Rights of Man* seemed to advocate a move towards republicanism in Britain. However extreme the logic of Paine's words, and despite the immediate hostility it aroused, the artisan radicals and many more besides devoured the book by the thousands. The figures are inevitably confusing — claims of upwards of 200,000 sold within the year are commonplace — but everyone was agreed that nothing quite like it had happened before.

The bitter complaints of Paine's enemies trace the trajectory of sales of the *Rights of Man*. One claimed that:

> not less than four thousand per week of Paine's despicable and nonsensical pamphlet have been issued forth, for almost nothing, and dispersed all over the kingdom. At Manchester and Sheffield the innovators bribe the poor by drink to hear it read.[17]

Walter Miller, a radical cabinet maker from Perth, told how he lent his copy to friends: 'they have already gone through about a dozen hands . . . I intend to spread them as far as my influence can go'.[18] For men like Miller and Thomas Hardy, men of independent education and radical sensibilities, Paine rapidly entered the pantheon of literary heroes and could be found on their bookshelves alongside Voltaire, Mirabaud and Shakespeare. Such literature formed the basis for local working-class self-education in succeeding decades.

Radical demands for Paine's book could scarcely be satisfied. From Sheffield came demands for 500 copies to be sent north 'by the flying Waggon'. To ease matters, groups published their own abridged versions for local consumption.[19] Few parts of the country seemed untouched by Paine's words; he was as ubiquitous as he was influential. In the Potteries, 'Paineite publications are in the hands of most of the people . . . particularly of the journeymen'.[20] By mid-1792 government and its supporters received regular and alarming reports of the degree of radical penetration. Moreover Paineite views had taken root and flourished, often without the existence of a local corresponding society. In Manchester it was claimed that the societies were affecting 'the minds of the lowest order of the people'. In Selby a group of men 'by their acts and conversations are doing what they can to disaffect the minds of their peaceable neighbours'. Even in rural parts disaffection was spreading among 'the lowest of the farmers and common people'. From Nottingham it was claimed that 'the minds of the people in the manufacturing towns . . . were . . . much disposed to embrace the levelling principles'.[21] There seemed no end to the damage caused by the tide of radical thought and activity which seemed to wash across the land in the course of 1792.

It was easy to find scapegoats. Most prominent were, inevitably perhaps, Dissenters and peripatetic preachers who, since the late 1780s, had been active both in the campaign against the slave trade and for the repeal of the Test and Corporation Acts. Symptomatic of this feeling, Gilray − that graphic barometer of the age − depicted Dr Price and Dr Priestley sitting in a room packed with gunpowder. Time and again Dissenters were blamed for spreading the radical word, as one man claimed from Cardiff where 'notions of disaffection is in great measure infused into the minds of the ignorant and unthinking by a sort of itinerant or dissenting minister'.[22] Sometimes the accusations were bizarre. In Liverpool it was claimed that Dissenting radicals consisted of 'schoolmasters and unitarian preachers of different Sectaries such as Presbyterians, Quakers and Jews'.[23] Dissenters were accused of distributing Paine in Wooton Underedge; in Plymouth the Presbyterians were blamed. From Hackney came complaints about 'certain Presbyterian Levellers'. In Huddersfield, apparently, the Methodists 'especially the lower sort' were to blame. Throughout the West Riding 'the followers of John Wesley . . . read and approved the works of Tom Paine'.[24]

Paine, naturally, was a marked man and on 21 May he was summoned to be tried the following month. On that same day a proclamation was issued against seditious writings.[25] In the short term the Proclamation gave the *Rights of Man* even more publicity and wider sales. The Home Secretary, Henry Dundas, thundered against Paine in the Commons; Paine replied with his *Letter to Dundas* which was, predictably, eagerly gobbled up by the reading public. The SCI alone distributed 12,000 copies to London, Sheffield, Manchester, Norwich, Cambridge, Derby, Great Yarmouth, Ipswich, Shrewsbury, Cheshunt, Maidstone and Portsmouth.[26]

What worried the government, as Dundas admitted in the Commons, was not so much Paine's book *tout court*, but its adoption by the reforming societies whence it was 'sedulously inculcated throughout the kingdom in a variety of shapes'. Waving resolutions from Sheffield radicals, Dundas told the Commons of the danger 'when great bodies of men in large manufacturing towns, adopted and circulated doctrines so pernicious in their tendency and so subversive of the Constitution and Government of this country'.[27] The government was clearly alarmed at the proliferation of artisan radical societies, and at their size, political stridency, and their political tactics. By the autumn societies in Norwich had 2000 members. In November there were forty separate radical groups in that town.[28] Founded late in 1791 by 'a working man[who] had read a great deal of history' the Norwich societies consisted mainly of 'the lower class'. A similar society in Derby in July was organised initially by two members of the SCI. A society in Nottingham — which raised 1000 names to a reform petition in a single week — was claimed to be the 'Poor Man's Virtue alone'. In Stockport the Friends of Universal Peace and the Rights of Man consisted of 'Yeomanry, Farmers, Manufacturers, Mechanics and Labourers', though their local opponents dismissed them as 'a small number of mechanics, servants in some of the cotton factories and labours [without] a man of respectability among them'.[30]

These and many more societies automatically turned to London, and initially to the SCI, for help and guidance, but by the autumn the LCS had become their main metropolitan correspondent and adviser. The government was quite right to think of that Society as the centre of a web of radically-minded clubs which were sustained by public disaffection and Paineite ideas. As if this were not serious enough, the corresponding societies began to turn to France.

The initial optimism invested in the early Revolution in France had rapidly dissipated by 1792. Early spring saw the formation of the emigré Doumouriez 'Patriotic Ministry', the French declaration of war on Austria and growing extremism in Paris. The Brunswick Manifesto (declaring a virtual state of war between the emigrés and the French people), the arrival of the Marseillais in Paris and the suspension of the king on 10 August were the prelude to the invasion of France, the September massacres and the abolition of the monarchy. At the centre of events stood the French Jacobin club. Yet, despite the violence and confusion, it was to France that the British societies now turned. Opponents of events in France were horrified to see large groups of lower-class Englishmen openly admire and liaise with French revolutionaries. In April 1792 two delegates from the Manchester Constitutional Society, James Watt and Thomas Cooper, were presented to the Jacobin Club by Robespierre. The address they presented from Manchester proved instrumental in converting English radicalism into English Jacobinism — at least in the eyes of their opponents. The Manchester men told the Jacobins:

> Our society will think itself happy to join its efforts to yours to spread the important principles of universal liberty, which alone can establish the empire of peace and the happiness of man on a solid and immovable basis.[31]

Replying, the President of the Jacobin Club seemed no less enthusiastic, declaring the

> English and French, reunited henceforth and for ever by the bonds of justice, humanity and the tenderest fraternity will fight together for the maintenance of their common liberties and the perfecting of their respective governments.[32]

The Manchester society, sensitive to the instant gale of criticism, issued a public reservation about events in France, but despite their disclaimers the result of the delegates' actions was to encourage other societies to follow suit. Moreover, Paine himself helped to focus attention on France, for he slipped away quietly to France to avoid prosecution. But he left behind his acerbic *Letter Addressed to the Addressers*. Tired of the circular and apparently fruitless pursuit of reform — courtesy of the parliamentary Whigs — Paine suggested the calling of a Convention to by-pass an obstructionist Parliament.

Elected by all men over twenty-one (no property qualifications needed), the Convention would draw up a new constitution. And on that radical note Paine took up his seat for Calais in the French Convention. Burke's early suggestion that the English radicals were in league with the French began to appear more and more convincing. Perhaps Burke was correct to think of the societies as 'Anglo-Gallican clubs', anxious to undermine British security. Even Pitt began to sympathise. The previously reforming chief minister declared in April 1792 (when discussing Grey's reform motion) that such a reform was 'a preliminary to the overthrow of the whole system of our present government'.[33]

The radicals' defence of France seemed ever more ambiguous. The SCI declared 'We now behold you a Nation provoked into Defence; and we can see no Mode of Defence equal to that of establishing the general freedom of *Europe*. In the best of causes we wish you success'.[34] A mere four months later this aspiration was fulfilled with the dazzling French military victories. There can be little doubt that the English radical societies were conscious of the importance and the success of the French radical societies. The Sheffield radicals, for instance, were keen to imitate the network of French clubs, 'for by this method France became so thoroughly united'.[35] They were even prepared to forgive the French their extreme measures. Had not the British had their own revolution a century before? The LCS was prepared publicly to justify the suspension of the French monarchy by arguing that the French 'like our brave ancestors of the last century . . . have driven out the family that would have destroyed them'. To their enemies this seemed to be a Paineite republicanism couched in terms of the (equally Paineite) right of resistance.

Radical sympathisers with France were given added reason for their support by the Brunswick Manifesto in August 1792 — a political mistake which helped to identify the king with the threat of a foreign invasion. The LCS remarked:

> If during this conflict with military assassins and domestic traitors, cruelty and revenge have arisen among a few inhabitants of the capital let us lament these effects of that bloody and tyrannous MANIFESTO.[36]

In August and September the LCS began a petition to the French. Signed by the LCS, the Manchester and the Norwich societies and the London Constitutional Whigs, the petition was handed to the

French ambassador, received by the Convention with acclaim, and widely circulated throughout France — all after the French had declared a Republic. In the process, the English radicals conveyed to the French a peculiar impression of English affairs:

> Information makes rapid progress among us. Curiosity has taken possession of the public mind; the conjoint region of ignorance and despotism passes away. Men now ask each other, What is Freedom? What are our Rights? French, you are already free, and Britons are preparing to become so.[37]

Not to be outdone, the SCI sent their own address to Paris carried by the attorney John Frost, who joined forces with the American, Joel Barlow. The intoxicating atmosphere of Paris clearly went to their heads, and in speaking to the Convention the SCI delegates outstripped their brief, declaring their belief that 'in a shorter time than we dare say, there will arrive from the continent addresses of solicitations to an English Convention'. The French responded in kind, declaring that 'doubtless the moment approaches when the French will felicitate the National Convention of Great Britain'.[38] English observers, always eager for news from Paris, could have been in no doubt that English radicals of all hues had openly admitted their ambition to imitate the French example. The SCI even resolved to send boots to the French army. And further petitions from radical societies continued to arrive in Paris.[39]

It is hard to imagine that throughout these friendly exchanges the *formal* political liaisons between England and France were disintegrating. It was the Convention which subsequently took France to war with Britain. Yet this was the same Convention which was so admired and praised by the radical societies. If further evidence were needed of the English radicals' apparently subversive intentions, the societies began to call for an English Convention. It was as if the radicals were intent on justifying Burke's worst forbodings.

In the face of such resurgent radical activities, the government did not remain idle. Regularly informed of the societies' activities by official spies and private informants, the government issued proclamations in May and December 1792 against seditious publications. They also prosecuted activists (most notably Paine), encouraged local action against radicals, and controlled an increasingly hostile press.[40] But all this proved inadequate. Dundas despaired:

unless something effectual can be done by Parliament to check the indiscriminate practice of association, they will spread the fermentation of the country to such a height that it will be impossible to restrain the effects of them.[41]

Pitt realised that, above all, the government needed political support from 'the higher and middling classes'.[42] The perfect answer took the form of the Association for the Preservation of Liberty and Property against Republicans and Levellers, founded in November 1792 by a government officer, John Reeves.[43] Though Pitt was unhappy with the idea of creating more public associations (even when they were loyalist) the Reeves Association and its hundreds of provincial counterparts were quickly organised by men of authority throughout the country. The loyalist movement ideally suited the government's purpose. Carefully expressed, organised and orchestrated, the Reeves phenomenon struck an amazing response in the English propertied class who were clearly anxious to strike a blow both for what they considered to be their beleaguered government and against the hitherto irresistable march of popular radicalism. The consequent loyalist associations which grew in much greater numbers than the radical societies themselves provided the enemies of radicalism with the means of beating the radicals at their own game. There was, however, no pretence that the associations would be democratic organisations — they were designed as small caucuses of local, influential men acting in the name of the 'public interest' to counter radical activity. This would, as Pitt told Dundas, 'have the Impression and Effects of Numbers on our Side' without the dangers of too much public agitation.[44]

However undemocratic, the loyalist associations were a remarkable phenomenon. Within months many hundreds had been established and had begun to overawe the radicals in the localities. They sometimes masked their proceeding with oaths of secrecy and resolved that local attorneys should not defend known radicals. Printers were intimidated; innkeepers were forced to close their doors to radical meetings. Loyalists even tried to persuade local magistrates (often, of course, their friends and fellow members) to extract oaths of loyalty from local radicals. They were in effect crude juntas of the local establishment — but this is not to deny their enormous success. In Manchester, for instance, Thomas Walker's political enemies formed an association, which survived until 1799

and which spawned no fewer than twenty-nine other loyalist associations in the area.[45] There was no doubt either about the social
groups the loyalist most depended on. One supporter confessed,
rather pathetically: 'I occupy too humble a situation in the community to presume at endeavouring to become a member of your
valuable Association'.[46] A familiar story unfolded across the country.
One association consisted of 'almost every gentleman and Yeoman'.
Another consisted 'principally of merchants'. Whatever their
origins, the associations fitted the political bill, as Reeves himself
confessed:

> they inspire confidence and they furnish strength to resist every
> attempt at disturbing the public peace and to aid the Executive
> power and the magistrates in preserving it.[47]

In order to neutralise the effects of radical literature the Reeves
Association published their own tracts (financed by public subscription) and, although the volume of these publications was impressive,
their quality was derisory and insulting to its potential audience.
Indeed the loyalist tracts tell us much more about their authors and
their views of the lower orders than anything else. Unattractive and
politically naïve as these tracts were, they signify the coming of age
of mass political literacy. Faced, after Paine, with the undeniable fact
of mass readership, the government and its friends, no longer able to
prevent or curtail popular reading, were obliged to try to channel
that reading into 'suitable' channels by providing the right kind of
literature. Hazlitt later wrote:

> When it was impossible to prevent our reading something, the
> fear of the progress of knowledge and a *Reading Public* . . . made
> the Church and State . . . anxious to provide us with the sort of
> food for our stomachs which they thought best.[48]

By the early months of 1793 men of authority were confident that
their activities had been successful in curbing radical enthusiasm.
The outbreak of war with France in February 1793 had greatly
helped the government's cause, for it restrained those radicals who
had previously admired and looked to the French. There were,
however, more specific reasons for a cooling of radical agitation in
1793. Local magistrates placed obstacles to radical meetings in public
or private. Newspapers refused to accept radical advertisements.
Thugs − and magistrates − brcke up radical meetings. In Man-

chester Thomas Walker had to repel a serious attack on his home launched by a loyalist–organised 'Church and King' mob. Nor was this violence exceptional, for from Novermber 1792 onwards organised mobs roamed the length and breadth of the country burning effigies of Tom Paine. By March 1793 there had been twenty–six such Paine burnings reported within twenty miles of Manchester.[49] Such incidents were often accompanied by violence, intimidation and general harassment of men known to be radical. Where local authorities were not active in organising and promoting the burnings, they stood idly by and watched the mob proceed with its activities. Local ministers, government officials, men of influence and substance all played their part (sometime paying the expenses) in supervising this populist outburst against local radicals. Yet there can be no doubt that these men were very successful in rallying large crowds against Paineite views and in favour of King and Constitution. There were undoubtedly large numbers of working men who, if not positively opposed to radical views, could easily be persuaded by anti–radical propaganda. Walker, a firm believer in the perfectability of man, thought that the loyalist violence was

founded upon, and comprized in, the want of a compleat and universal system of public education, why are the mass of the people, the poorer class, the swinish multitude, as Mr Burke contumeliously terms them, so generally adverse to their friends, so blindly the dupes of their oppressors? Because they are ignorant.[50]

When war was declared in February 1793, the enormous radical gains of the previous year seem to have been arrested; all that early buoyant optimism had been deflated by the joint pressures of formal government harassment and the orchestrated intimidation of the loyalists. In this process the country had become divided — more sharply indeed that at any time in living memory — between those who clung to an unchanged political system and those who sought to reform it. In the words of one loyalist tract: 'There is now a sort of line by which the friends of the Constitution may be distinguished from its enemies'.[51]

This was, of course, the ambition — and the achievement — of the Reeves movement: to single out, isolate, overawe and castigate their radical opponents as the enemies of the constitution. And as if to confirm these unrealistic views, the radicals continued, even after the outbreak of war, to appear to be influenced by the patterns of events in France. To the uncritical mind, there seemed ample evidence to think of these radicals as English Jacobins.

Chapter 4

ENGLISH JACOBINS

The corresponding societies were unsure about how to proceed with their agitation, but Paine in his *Letter Addressed to the Addressers* of September 1792 had already suggested a new tactic. Paine's belief was that 'a Convention of 1000 Persons, fairly elected, would bring every matter to a decided issue'.[1] In fact as early as May 1792 the Sheffield democrats suggested that

> the most likely and effectual plan will be to establish a Convention in London by delegates from each county or district, by which means the sentiments of the nation may be obtained without any confusion or disorder.

And this idea was further taken up by the Stockport radicals in September.[2] There was however nothing original in this concept. The Restoration of 1660 and the replacement of James II had been the work of Convention parliaments, while more recently the American Convention had been the forum for recasting the fabric of American politics. More directly the idea had been embodied in James Burgh's *Political Disquisitions* when he called for 'a GRAND NATIONAL ASSOCIATION FOR RESTORING THE CONSTITUTION'. Burgh's book and idea were extremely influential and can be seen more especially in Major Cartwright's *Take Your Choice* (1776) and in the Association movement of 1779–80.[3] Moreover, Burgh's influence went beyond his publication; tutor to Thomas Walker, friend and associate of Dr Price, his work was quoted liberally and reprinted by the SCI. Thus the concept of a radical extra-parliamentary gathering — whatever its title — was well-founded long before Paine gave the idea a new impetus and direction.

It was the calling of the French Convention (where Paine was a deputy) that seems to have been crucial. Six days after the French Convention held its first meeting, Stockport democrats suggested that they should follow suit. As a compromise however the corresponding societies opted merely to address the French — with all the attendant confusion and misunderstanding. But the most important step towards a Convention was taken in Scotland. There a

distinctive struggle for burgh reform had continued since 1784
which, as in England, had been transformed by Paine's *Rights of
Man*. The result was the proliferation of local radical societies,
headed by the Edinburgh Friends of the People.[4] Henry Dundas,
whose family dominated Scottish politics, was disturbed by the turn
of events in Scotland and his visit there in the autumn of 1792
stiffened his resolve. He saw two demons at work: the influence of
France and the political emergence of lower social groups.

> The success of the French democrats has had a most mischievous
> effect here. Did it go no further than give occasion for triumph to
> those who entertain the same sentiments here, there would be
> little harm, for they are very few in number, and but two or three
> of them possessed of any considerable influence or respectability.
> But it has led them to think of forming societies for reformation in
> which the lower classes of people are invited to enter.[5]

Despite Dundas' efforts some 260 delegates from eighty radical
societies met in a Convention in Edinburgh on 11-13 December
1792. Dominated by Lord Daer, the style and tone of the Convention
were unashamedly French. Deciding to adjourn to 19 April 1793,
members of the Convention passed a motion that 'all should take the
French oath to live free or die'.[6] The Scottish Convention thus
offered an example to its English friends – but it also further alarmed
the government about the apparent Frenchness of the emergent
British movement.

In England, however, in the spring of 1793 the impact of the
loyalists had severely hampered the radical cause. Not surprisingly
there was little enthusiasm for an English Convention. Instead, after
long correspondence between the societies, it was agreed to petition
Parliament; the abolitionists had after all been able to build up
enormous support by this means.

The reform petitions provided the opportunity to rally the radical
faithful in the spring of 1793. In May the societies rained their
petitions on Parliament. The LCS petition alone contained 6000
names; that from Sheffield 8000. The Edinburgh petition was 'the
whole length of the house'.[7] Though the societies were pleased with
their efforts, the number of petitions – and the names attached –
were far fewer than the abolitionists had mustered recently. The
outcome was, however, as predictable as it was depressing, and only
forty-one MPs could be found to support Grey's reform motion.
Democrats in Norwich asked the LCS how best to proceed: 'An

address to the King — futile; a petition to Parliament (as a conquered people) — tolerable; a National Convention (if circumstances admitted) — best of all'.[8]

Capturing this mood, Joseph Gerrald, a prominent LCS member, published a timely pamphlet, *A Convention, The only Means of saving Us from Ruin.* Gerrald, a former pupil of Dr Parr, had come to the LCS by way of the SCI. His pamphlet was direct and assertive, arguing that 'population not property is the basis of our plan'. His Convention would be elected by 'Everyman of the age of 21, who is neither a criminal, an idiot, nor a lunatic'.[9] Though his pamphlet gave Paine's earlier ideas a new impetus, it was events in Scotland in 1793 which gave reality to this rather abstract debate about a Convention. Although the English were now accustomed to intimidation, they were shocked by the subsequent trials (for sedition) of prominent Scottish radicals. Thomas Muir, perhaps the most influential Scot, was given a staggering fourteen years' transportation; he was followed by Thomas Fyshe Palmer, a Unitarian minister who received seven years.[10] Both were gifted, courageous, and moderate, men, transported for 'offences' which were committed daily by English democrats.

The sentences helped revive the English societies and forced Scottish and English radicals into each other's arms. When, later in the year, the Scots began to plan a further Convention, the English democrats, led by the LCS, made arrangements to send their own delegates. The LCS sent Gerrald and Maurice Margarot; the SCI Charles Sinclair; and Sheffield, Matthew Campbell Brown. Their task was daunting, for by crossing the border they exposed themselves to a more severe legal system. But to their enemies the most significant fact was that the Edinburgh Convention, when it reconvened in October 1793, labelled its proceedings 'First Year of the British Convention'.[11] Furthermore, the social composition of this gathering was different from the first; now, weavers, tailors, cobblers and other artisans characterised the ranks — and their political style seemed more extreme. Adjourning to April 1794 after a brief gathering, the Convention was hastily reconvened in November when the English delegates arrived. Later two delegates arrived from the even more radical United Irishmen in Dublin.

As soon as the Convention re-opened, Margarot and Gerrald emerged as its leaders. But it was, again, the style and vocabulary of the Convention which most alarmed observers. According to the

Report of the Committee of Secrecy of 1794, the Convention, 'in almost every Particular, assumed the Stile and Mode of Proceedings adopted by the National Convention of France'.[12] Delegates to the Convention conveyed a sense of 'Frenchness', and both LCS men were seized with the radical vice of self-dramatisation. In their minds there was no doubt at all that the Convention represented the people — a fact much emphasised by the prosecutions in the subsequent trials. And they resolved, should the Convention be interfered with, or foreign troops landed, that it would be 'a Signal to several Delegates to repair to such a place as the Secret Committee of this Convention shall appoint'.[13]

From the first, spies kept the government informed of the Convention's proceedings and it was but a matter of time before it was broken up and its leaders arrested. Gerrald, Margarot and William Skirving were charged with sedition. The new trials merely repeated the travesties of the Muir-Palmer proceedings, but with the added accusation of imitating the French Convention. Despite Skirving's natural humility and Margarot's flamboyance, both men were sentenced to fourteen years' transportation.[14] Convictions which, though hardly unexpected, persuaded the English societies to press for their own Convention.

The democrats had clearly begun to lose faith in Parliament. The LCS had come to learn 'not to expect grapes from thorns, nor figs from thistles'.[15] Many non-radicals were horrified by the Scottish sentences and other waverers began to drift back. Membership rose and divisions flourished. It was noticed within the LCS that 'the Rich now begin to come among us and to sit down with pleasure among the honest men with leathern aprons'.[16] Increasingly, the political debate centred on the question of a Convention and attracted ever more support. But of all the factors which propelled men back towards the societies perhaps the most important was hunger and distress, mentioned time and again in radical correspondence. Trade was depressed, work scarce and badly paid, and there was a notable decline in real wages. Whatever the objective realities, contemporaries blamed this deterioration on the war — a war, furthermore, waged against a country the democrats admired. Inevitably the war entered radical complaints and by 1794 anti-war sentiment had become a common theme in radical meetings and publications.[17] The Sheffield radicals complained that it was 'destructive of the Happiness, Commerce and Liberties of this Country', and hoped that peace would be followed by an alliance with France. Even government supporters could not deny the economic and industrial dislocation it caused.[18] There seemed little doubt that the war helped to complete the crude polarisation of English politics.

In the spring of 1794 another Convention seemed a perfect opportunity of rallying the radical discontent and feeling. Consequently on 14 April, 1794 the LCS held a massive meeting at Chalk Farm where for hours, on a hot sticky day, a massive crowd listened patiently, notably to the lecture by John Thelwall. They resolved to call a Convention and, less cautiously, passed resolutions which were destined to be misinterpreted. Their claims that any further infringement of the law 'ought to be considered as dissolving entirely the social compact between the English nation and their governors'[19] seemed to be a call for resistance to government authority. Government officials convinced themselves that spring that the language of the LCS had veered towards the violent, while their spies told of certain LCS divisions giving their members arms training.[20]

What worried the government in those months was not simply organised radical politics, but also the impact of radical literature and lectures. Three booksellers, Daniel Isaac Eaton, Thomas Spence and James Ridgway — all members of the LCS were, it was alleged, more frequented than any other bookseller's shop in London. But it was the amazing success of Thewall's lectures which provided an object lesson in successful radical agitation. Designed initially to raise funds for the LCS delegates to Scotland, so successful were they that they became a nightly feature in the winter of 1793-4, with capacity audiences wherever Thelwall spoke. Throughout, he had to contend with spies, magistrates and thugs. And his words reached an even wider audience in published form. Moderate in his demands for reform ('This then is the equality I mean; the equality of rights not of property'), Thewall's style and occasional outburst conveyed a much more revolutionary image. He claimed for instance to appeal to those who 'may be called the *Sansculotteries*', and proclaimed himself to be 'the only avowed *sans culottes* in the metropolis' and, further, 'in plain truth I am a Republican, a downright *sansculottes* though I am by no means reconciled to the dagger of the Maratists'.[22] What alarmed the government was his success in appealing to the 'lower orders'. Thelwall, it was claimed, proposes more to instruct the lower classes, than appeal to the reflecting part . . . hence the poison of this doctrine is more likely to be extensively propagated.[23]

Spies reported that his audiences, though 'by no means to be ranked with the lowest orders of people' none the less 'seem to be chiefly Tradesmen and artificers of a low description'.[24]

For such men there was an abundance of cheap literature written and published by men in and around the societies, all helping to further the democratic debate. Eaton's *Politics for the People*, for instance, contained some of the best radical journalism of the decade; irreverent, ribald, iconoclastic, it none the less made some of the most telling political criticisms of the 1790s. Anti-aristocratic and anti-monarchic, it often bordered on the revolutionary; 'Let them have rope enough and it may save us a deal of trouble'.[25] More sinister — to the government — were Eaton's frequent quotations from Robespierre.[26] Despite three prosecutions, Eaton refused to staunch the flow of biting radical ideas from his press. Yet even more trenchant was Thomas Spence who issued a stream of tracts, *Pig's Meat* and the *Poor Man's Advocate*, from 'The Hive of Liberty' in High Holborn. More extreme than Paine, Spence advocated the ideal of abolishing private property. Arrested four times, arraigned before three grand juries, Spence was only effectively dealt with when habeas corpus was suspended.[27] Harassed, yet irrepressible, Spence was eventually forced to sell his wares from a barrow.

London was, of course, the centre of the nation's publishing, but it was dispiriting for the government to realise that radical outpourings were issuing from all parts of the nation. The democratic spirit was generated — and was itself furthered — by a new brand of sophisticated radical journalism, notably in Sheffield, Manchester, Leicester and Cambridge. Overlooking the distinctiveness of these newspapers, which combined shrewd local interest with general radical zeal, the government preferred instead to regard them as being 'in the pay of Jacobins'.[28] The government thus did its best to bribe, sponsor and cajole the press (though this was not of course new) and to publish an outpouring of loyalist and sympathetic tracts.[29] Indeed nothing highlights more sharply the profound impact of popular radical literature than the enormous government efforts to counter it. Yet radical literature often flourished in direct proportion to the efforts made to hinder it.

In the spring of 1794 the government was clearly concerned about the radical drift of events — and the proposal to call yet another Convention. And there were even more alarming developments to consider: in Paris there were calls for an invasion of England, while spies reported arms training among London radicals. At the same time the government learned of a secret mission to England and Ireland by a British *emigré* in Paris, William Jackson, to assess the prospects for a French invasion. Jackson's correspondence and contacts were instantly available to the government and, despite his reassuring picture of a fundamentally loyal Britain, the very existence of this bizarre and utterly unrealistic mission proved the final straw for an alarmed government.[30] The government hestitated to act until it heard that Jackson's enquiries in Ireland had yielded encouragement from the United Irishmen. It was commonly appreciated that Ireland was *the* weak link in Britain's defence. If disaffection were ever to break out it seemed certain to erupt in that troubled island where the United Irishmen reflected the structure and ideology of the English democratic societies — though with the added bitterness of Irish separatism.

Late in 1794 the government arrested Jackson and his London contact, William Stone, a coal merchant known 'to be a man of Jacobin principles'. Stone's subsequent examination by the Privy Council merely proved what the government already knew but, more important perhaps, it gave substance to their long-standing but unproven suspicions that French invasion plans hinged upon an element of popular support in Britain.[31] In fact the evidence was unimpressive and came from a mere handful of uninfluential men. Whether or not, as has been claimed, the ministers were in the grips of a collective psychosis, they were forced to conclude that the English democratic movement was not only influenced by France but that it was also vital to French invasion plans. The Jackson mission clinched the government's case against the radicals. Unable to curb and silence the progress of democracy by traditional means, it used the pretext of French invasion to suspend constitutional safeguards and to break the back of the radical societies. Early in the morning of 12 May 1794, government officers began a sweeping arrest of prominent men in the LCS and SCI.

Thomas Hardy's home was ransacked and all the LCS papers seized; so too were those from the SCI. Hours later, a Royal message to Parliament noted that the societies intended to call a pretended Convention of the People . . . directly tending to the Introduction of that System of Anarchy and Confusion which has fatally prevailed in France.[32]

The Commons responded with a Committee to investigate the alleged conspiracy by examining the impounded papers. It was, sniffed Fox, 'made up of two characters; men who were dupes themselves or men who were willing to dupe others'.[33] Predictably, the Committee agreed that there was a conspiracy afoot — an opinion which swayed Parliament into suspending habeas corpus.[34] Thelwall, Tooke and other prominent members of the LCS and SCI were imprisoned; within two weeks thirty men were in gaol on suspicion of treason; eleven more were added later, and ten were arrested on less serious charges. A similar story unfolded in other cities where the societies flourished; some men fled to the USA, others were arrested, then released. The lesson was clear. Radical activity would lead to arrest, indefinite detention and resulting hardship for one's family.[35]

One by one the arrested men were paraded before the Privy Council (some of whose members were also on the Committee of Secrecy) and subjected to browbeating and ministerial bullying. Many proved more than a match for their inquisitors, others, understandably, wilted. Tooke was aggressive; Jeremiah Joyce refused to answer questions; while Thewall asserted 'It is not part of the law or constitution of this country that I should answer the questions of the Privy Council', and promptly turned his back on the gathering.[36] Spence predictably took the offensive, telling his inquisitors that 'If the burthens and grievances were not attended to they must look to the consequences'. While these examinations went on, the Committee of Secrecy poured over the impounded papers, issuing a Second Report in June associating the LCS with the arming of its members and with the Revolution in France.[38] In truth the Report was a politically-motivated jumble of assertions, but its effort was calculated, and successful. To *The Times*, the Report established

> most incontestably the real existence of a PLOT ripened for the execution, to bring about revolution in this country with a view to destroy under the artful pretext of reform in Parliament, the Constitution of Great Britain.[39]

Newspapers throughout the country had been claiming much the same all summer.[40] The apparent virtue of the Report was that it gave documented proof to inchoate suspicions and fears. Thereafter opponents of the radical cause could merely point to the Report as evidence and proof that the societies were subversive and acting in slavish imitation of the French — if not in their pay.

Not surprisingly, the arrests alarmed the democrats and they were afraid to meet. The SCI disappeared completely, to re-emerge on only one future occasion. By mid-summer the LCS was in disarray, with only sparsely-attended meetings, though their proceedings were instantly reported to the government by spies.[41] But the remnants regrouped, re-organised the society's structure and issued new reform proposals, arguing for equal constituencies and universal suffrage. In fact these ideas were now very close indeed to the proposals of the Sub-Committee of Westminster first published in 1780, and later reprinted by the SCI and LCS.[42]

The LCS was afraid of spies and collaborators; 'BEWARE OF ORATORS' was placed above the president's chair and they even devised an elaborate system for trying suspected traitors in their midst. The first proceedings under this new system against the spy Groves resulted in his acquittal: his first act was to inform his ministerial pay-masters.[43] From that time forwards, and for the next half century, the government spy, agent and *provocateur* was to be a recurring feature in radical and working-class movements, debilitating their strength and distorting their image in the eyes of successive governments.

The future of the radical cause — to say nothing of the arrested men — clearly hinged on the forthcoming treason trials. The presiding Lord Chief Justice decided *before* the trial, however, that 'the parties were guilty of high treason'.[44] The prospects seemed gloomy when on 28 October 1794 Thomas Hardy's trial began at the Old Bailey (though not before prolonged efforts to secure a 'reliable' jury).[45] Hardy faced nine indictments detailing the charges that he had planned the king's death. The opening prosecution speech took nine hours to deliver and the trial lasted nine days. Throughout, LCS papers were misrepresented by the prosecution. Paine's name was frequently used and much play made of the contacts with France and the plans for a Convention. However the prosecution case was, at best, only circumstantial and was, along with their witnesses, thoroughly discredited by the brilliant defence offered by Thomas Erskine.[46]

The populace of London summoned up their traditional radical fervour, hemming in the court building and packing its public benches throughout the trial – abusing and vilifying the prosecution. Local officials in the capital were alarmed at the prospect of a conviction, for there were, they claimed, 'a great number of jacobins from the Country Societies who added to these in Town are ripe for any disturbance or mischief'.[47] The verdict of not guilty (the jury foreman promptly fainted) produced massive scenes of celebration on the streets of London. Boisterous crowds swept Hardy away in triumph, and in the day's ensuing turmoil twenty-six were arrested, mainly 'of a middling and inferior Condition of Life . . . of the whole number only one of a low cast'.[48] The news spread throughout the country, and newspapers gave the result the sort of coverage they normally reserved for military victories.

Convinced the Hardy's acquital was due to 'some accidental feeling, prejudice or misapprehension, in the breasts of those particular jurymen, or some of them',[50] the government decided to press on with the other prosecutions. They ought to have known that Hardy's acquittal had set a precedent. Twelve days after Hardy's acquittal, Tooke's trial began. Both sides remained much as before, and again Erskine's defence was outstanding, though not as memorable as Tooke's own behaviour. Throughout the defendant conducted himself

> with a great air of unconcern, and passing his snuff-box about the court, was sometimes disposed to be sarcastic upon the law officers of the Crown and upon the Bench itself.

At one point the Attorney-General was literally reduced to tears. Pitt – called as a witness – cut a very sorry figure in Court.[50] After eight days, the jury took only six minutes to reach their verdict of not guilty. It was received with a 'roar, or rather *convulsive scream of joy* . . . The cheering soon was caught by the attendant populace without, on whom it had an electric effect.'[51] Despite this second rebuff, the ever-optimistic government pressed on with Thelwall's trial which followed the by-now familiar routine, though shorter. His acquittal was expected.

The other prisoners were now released, signalling an end to the government's attempt to halt the democratic movement by legal proceedings. In the process the societies had, however, been halted in their tracks, the prisoners subjected to intolerable conditions in prison and their families reduced to penury. It was a high price to pay for demanding no more than Pitt himself had advocated a mere decade before. It seemed bitterly ironic that men who (rightly) viewed their proposals for reform as rootedly and immovably British should find themselves tarred with a French Jacobinical brush. They may have been careless and naïve in their praise for and dealings with the French, but these were hardly offences which warranted the charge of treason. Yet we need to remember that the shadow of France was largely responsible for transmuting English democrats into English Jacobins and for distorting the judgement of the government and its friends. It is hard to deny however that those outsiders who best knew the true nature of the democratic societies — the government officers with access to regular spies' reports and, later, to the societies' own papers — chose deliberately to distort the evidence before them in order to destroy their domestic political enemies.

The euphoria of the acquittals soon evaporated, but to Francis Place, a young breeches maker recently won over to the LCS (and whose views and documentary collections have so shaped historical perceptions of that society), thought that the society had been greatly improved by these purges: 'as most of these who joined it were of decided character, sober, thinking men, not likely to be easily put from their purpose'.[52] In fact the society had very few members, but nature came to the society's assistance. The fearfully cold winter of 1794-5, followed by a hot summer, led to a disastrous harvest, and hunger and starvation spread throughout the country. By the summer of 1795 ever more hungry men turned once again for redress to the LCS. Across the land, with regional variations, the hunger in the summer of 1795 brought violence in its train. Time and again local crowds (sometimes aided by the very troops deployed to control them) seized foodstuffs and sold them at what they considered to be a 'fair price'. The tenuousness of government control was once more starkly revealed, nowhere more so than in London where memories of 1780 still haunted the propertied mind. Charitable effort did little to alleviate the hunger, helping instead to highlight its extent.[53] Not surprisingly the LCS began to register this distress both in its political pronouncements and in its accumulation of new members. In May 1795 Place thought that some 2000 men attended; by the end of that summer there were sixty-five divisions. The actual membership may have been anything between five and ten thousand; but whatever its size, it is also clear that its meetings were swollen by even greater numbers of interested by-standers.[54]

Thelwall was back at his best, hectoring vast crowds with highly effective lectures which later appeared in *The Tribune* (running from March 1795 to April 1796). In the troubled climate of 1795 his words struck home in audiences anxious to hear their complaints articulated by so powerful and telling a critic. But like the LCS (and indeed like most of the press until the autumn of 1795), he believed that the prevailing hunger was man-made. Opinion began to shift in the autumn when it was finally appreciated that a genuine food shortage did actually exist.[55] Long before then the LCS had taken its grievances to the public in the first of a series of mass public meetings which marked a shift in the style and potential of radical politics.

Large public meetings had been organised earlier by the LCS but in the main the society had concentrated its politics on internal debate, lectures and publications. To appeal to a wider public, in such volatile conditions, was to raise the political tempo and heighten government concern about both radical politics and public safety. In late June a crowd, 'the largest ever assembled on any occasion', gathered in St George's Field to hear LCS speeches. Chaired by John Gale Jones, a 'shabby genteel' surgeon, the meeting attacked the war, the government, and even the king, blaming the food crisis on the war and avarice. The crowd was told 'YOUR CHIEF, PERHAPS YOUR ONLY HOPE, IS YOURSELVES'.[56] Confidence flowed back to the society, and to the provincial societies who picked up their correspondence with the LCS. The story was the same everywhere; local radicals determined to tap the groundswell of discontent but were often overawed by 'a banditti of armed ruffians [so] that the least word spoke in public is dangerous'.[57] It seemed like a reprise of 1792, though now the situation was much more explosive. Throughout there was of course that plethora of radical publications which flew off the London presses feeding the popular appetite for cheap radical information and criticism. Place, meanwhile, struggled within the LCS to maintain the image (and the reality) of peacefulness and moderation. Ultimately however his efforts were simply overwhelmed by hungry desperation. It is significant that irreligion and freethought now featured in LCS affairs; this was after all the year of Paine's *Age of Reason*, published by Eaton and designed as a blast against organised religion and priestcraft. The power of irreligion within the LCS became so strong as to drive out colleagues who felt their religious sensibilities offended.

In the autumn of 1795 the LCS narrowly decided once more to appeal to the public and on 26 October at Copenhagen Fields from 9 am to 5 pm LCS speakers addressed a crowd of between 100,000 and 150,000, all of whom remained peaceful throughout.[58] They passed a remonstrance to the king calling for reforms, but it was Thelwall's lecture which particularly captured the mood. Denouncing the recent food riots, he argued.

> It is not a crimp, it is not a baker, a miller, or a maltster no nor even a few despicable and avaricious monopolisers — those are not the authors of your sufferings . . . It is therefore the system you must reform.

What Thelwall argued for was straightforward enough:

> if you procure that weight and balance which you ought to have in the representation and legislation of your country — if you obtain annual parliaments and universal suffrage it will be no longer in the power of a worthless set of beings to crimp, starve and murder you.[59]

No dissenting voice was heard from the vast crowd listening to Thelwall and it is clear that, once again, the LCS had stepped forward to speak for the distressed and the dispossessed. It was as if those beyond the political pale had found their political voice in the LCS; a voice moreover which, in increasingly strident tones, offered a case for reform which was both rational and convincing. Indeed it was these qualities of rationality and reasoned argument which particularly disturbed opponents who were accustomed to characterising the common people as brute and irrational. The LCS thus marked a profound transition in British politics, for it registered for the first time in modern history the emergence of an articulate political voice from below.

The democrats had been able to campaign publicly in 1795 because in July of that year the suspension of habeas corpus had lapsed. An opportunity once more to curb radical agitation presented itself only three days after the massive LCS meeting. The king on his way to open Parliament was hissed and booed. A stone hit his coach and he was forced to return home in a different carriage. It is quite clear that the crowds were demanding food and peace, but this incident provided the opportunity the government needed. A proclamation was

issued against seditious assemblies and the 'Two Acts' were introduced specifically aimed at the societies, banning all meetings of
more than forty people and licensing lecture halls. It was, as Gwyn
Williams has written, 'the most serious invasion of liberties since the
Stuarts'.[60] Try as they might to deny any connection with the attack,
the LCS was damned, in official eyes, as the agent of unrest which
had, in some indefinable and unspecified way, encouraged an
'attack' on the king.

In November and December 1795 radical and liberal sympathisers
rallied to the (forlorn) task of resisting the passing of the Two Acts.
Fox was indefatigable in leading parliamentary opposition. Even the
SCI and Wyvill joined the struggle. Coleridge, far from London,
was conscience-striken about his own inactivity:

> Was it right
> While my unnumbered brethen toiled and bled
> That I should dream away the entrusted hours
> On rose-leaf beds, pampering the coward heart
> With feelings all too delicate for use?[61]

The 'attack' on the king also revived loyalists who responded with
meetings, pamphlets and protestations of loyalty, though on nothing like the scale of their radical opponents. Nothing however quite
caught the public eye like the LCS, whose public meeting of 12
November drew a still bigger crowd. The throng was addressed
from three tribunes, Thelwall moving from one to the other. The
meeting denied any connection with the attack, and petitioned
against the Two Acts. As before, the massive assembly dispersed
peacefully.[62]

Agitation against the Acts produced a united front among groups
long separated by the repercussions of the war. There emerged, for
all too brief a period, a unity of middle-class parliamentary reformers and plebeian agitators. A debate was organised on the
question 'Are not the most probably means left of saving the
Country from the Despotism of the Minister — an immediate junc-
tion of the Whig Interest and the Corresponding Society?'[63] It was,
however, an aspiration which — with the exception of the campaign
against the slave trade — was not to be fulfilled for more than three
decades. Some radicals were unhappy about taking politics on to the
streets of London. William Godwin, whose *Political Justice* of 1793
(though not as important as Paine's work) had made a greater impact
than is sometimes allowed, took the LCS and Thelwall to task for

collecting of immense multitudes of men particularly when there have been no persons of eminence, distinction and importance in the country, that have mixed with them, and been ready to temper their efforts.[64]

For their part the LCS felt that 'there is not but one alternative, Liberty and Reform or Encroachment and absolute Despotism'.[65] They convened yet another public meeting to petition the king. On 7 December another huge crowd assembled in Marylebone Fields where Thelwall, though 'emaciated and labouring under severe indisposition', again played a crucial role.[66] Once again, 'The conduct of the multitude was temperate and orderly. They signed the papers in great numbers and separated in good order and without the least tumult'.[67] Eleven days later, however, the Two Acts received the Royal Assent, instantly rendering illegal the existing tactics of popular politics.

These measures were to be the cornerstones of future repressive legislation against democratic and working–class organisations, stretching through the Four Acts of 1817 and Six Acts of 1819, as far as the conviction of the Tolpuddle Martyrs thirty–eight years later. Understandably the Two Acts entered into the demonology of English radicalism and into the bitter memories of working–class politics. The government had tried every means at its disposal to curb the popular radicalism which centred on the corresponding societies. Despite legal and social intimidation, restrictive proclamations, legal proceedings, contrary political pressure and manipulation, Pitt's government had failed to staunch the radical tide. Indeed in many respects its tactics had been counter–productive. Moreover the dislocation of the war and the hunger of 1795 had given added drive to the radical cause. Ultimately, however, it was only the force of repressive legislation (and the willingness of the radicals to accept the rule of law) which purged the nation of the most obvious manifestations of radical agitation. Yet the radical experience of 1791-5 could not be utterly erased by legislation, even if driven underground. But for the time being the results of the Two Acts devastated the radical movement. Within weeks the LCS disintegrated:

the number of members rapidly declined and the whole of the labour and expense fell upon a comparatively small number. The consequences were the same all over the country, the reformers were disappointed in their expectations, no reforms had been obtained, some thought it dangerous, others that it was useless to meet again, and the whole matter fell rapidly into decay.[68]

English democrats had been damned as English Jacobins. Wilberforce — active for Pitt in his Yorkshire bailiwick — expressed the feeling perfectly, claiming that the radical had excited

> a contempt for the British Constitution and an attachment to those false principles of liberty which had produced such extensive mischief in a neighbouring country; nor was it only French politics which they imported into this country, but French philosophy also; in the numerous publications by which their opinions were disseminated, there was a marked contempt for everything sacred, an avowed opposition to the religion, as well as the constitution of Great Britain.[69]

British radicals must have despaired. Would they and their arguments never be viewed on their own merits? Were they always to be dismissed so haughtily as the spokesmen of French abstractions and to be consigned into illegal limbo for events they had no hand in? By Christmas 1795 the English radical movement, so powerful, promising and original, lay in pieces and, although no one could have known it at the time, it would be a full generation before anything comparable would again surface in British politics. Despite the democrats' efforts, reform seemed further away than ever.

Chapter 5

MUTINY AND REBELLION, 1796–9

The democratic movement collapsed after the passing of the Two Acts. By March 1796 the LCS had fewer than 700 members on its books; and by the end of the year only 200.[1] Very few members attended meetings and it is scarcely surprising that those tough-minded men who, in the teeth of legal danger persisted in their radical activities, were generally untypical of the former membership. In the truncated remnants of the Society the voice of moderation was silenced and the Society's proceedings became more reckless. But the LCS was also unlucky. To contact provincial democrats the LCS sent out delegates – John Gale Jones to Kent, and an Irishman, John Binns, to Portsmouth. These journeys were to take on a totally different complexion when, within the year, naval mutinies broke out from the bases visited by the LCS delegates.

Prominent democrats faced difficult and harrowing times. Thelwall was assaulted and hounded in East Anglia, the Midlands and the North before quitting for the peace of Wales.[2] Coleridge chose to publish a radical literary journal, *The Watchman*, but his journey through the Midlands and the North left him with little hope for the democratic cause.[3] In the Midlands Jones and Binns had better fortunes, though the crowds they attracted to various Birmingham taverns clearly infringed the restrictions of the Two Acts. They were inevitably arrested and had to wait twelve months for their trials: Jones was gaoled, Binns acquitted. Their arrests however confirmed that the only safe, surviving outlet for radical activity was publishing. Yet even this was precarious. It was costly to publish, difficult to sell, and almost impossible to distribute, as Coleridge had discovered. The LCS, none the less, decided to launch its own publication, *The Moral and Political Magazine*, which ran from 1 July 1796 to May 1797.[4] The magazine, however, merely compounded the Society's financial problems. Ironically, the Society's desperate search for money – to finance both the ill-fated publication and the defences of Binns and Jones – revealed a heartening degree of radical activity in the provinces.[5] Yet little could be done to provide these men with help and leadership from the capital.

War and internal security continued to dominate political and social life. Though the government had initiated tentative peace negotiations, these collapsed in April 1796. French armies swept into Italy, where Napoleon first revealed his remarkable talents. The British for their part could take little comfort from their successes in South Africa and Asia — and none at all from the disasters in Haiti. In Europe the French were in astonishing and apparently unstoppable ascendancy and, though the threat of a French invasion of Britain seemed remote, it was a nightmare which haunted the British government. Accordingly, in the autumn of 1796 the government launched a military expansion to resist any threat of invasion — or internal upheaval. After yet another abortive attempt to negotiate peace through Lord Malmesbury, the country settled into a gloomy mood, expecting the worst from the inevitable sharpening of hostilities.[6] The last weeks of 1796 proved dreadful. Malmesbury's failure coincided with a financial slump (the worst since the American War), a run on the Bank of England, discontent in the army, and the first signs of serious trouble in the navy — to say nothing of the threat from Ireland. In the words of the *Annual Register*, 'the wild and darkening forest threatened to close around us'.[7] Persevering democrats who demanded peace found their pleas rejected both in times of peace negotiations and when the government rededicated itself to war; in the one, their demands were said to jeopardise the negotiations, in the other they were alleged to be sympathetic to the enemy.

The French seemed to come to the assistance of the government's argument. On 21 December 1796 a French invasion fleet of thirty five ships and 12,000 men appeared off the south-west coast of Ireland. The expulsion of the English and a French-inspired republic in Ireland would have left mainland England outflanked and exposed. Fortunately a 'Protestant Wind' scattered the fleet within sight of Bantry Bay and the ships returned to France. But the lesson was patently clear to the British government.

In the spring of 1797 the critics of government were in total disarray. The LCS for instance was reduced to a few dozen members.[8] Fox had abandoned Parliament completely, and there was no clear focus for opposition to the government and its policies. What opposition did exist was scattered by subsequent events in the navy. In the spring of 1797 mutinies broke out at the Nore and at

Spithead, coming perilously close to destroying the defensive shield which kept out the French.

Trouble in the navy was endemic. Harsh conditions, poor pay (always in arrears) and draconian punishments were commonplace. But these problems were accentuated in the war years by the rapid build-up and expansion of the service. After 1793 there was a massive growth in the numbers of ships and a consequent over-crowding of vessels. The influx of 'quota men' large numbers of whom were Irish — in conjunction with the overall deterioration in conditions provided all the necessary ingredients for trouble below decks. By 1796 the Admiralty was receiving regular reports about the extent of naval disaffection — but nothing was done. In April 1797 ships at Spithead mutinied, petitioning for better conditions, and a month later, and more seriously, the fleet at the Nore joined in. The essence of their case was clearly 'industrial', but the style of their behaviour and the language they adopted were redolent of the corresponding societies and popular democracy. Doutless there were many in the navy who, in the age of the rights of man, saw no reason to abdicate their rights simply by serving at sea. But to their opponents, the connection seemed even more direct. Had not Binns and Jones, still waiting trial in Birmingham, tried their corrupting tactics at Portsmouth and the Medway towns? Had the sailors not used the radical device of petitioning? In June 1797, Pitt hinted that 'Our indignation should be more active against the seducers than the seduced and the misguided'.[9] Years later, Binns did indeed admit that he had 'visited the dockyards, naval depots and some of the largest ships afloat and on docks, naval and mercantile', while Jones confessed to visiting one ship on the Thames.[10] But it is incon-ceivable that the mere visits and words of these minor figures could have produced such far-reaching consequences. Democracy and even revolutionary ideas were often discussed in the nation at large, and there is no reason to suppose that the navy could remain immune from the debate, especially in the light of the influx of new men.

The LCS was instantly suspected of fomenting the troubles; the mutineers used the terms 'delegates', symptomatic, it was thought, of LCS influence. A government investigator, despatched to Ports-mouth to probe the matter, could find no direct link.[11] It is true, as the spies told the government, that sympathy for the mutineers was widespread within the LCS, but this was as understandable as it was insignificant.[12] The conclusion of the investigating magistrates was crisp and assertive: they did not believe that

> any club, or society in this kingdom or any of those persons who
> may have found means of introducing themselves to the delegates
> have in the smallest degree been able to influence the proceedings
> of the mutineers, whose conduct from the beginning seems to
> have been of a wild and extravagent nature not reducible to any
> sort of form or order and therefore capable of no other mischief
> than was to be apprehended from a want of the fleet to serve
> against the enemy. [13]

It was not in the government's political interest, however, to explain
to the public that the mutinies were merely industrial. It suited its
purpose to develop the by now well-worn theme that the country
was dangerously beleaguered at home and abroad, surrounded by
the agents of international Jacobinism on all hands. This was the
view concisely expressed by the 1799 Report from the Committee of
Secrecy, which saw in the mutinies

> a spirit, in itself so repugnant to the habits and dispositions of
> British sailors, which must have had its origins in those principles
> of foreign growth, which the societies of the conspirators have
> industriously introduced into this country. [14]

It was hoped to purge the naval distempers by exemplary punishments of the ringleaders. Richard Parker, the most prominent and in
many respects most gifted man, was hanged on 30 October. In
subsequent weeks, he was followed by thirty more; others were
flogged, twenty four imprisoned and 180 consigned to the hulks. [15]
And yet, in that same month, the fleet put to sea and destroyed the
Dutch fleet at Camperdown, removing, for the time being, the
threat of invasion. Thus in the winter of 1797–8 England appeared
safe. But what a remarkable transformation had taken place — only
six months before the navy had seemed to be the weak link in the
defensive chain.

It seems strange that the government should continue to worry
about the democratic societies in 1797 for they had, as the spies
clearly told ministers, ceased to be of any real significance. When in
July the LCS decided to call another public meeting, the gathering
was watched over by 200 constables and 6000 soldiers. [16] The leaders
were arrested before anything of significance had taken place. None
the less, *The Times* alleged of them that 'though acquainted with the

elements of their native language they are minutely skilled in the motley jargon of Revolutionary cant'.[17] The surviving active democrats were keen to show their continuing commitment to reform, but the government knew full well that the LCS was minute, divided and insignificant. Social and economic conditions ought to have revitalised the society, as they had in 1795, but the fact that no one was able to capitalise on current unrest is indicative of the effectiveness of the Two Acts in undermining popular radical politics.

By the end of the year the LCS was shorn of its moderate men and had fallen into more desperate and sometimes cruder hands. There was a widespread suspicion that the Society had dabbled in the naval mutinies. Another member, Henry Fellowes, had been convicted of circulating seditious literature among troops in Kent. And, to cap it all, the society seemed to have been taken over by Irishmen more concerned with Irish freedom than parliamentary reform. Just when the country seemed rid of its naval dangers the problem of Ireland once more presented itself as the most serious threat to the security of England itself.

The Irish had long been a feature of British urban life. As often as not they lived in desperate straits in the poorest quarters of the cities, the object of traditional English ridicule and antipathy. Unable to survive on their own land, much of which had been appropriated by Englishmen, the Irish were rarely able to do more than scratch a minimal survival from the harsh work they found in English cities and at harvest-time. Moreover thanks to English policies and land-holdings, the Irish had been rendered alien and alienated in their own country, a fact which dominated Anglo-Irish affairs in 1798. Of course the origins of the long-standing Irish troubles were complex, but in the short term they were transformed in the years of the American revolution. American privateering, threats of a French invasion and the English inability to raise troops for Ireland (the bulk being tied down in America) forced the English to admit Irishmen into local defence units in 1779. By 1780 there were no fewer than 100,000 such 'Volunteers'. In those politically sensitive years, the Irish began to demand their own rights and, though the Catholic Relief Acts of 1779 and 1782 gave some satisfaction, the most pressing problem for the Irish remained the harshness of daily life itself. Irish Protestants however, alarmed at what they took to be the rise of Catholic demands, began to edge towards the English government.

Thus Protestants and Catholics began to form their distinctive political groupings. Protestant secret societies, the 'Protestant Boys', forced the Catholics to establish their own defence groups, 'The Defenders', with consequent ghastly terrorist and intimidatory tactics used by the one side against the other. Political sectarian feeling ran high, but beneath it all slumbered the long suffering, oppressed peasantry beset by conditions unparalleled in western Europe.

The news of the French Revolution and the impact of Paine transformed the Irish political scene. Belfast Protestants, led by Wolfe Tone, created the Society of United Irishmen in 1791 to press both for full Irish nationalism and for reform. In June 1792 the Society's paper, the *Northern Whig*, declared:

> Although Ireland will be the great object of the paper, yet *America* and *France* shall not be forgotten — America and France long suffering under the arbitrary supremacy of Britain, and with a generous concern did Irishmen anxiously attend to the conflict that established American freedom.[18]

Perhaps the most striking feature of the initial United Society was the alliance of Catholics and Protestants. It was, however, a fragile unity which camouflaged the painful divides so exacerbated by the secret societies in the 1780s. There was, none the less a unity of sorts, based on a democratic sensibility which aimed at an extension of the franchise, Catholic emancipation, and an end to English domination — though this last point was played down. The United Society aimed, in the words of Napper Tandy, one of its early leaders, 'to make a United Society of the Irish Nation; to make all Irishmen Citizens, all Citizens Irishmen'.[19]

The war in 1793 polarised feeling even more sharply. Pitt, understandably, was determined that the Irish discontents should not be exploited by the French. Yet it was the Irish, not the French, that he needed to look to. Independent of the democratic movement, the Irish peasantry had begun to stir itself, goaded both by the worsening conditions, and by the persecutions suffered by the Catholics at the hands of the newly-created Orange lodges. Defenders became bolder, more desperate and more savage, and in 1792–3 sectarian attacks, reprisals and judicial revenge cast a deathly shadow across Ireland. Thousands of Catholics fled south from Ulster, and by 1796 the Lord Lieutenant of Armagh could write: 'It is no secret that a persecution with all the circumstances of ferocious cruelty . . . is now waging in this country'.[20] Under such pressures, the initial, though admittedly tenuous, bi-partisan political democracy crumbled away, though some assumed that this was the deliberate work of the government. Yet much of the violence and bitterness between the two sides (and against the English) took place quite independently of the United movement. Indeed, though the movement was similar to the English corresponding societies, the government — regularly informed by its spies — was aware that soon after the outbreak of the war, the United movement was at a low ebb. As in England, however, the significance of the movement was transformed by its dealings with France.

Agents from France had regularly reported to Paris on the state of Irish disaffection, though they were generally too optimistic about the potential for revolution or independence. But it was the Jackson mission of 1793 which so damned the United Irish, as indeed it did the English societies. The result of Jackson's arrest was the flight of a number of prominent members, the establishment of an efficient spy system, and mounting government propaganda against the Society. The United Irishmen were henceforth declared illegal, and the cause of Irish reform and democracy rendered impossible by legal means. From the fragments of the old movement there emerged, in 1794-5, a qualitatively different United Society — one pledged to seek 'A Republican government and separation from England'.[21] They knew, however, that their best hope lay in securing French assistance. After all had not the French already toppled the *ancien régime*, not only in their own country but throughout Europe? The Irish sectarian groups agreed in 1795-6 to unite their feuding members against the English. Now, however, the English felt themselves threatened not so much by the Irish, as by the French.

Wolfe Tone landed in France from the USA in February 1796 with a brief to recruit French support for the Irish cause. Though faced by enormous difficulties and frustrations, Tone's persistence and energy caught Carnot's attention, though the French were also negotiating with other emigré groups. By July the French had begun to prepare an invasion under General Hoche. In the event, as we have seen, the threatened invasion was thwarted by bad weather. The experience of Bantry Bay frightened the English who embarked on a repressive policy in Ireland throughout 1797. While apparently effective in the short term, it did little but contribute to that spiral of terror which was to lead within the year 'to the worst display of savagery Britain had witnessed since the wars of Cromwell'.[22]

When the next French invasion fleet sailed it did so from Toulon — to Egypt; but the earlier prospects of French help, and the subsequent English repression, had helped to stiffen Irish resistance to the English. From first to last, the government's spy network kept the governments in Dublin and London informed of the activities of the United men. Inevitably perhaps, it was widely believed that the French lay behind the troubles. Pitt was informed that, 'This cause is an attachment to French principles in politics and religion . . . and an ardent desire for a republican government'.[23] The truth was quite different. The Irish problem was made worse in 1797–8 by the fearful rapaciousness of the English army (which consisted largely of Irishmen). Throughout the spring of 1798 reports to the government uniformly spoke of the spread and severity of disaffection and of the grip of the United Irishmen. Often, however, the Society's leadership had little control over the course of events in the localities, particularly among the peasants. What erupted in 1798 was in fact an unprecedented outburst of popular, violent discontent.

In the spring of 1798 the United Irishmen were spurred on by rumours of yet another French invasion plan. The Society was put on a more organised military footing by the romantic Lord Edward Fitzgerald, using the political structure of the earlier years (so similar to the English corresponding societies). From an early date there had been a close connection between the LCS and the United Irishmen and in January 1798 the remnants of the London society published, an *Address to the Irish Nation* which expressed sympathy for the movement and for Ireland.[24] Not surprisingly, throughout Britain there were groups of Irishmen who supported the United cause and it is quite clear that a chain of activists linked radical groups in the mainland cities with their more desperate comrades in Ireland.[25] Moreover, in the spring of 1798 invasion by France seemed to threaten England as much as Ireland, and even the English radicals debated what their response should be in this event. The LCS, for instance, declared that its members would join the local Volunteers. But in the middle of this debate, in April 1798, the remnants of the LCS were arrested by the Bow Street Runners.[26] That the government should even concern itself with this tiny handful of men seems strange unless we recall that they were closely associated with the

Irish and the Irish troubles.

Thomas Hodgskin, an LCS member arrested in 1798, said the government believed the LCS 'occasionally assumed a different name, *viz*. the United Englishmen'.[27] And it was this 'takeover' of the radical movement — or rather what was left of it — by the United movement which caused such alarm. In the summer of 1797 there had been evidence of fugitive Irishmen, perhaps 600 strong, in a society in Liverpool, with sympathisers in Stockport.[28] The news got progressively worse for the government. Early in 1798 they heard about the mission of Father O'Coigley, travelling on behalf of the United Irishmen between Liverpool, Manchester, London and Europe. Meeting members of the corresponding societies, O'Coigley was heading for France. The information painted a gloomy picture: sixty-seven divisions of United men in Manchester; delegates travelling to Scotland and Ireland; fund-raising in Liverpool and Stockport.[29] O'Coigley also met men in the LCS (in a division renamed a United English division) and there seems little doubt that by early 1798 some of the former LCS men and groups had gone over to the United cause.[30] But the English United men seemed strongest in and around Manchester and, with the threat of invasion in the air, reports about radical activities became ever more alarmist. There were stories of Jacobins in Bolton ('even our Sunday Schools have become in some instances the Seminaries of Faction') while in Manchester it was claimed there were 20,000 United men.[31]

Uncertain of these reports, the government sought clarification from Thomas Butterworth Bayley, a local magistrate, luminary, and former Wilkes supporter. Initially sceptical, Bayley soon changed his mind. Interrogating a local informer, Bayley was told of eighty divisions of the LCS United movement in Manchester, with delegates travelling to friends in Leeds, Halifax, Sheffield, Nottingham, Bolton, Preston, Kendal, Carlisle, Glasgow, Norwich and London. It was claimed that delegates from Manchester went as far afield as Cornwall. There was even talk in Stalybridge and Audenshaw of killing the king — though it seems unlikely he would ever pass that way.[32]

Much of this evidence seems fanciful — the traditional, inflated work of informers whose credibility often depended on exaggeration. Yet, given the ease with which O'Coigley travelled and the friendly reception he received, the government was unwilling to remain doubtful. On 18 February O'Coigley was arrested, along with Arthur O'Connor of the United Irishmen and John Binns of the LCS, when about to embark from Margate for France. Among their papers was discovered an address to the French Directory from the 'Secret Committee of England' pleading for a French invasion and promising that 'Englishmen will be ready to second your efforts'.[33] O'Coigley paid with his life. In the time between his arrest and execution (February–June 1798) Ireland erupted into open revolt.

The Irish soldiers of the English army broke the back of the United movement in Ireland by systematic terror, using horrendous floggings of innocent and guilty alike to extract information. These floggings, which literally tore the victims to pieces, and the wide-scale attacks on property, forced men into open revolt. But, as ever, informers fed back to the government the daily plans of the organisers. On 24 May the Dublin leadership gave the order to rise, but the resulting revolt was fragmented, ill-planned, uncertain, divided and doomed to failure. The army's retribution was terrible and lucky were the people who died quickly in a military engagement. Wherever revolt — or support for it — broke out, the army unleashed the worst horrors of a punitive civil war. Moreover, it was unleashed indiscriminately on anyone within reach. The armed forces were seized with a blood-letting which was to leave an indelible memory on the Irish nation.[34] The rising in Wexford was perhaps the biggest of all, led by a marauding and aimless army of 3000. Inevitably, they meted out to their enemies a savage punishment which reflected the bestialities they had experienced from the government forces. The insurgents' bravery was to prove no match for the more disciplined forces of the government. The rebels were finally and bloodily cowed at the Battle of Vinegar Hill late in June 1798. There followed, again, the sickening tale of reprisals. Throughout the rebellion it is quite clear that many more people died in cold blood than were killed in military action.

Throughout those terrible months the government received disturbing news about sympathisers in England; someone even tried to persuade ministers of an arms cache in Wigan.[35] More worrying still, they were told that the United movement had even penetrated the armed forces — a worry all the more acute in the light of the naval mutinies.[36] In April therefore the suspected men were arrested, but their activities subsequently proved to have been much less significant and widespread than feared. In London, as we have seen, the remnants of the LCS were rounded up. The results of those arrests, as Duke of Portland wrote, were 'the dispersion of those Societies and the seizing of so many of their leaders'.[37]

Even then, spies' reports continued to tell alarmist stories of LCS and United activity throughout 1798 in London (including stories about arms and drill practice). Rumours of 15,000 Irishmen in London keen to contact 'Jacobin societies of Englishmen and Scotsmen', may have seemed absurd,[38] but given the ability of Irishmen to melt into their protective ghettoes, who could ignore such rumours? Moreover, the government received numerous reports from an agent in Hamburg telling of Irishmen and Frenchmen crossing to Britain, often with plans for disruption.[39] On the whole, however, the government was kept abreast of events, thanks to their spies and agents reporting from Ireland, Paris, Hamburg and, of course, from the Irish haunts in London. These years confirmed the government in the justice of using and persisting with its spy networks. For all its failings — mainly those of exaggeration — it provided the government with a regular supply of information. Thus there evolved a system of political espionage which, in the changed circumstances of the next century, was to develop into an abused and utterly misleading instrument of political investigation and manipulation. In the 1790s, as a wartime measure, however misconceived, wrongheaded or simply inaccurate, this flow of information meant that the government was rarely more than one day behind events in the radical societies.

If, in retrospect, the number of suspects and the degree of subversion reached nothing like the scale predicted, it was perhaps understandable that the government, in the fearful climate of 1798, should expect the worst. At the time the government thought itself hemmed in by a series of related threats — Ireland in revolt, gaps in the armed forces, peripatetic agents linking Ireland, England and France. Indeed, the fear of French invasion together with support for that idea in Britain, was, in essence, the same much feared connection between France and the British democrats which Burke had first spelled out and denounced in his *Reflections*. The United movement, however distorted by the spies, seemed to add further strength to this traditional fear. In the words of the *Anti-Jacobin Review*:

> The existence of a Jacobin faction, in the bosom of our country, can no longer be denied. Its members are vigilant, persevering, indefatigable; desperate in their plans and daring in their language.[40]

In fact this 'Jacobin' faction was insignificant and was, in any case, swamped by a wider and contrary nationalistic feeling which united the nation in the face of a French invasion threat. So confused had the political issues become that the term 'Jacobin' was used to describe all forms of dissent, no matter how insignificant. Even the Irish revolt was dismissed as 'nothing more nor less than a mere *Jacobin* conspiracy'. One corollary to this view was that anti-French sentiment was a patriotic duty:

> To cherish an Anti-Gallican spirit has, in all times, been deemed an effort of genuine patriotism, a mark of love for one's country, which distinguishes the true-born Englishman from the mongrel cosmopolite.[42]

The events of 1798 paved the way for the complete outlawing of organised radical politics throughout Britain, for it seemed clear to the government and its friends that, despite the arrests, there was a continuing rumble of discontent which found expression wherever Irishmen gathered in English cities. Moreover, they continued to meet and aspire to political organisations which seemed to be modelled on the corresponding societies. Despite the fact that theirs was a political twilight world, unable to act publicly and incapable of real political action, it was the very existence of such organisations which alarmed the government. Keeping a close watch on their proceedings was clearly not enough; the government would be much happier to erase all traces of radical politics. Thus in March 1799 yet another Report from a Committee of Secrecy set the scene for a final legislative attack on the democratic movement.

The thrust of their argument was to claim that France had manipulated the British radical movement in order to undermine the British constitution. Reviewing the past decade, the Report asserted that every form of dissent and unrest was attributable to the sinister influence of the corresponding societies and the United men. Wisely, the Committee refused to cite the evidence for such assertions. The conclusion was predictable:

> they cannot forbear particularly and earnestly pressing their unanimous opinions, that the system of secret societies . . . cannot be suffered to exist in these kingdoms.[43]

Parliament, of course, agreed and in July 1799 passed the Corresponding Societies Act:

from and after the passing of this Act, all the said Societies of United Englishmen, United Scotsmen, United Irishmen, and United Briton, and the said Society commonly called the London Corresponding Society, and all other Societies called Corresponding Societies, of any other City, Town or Place, shall be and the same are hereby utterly suppressed and prohibited, as being unlawful Combinations and Confederacies against the Government of our Sovereign Lord the King, and against the Peace and Security of his Majesty's liege subjects.[44]

As effective as this legislation proved to be, events were to show that the democratic experience of the past ten years had left a mark on British society which could not be easily erased by mere legislation. Of course the social and economic conditions which had nurtured the democratic movement also survived. But those men who wished to register a dissenting voice and who wanted to argue the case for democratic change knew that their formal complaints would now be illegal. Henceforth, and for the best part of a whole generation, popular radical activity entered a secretive subterranean phase which was to last until the even more troubled years of post-war dislocation after 1815.

Chapter 6

THE TRADITION PRESERVED

The repressive legislation introduced at the end of the 1790s to counteract the 'Jacobin' agitations of that decade hampered but did not totally destroy the reform movement. Open political action could not entirely be suppressed so long as the electoral system, however restricted, continued to operate; but the effect of the legislation on the more radical reformers was to drive them underground, where their ideas and organisations were subject to infiltration by both revolutionaries and spies, who filled the government with alarm. At the same time the economic distress usually associated with high food prices was being compounded by the effect of the long war on the economy, and by the transformation of industry through the introduction of new machinery and the extension of capitalistic control over labour processes. In the quarter of a century which followed the publication of Burke's *Reflections* and Paine's *Rights of Man*, Britain experienced rapid social change. The foundations of a new industrialising and urbanising society were laid; class was born; and democratic politics were rooted in the fertile soil of economic and social protest. By the end of the war the reforming tradition of the years of the American and French Revolutions had not only been preserved but also changed and enriched.

The resignation of William Pitt in March 1801, the ending of the suspension of habeas corpus, and the Peace of Amiens in March 1802 inspired reformers with new hope, and the general election of 1802 gave some slight comfort to the Foxite Whigs but any optimism expressed at this time was premature. The war — and Pitt — soon returned, and it was not until the change in ministry following Pitt's death in 1806 that Whig ministers, open to considering some moderate degree of reform, briefly obtained power. This Grenville-Fox 'Ministry of All the Talents', though, was a half-hearted affair with the Grenville Whigs unable to accept the need to reform Parliament, and the Foxite Whigs unwilling to press the issue. The chief advance came in the matter of the slave trade when Parliament was brought to accept the principle of abolition following the revival of the agitation against the trade in 1804. Fox's death in September, however, followed shortly by the dissolution of Parliament, gave an opportunity to the political reformers to express themselves at the polls.

Fox had sat for the City of Westminster, and the radicals had hopes that Sir Francis Burdett would stand. Burdett had been elected for Middlesex in 1802, but had then been unseated on petition, and had narrowly been defeated in a by-election there in 1804. He declined to stand in 1806 at the Westminster by-election, and the radicals were outmanoeuvred by the Whigs into allowing the government candidate, Lord Percy, an uncontested victory. At the general election a month later things were to be very different. The subsequent events of 1806 and 1807 were to mark a turning point in the development of the reform movement.[1]

First, Burdett emerged as the leading representative of popular radicalism in the Commons. His experiences as MP for Wilkes' old seat of Middlesex had disillusioned him with the Whigs, from whom he now broke completely. Secondly, the events of the by-election of 1806 stirred William Cobbett to write in his *Political Register* an influential open letter critical of the Whigs and challenging to the radicals. Cobbett had been pro-war and tory in outlook, but since 1804, when he had been prosecuted for libelling the Lord Lieutenant of Ireland, had become more openly hostile to the government and to those features of the political system which he identified as 'corruption'. At the general election of 1806 he offered himself at Honiton, where the gross venality of the small electorate convinced him of the need for parliamentary reform. Thirdly, the fiasco of the Westminster by-election, and the sight of the Duke of Northumberland ladling out beer to the mob, brought Francis Place back into politics. With the collapse of the London Corresponding Society into extremism under Thomas Evans' leadership in 1797, Place had retired to concentrate on his business as a tailor, which since 1801 he had been building up at his shop at 16 Charing Cross Road. Now Place, Cobbett and Burdett were all moving into a formidable partnership.[2]

Westminster was a scot-and-lot borough with a relatively open constituency of some 10,000 electors. At the 1806 general election Burdett himself nominated James Paull as the radical candidate in opposition to the Foxite Whig, Sheridan. Paull had become established in the popular esteem for his attempt to impeach the Marquess

Wellesley for his treatment of the Nawab of Oudh. Burdett stood again for Middlesex, this time as an independent, anti-corruption candidate, spending nothing on his own campaign — in marked contrast to the fortune he had spent in 1802 and 1804. Neither he nor Paull was successful. Nationally the position of the Whigs was strengthened, and they put forward moderate proposals to extend the civil rights of Roman Catholics. Such a policy was anathema both to the Tories and to the Court, and in something of a palace *coup* Grenville's ministry was replaced by one headed by the Duke of Portland. To strengthen his position the latter called a further general election in 1807.

This time, after some hesitation, Burdett agreed to let his name go forward for Westminster. With the full support of Cobbett's *Political Register* and Place's organising genius, Burdett was overwhelmingly successful, amassing more votes than the three unsuccessful candidates put together, despite the fact that he himself fought no personal election campaign at all. This was done for him by the Westminster Committee, largely Place's creation, which organised the support, brought out the voters, collected funds, and secured the result. The beginning was not auspicious. Paull, who was to have contested the other Westminster seat, quarrelled with Burdett, the two men fought a duel in which both were injured, and Place's committee was forced to drop Paull who not long afterwards committed suicide. Support was given instead to Lord Cochrane, an independent Whig. At first Burdett trailed in the polls, but gradually Place was able to rally the radical voters, and their candidate edged ahead. His popularity was undoubtedly great: in 1798 he had taken up the cause of the political prisoners held without trial in Cold Bath Fields prison, and his unseating from Middlesex, reminiscent of the Wilkes affair, was popularly attributed to corruption in Parliament. His victory in 1807, with the second seat going to Cochrane, thus excluding both Whig and Tory candidates (and Paull), made the Westminster Committee an inspiration to the revival of independent radicalism throughout the country. For example, a resolution of support came from Bristol where Henry Hunt marked his entry into radicalism by chairing a dinner to celebrate Burdett's victory.[3]

Burdett, like Wilkes, occupied an ambiguous position with respect both to his popular followers and to reform. He was rich (having married the heiress Sophia Coutts), proud, unpredictable and disdainful; but like Wilkes he also had the ability to seize on issues which would feed his popularity. This had been true of his support for the political prisoners and was again exemplified in 1810 when John Gale Jones, one of the militants of the London Corresponding Society, was committed to Newgate by the House of Commons for breach of privilege. Burdett moved in the House for his release, and published his criticism in Cobbett's *Political Register*, itself an act which the Commons condemned as a breach of privilege. But rather than submit to the Commons, Burdett barricaded himself inside his house in Piccadilly and declared that the Speaker's warrant was illegal. Crowds of supporters gathered in the street, troops were called, and Cochrane dreamed up a hare-brained scheme for rescuing the beleaguered MP by force, while Place conceived a peaceful plan for using the City authorities against the government as Wilkes had done. But before this could be tried the troops had broken into the house, seized Burdett (who was busying himself reading Magna Carta with his son!) and carried him off to the Tower. The similarity to Wilkes' case was ended only when the government wisely refused to declare Burdett's seat vacant. While in prison he managed to quarrel with Place over a misunderstanding which led him to believe that Place was a government spy, and the two men were not reconciled until 1819. Despite this, Burdett and Cochrane were returned, unopposed, at the 1812 general election, and 'the people' retained their two eccentric and rather dubious parliamentary champions.[4]

Fortunately the reform movement in parliament was not left entirely in their hands. Not all the Whigs were as lost to the cause as radicals like Burdett sometimes believed them to be. Samual Whitbread, Charles Grey's brother-in-law, who had been left out of Fox's ministry in 1806, and who was then passed over for the leadership of the Whigs in the Commons on Grey's elevation to the Lords, was an independently-minded opponent of corruption in government and an advocate of educational and Poor Law reform; while Sir Samuel Romilly, who had been Solicitor General in the 1806 ministry, was a noted legal reformer. There was also a group of mainly Tory Evangelical reformers, led by the Pittite William Wilberforce, who sought the abolition of slavery and the reform of public morals.[5]

Place's shop in the Charing Cross Road was only one of the forums where the worlds of parliamentary and extra-parliamentary pressure-group radicalism met. Another was Jeremy Bentham's house in Queen's Square Place. Here the circle of Philosophic Radicals extended not only to Romilly and to James Mill, but also to

Place whose intellectual development in the nineteenth century was much influenced by the connection. Bentham did not believe in 'natural rights', but his theories could lead to a democratic programme of reform and a critical questioning of every institution in the land — parliament, the Church, the universities and the legal profession — which put the Benthamites among the most radical of all reformers. They were certainly more radical than an old traditionalist like Major Cartwright or even a younger one like Cobbett. Yet there were also profound differences between the Philosophic Radicals and the growing popular radical movement, and Place (sometimes uneasily) acted as a bridge between the two.[6]

Events in London and Westminster, however important in the development of the reform movement, were not the whole story, though, for that provincial opinion which had emerged in the later eighteenth century was becoming increasingly uneasy about government wartime policy. An early expression of this new provincial opinion had been the General Chamber of Manufactures of 1785, formed to represent to Pitt the manufacturers' views on commercial policy, and in the period 1811-12 this tradition was continued with a successful campaign to secure the abolition of the East India Company's monopoly of the India trade. Neither of these issues transcended matters of commercial policy to infringe upon politics, though some of the leaders, such as the Birmingham banker Thomas Attwood, were shortly to become prominent radicals. But this was less true of the agitation conducted against the war itself — and particularly against the Orders in Council — which reached a crescendo in 1811-12.[7]

Radicals who had denounced the war in 1793 had been regarded as unpatriotic Jacobins, but by 1796 stagnation in trade had brought some manufacturers to oppose the war too and by 1800 Wilberforce could gloomily estimate that three-quarters of West Riding manufacturers were in favour of peace.[8] New taxes, such as the duty imposed on raw cotton (1798) and imported wool (1803) were very unpopular, but despite such grumblings British manufacturing industry was generally expanding and trade was flourishing. All this seemed threatened in 1807 when the Orders in Council were introduced in the economic warfare with Napoleonic Europe. Not only was European trade threatened but also, because of the implications for West Indian trade, there was friction with the United States which led to a closing of the American trade in 1811. This was a disaster for both employers and their workforce, with important implications for radicalism at all levels. In 1808 an agitation against the Orders, in which Henry Brougham took a leading part, was unsuccessful, but by 1811 there was a severe recession coinciding with famine-level food prices after a run of bad harvests. Brougham and Attwood led the campaign, and in June 1812 the Orders were revoked – too late, however, to prevent a war with America which was not ended until 1814.

This agitation had been political in the sense that it had aimed to change an item of government policy, but most industrialists had not yet reached the conclusion that Parliament itself needed reforming. When Christopher Wyvill had called a County Meeting in York in 1795 to protest at the Two Acts, the clothiers had been loyal to the government, and this situation was changing only slowly, *pace* Wilberforce's alarm in 1800.[9] One straw in the wind came in Leeds where, in 1801, Edward Baines acquired the *Leeds Mercury* and made it the mouthpiece of the new industrialists who, unlike the older generation of Tory merchants, were inclined to be Whig in their sympathies. Gradually Baines became convinced of the need for reform, though he had the wisdom not to advocate it openly until after the war, bearing in mind the fate of such journalistic critics as James Montgomery of Sheffield in the 1790s.[10] In Sheffield itself, with its much more forceful tradition of radicalism, the Burdett riots of 1810 led to a petition of 8000 signatures condemning the House of Commons; while Daniel Sykes of Hull, who chaired a reform meeting in Sheffield, wrote to Wyvill in May 1810 that the Burdett affair 'has excited now for the first time in all the populous parts of the nation a wish for reform'.[11]

The popular demand for reform had never been entirely quelled by the legislation of the 1790s, and it was soon to re-emerge when favourable opportunities presented themselves. Reformers like Wyvill and Cartwright were still active, though the former, representing the old 'country' attitude to reform, was highly suspicious of the lower orders and democratic notions of reform. Less open and less easy to detect was the surviving tradition of revolutionary activity associated in the late 1790s with the United Irishmen, which emerged briefly in such episodes as the Despard conspiracy of 1802 and the Luddite disturbances of 1811-12.

The significance of the Despard affair is unclear, and historians have been much divided in their interpretations. Some see it as an isolated attempt at a *coup d'état* planned by a disillusioned former army officer — the last dying twitch of the revolutionary fringe of the 1790s.[12] Others see it as much more serious — merely a part (and not even the major part) of a more widespread and organised revolutionary conspiracy, and the beginning of a new form of physical-force radicalism which was to re-emerge at intervals over the next half century.[13]

Edward Marcus Despard was an Irishman, born in 1751, who rose through military service to become Governor of Honduras in 1784. Six years later he was recalled and dismissed without compensation, having found himself on the wrong side from Lord Grenville in a dispute among the settlers. Nursing his grievance, Despard became associated with the United Irishmen, and in April 1798 was arrested and held in Cold Bath Fields prison during the suspension of habeas corpus. His case was one of those taken up by Burdett who stood surety for him on his release. On 19 November 1802 Despard and a group of about thirty conspirators were arrested at the 'Oakley Arms' in Lambeth. He was charged with high treason and, on the evidence of some of the conspirators who had turned King's Evidence, found guilty. Despite a character reference from his former colleague-in-arms, Lord Nelson, and despite a rider from the jury on this account recommending mercy, Despard was executed on 21 February 1803. Many radicals, including Henry Hunt, believed him to have been innocent, the victim of *agents provocateurs*.

Behind this Despard story, which might superficially be represented as the tragedy of a demented and embittered man, lay a much more complicated series of events. There is evidence that as early as June 1797 Despard held some sort of organising position between the Irish and the French, though it is unclear whether he was actually a French agent. At the time of his arrest in 1798 he was a member of the central committee of the United Britons, involved in the plan for risings in Britain and Ireland to assist an invasion by the French. After the collapse of the Irish rising in 1798 and the failure of the French invasion plan, the United Irishmen continued to hope for a simultaneous rising in both kingdoms. This was encouraged by the growth in popular unrest during the grain crisis of 1800–1, and by the release of political prisoners in March 1801. Among those who now resumed their revolutionary careers was Thomas Evans of the London Corresponding Society and, possibly, Despard.

Despite the Peace of Amiens, plotting continued for risings in support of a French invasion. Despard, who had apparently retired to his family estate in Ireland on his release, returned to London and was seen in several public houses among company not normally associated with a gentleman of his position. As a former soldier he appears to have been given the task of spreading disaffection among the troops who guarded Windsor and the Tower. Some of the guards seem to have been won over and been eager to make a start on the revolution. Despard appears to have been persuaded to abandon the plan for a co-ordinated rising and instead agreed to lead a *coup* to coincide with the opening of Parliament on 23 November. By this time, though, his conspiracy had been detected by government agents and hence Despard and his fellow-plotters were arrested on 16 November. These events probably upset the plans of other English revolutionaries, though the Irish persisted until their rising, led by Robert Emmett, went off early in July 1803 while a French invasion force was still mustering at Boulogne. None of this wider context to Despard's conspiracy was mentioned by the prosecution at the trial, though the evidence for it now seems substantial. One reason for this, suggested by Edward Thompson, is that the government was anxious to avoid any embarrassing details which might endanger the cover of spies or the fragile peace with France. Something else which was not made clear at the time, though magistrates' spies were aware of it, was the extent to which the conspiracy reached beyond London and the Irish to the English provinces which Despard had hoped his *coup* would inspire to general revolution in 1802.[14]

Lancashire had been a centre for the United Britons in 1797-8, when a native local leadership seems to have emerged including such men as William Hanson of Bolton, William Cowdry of Manchester, and William Cheetham who was sufficiently important to be detained during the suspension of habeas corpus. The background to continued radical activities in Lancashire was the unrest associated with high price of provisions in 1800-1, and the plight of the cotton handloom weavers whose real wages had fallen since the start of the war.[15] Magistrates, alarmed by the reports of their spies, were expecting a rising in the summer of 1801. There is evidence of continued organisation amongst former United Britons in both Lancashire and Yorkshire on which Despard pinned his hopes, and these extreme radicals appear to have infiltrated the wider organisations of labour which existed for trade purposes. The Combination Acts of 1799 and 1800 played into the hands of these extremists by emphasising the common illegality of both political and trade organisation. 'The republicans are drinking Mr Pitt's health', reported one government spy in 1799, as they seized the opportunity to channel economic grievances into the cause of political reform.[16]

Much of the evidence for a widespread conspiracy in the provinces is circumstantial or suspect. The evidence of spies is notoriously unreliable but not *ipso facto* untrue. Undoubtedly there was some activity of a revolutionary nature amongst former United Men, but the extent and significance of this is disputed. Edward Thompson tentatively gives credence to the possibility of a revolutionary conspiracy in Yorkshire, and this has found some support in evidence relating to Sheffield where, after the uncovering of the Despard conspiracy, two men, William Lee and William Ronkesley, were arrested and later transported.[17] In themselves these events might not seem significant, but the plotting in Yorkshire appears to have been inspired by the better organised men of Lancashire; there does seem to have been some awareness of what was happening in London; and the whole can be put within the wider Franco–Irish context of invasion and rebellion. What, then, emerges is a very real threat to the domestic peace, though hardly sufficient within England itself to constitute the basis of a widespread popular rising. Despite the material hardships of the poor and the reality of the revolutionary underground, such extremist physical–force activity was to persist only on the fringes of English political life, fed from time to time by the more serious revolutionaries of Ireland.

What lends the events of 1802–3 additional significance is the existence of later evidence linking men who had been involved with Despard with renewed attempts at subversion after 1815, and even with the clouded events of Luddism during 1811 and 1812.

Luddism, which at its peak coincided with the agitation against the Orders in Council and the worst provisions crisis of the entire war period, is as difficult to interpret as the wider ramifications of the Despard conspiracy, and historians have been no less divided. The basic question is, were the Luddites engaged in a purely industrial struggle, as Malcolm Thomis amongst others has argued, or were they part of a wider revolutionary political movement, as Edward Thompson has suggested?[18]

At the heart of Luddism lay not only opposition to new textile machinery but also disquiet among workmen who felt they were losing control over their own labour even in their own homes, and frustration at the apparent indifference of the government to their deteriorating position. The precise form which these grievances took varied according to which branch of the textile industry was concerned, but the reaction was similar throughout the main areas of activity in the east Midlands, south Lancashire, and west Yorkshire. Everywhere working men met in secret, in public houses or on the moors, took oaths, smashed the machinery of notable offenders against their code, and then merged back into their sympathetic communities leaving few clues, for either contemporaries or historians, as to what was going on. The hosiery industry of Nottinghamshire, Derbyshire and Leicestershire experienced no new technology, and remained based on the domestic outwork system until the middle of the nineteenth century. Nevertheless the domestic framework knitters were as much the employees of the capitalists from whom they rented their frames and received their raw materials as were the lace-workers whose industry was rapidly being transferred into factories after 1780. Both the lace and stocking industries were suffering from intense competition leading to cost-cutting and the production of inferior goods. The workmen chose as their leader Gravener Henson, a fellow framework knitter and a largely self-educated man, who attempted to organise the workers in both the lace and stocking trades into a union. A strike was attempted in 1810 but failed as the depression associated with the Orders in Council cut demand and employment, and the union then turned to Parliament for protection against those abuses to which they attributed so many of their troubles. The Statute of Artificers (5 Elizabeth c.4), on which many prosecutions of strikers were based, also contained clauses governing apprenticeship and the level of wages, and this created the expectation that Parliament would legislate in a paternalistic way. As recently as 1765 and 1773 Acts of Parliament had been passed which fixed piece-rates for the Spitalfields silk weavers and empowered justices to enforce them. In 1811 the framework knitters, led by Henson, formed a nationwide society to secure parliamentary relief, with a central committee based in Nottingham, which asked for legislation fixing piece-rates, forbidding 'truck' payments, and outlawing such abuses as the production of 'cut-up' stockings, made in one piece and then cut to the required shape. Their Bill was emasculated in the Commons and destroyed in the Lords by a Parliament which shortly afterwards did pass another Bill favourable to the masters which made frame-breaking a capital offence. Frames were smashed in 1811 and again on a large scale in 1814, though it is unclear whether Henson and the central committee were behind these outbreaks of Luddism. Circumstantial evidence suggests they could have been: the outbreaks followed the failure of the attempt to secure a political remedy, though Henson did not give up trying, and he could easily have been drawn into the violence; his own deliberate silence on the matter is suspicious. Whatever the truth may be, nothing could save the poor stockingers. The change in fashion from knee-breeches to trousers was undermining the market for high-quality products and accentuating the emphasis on cheap, low-quality goods. The framework knitter was fighting and losing a long drawn out and bitter battle for survival. He provided the anger behind Luddism and support for those who taught him that the only remedy for his problems was a thorough reform of Parliament.[19]

In Lancashire the cotton handloom weaver was entering a similar struggle. An attempt to secure some kind of wage-bargaining machinery with the Cotton Arbitration Act of 1800 had largely failed by 1804, and by 1807 the weavers were applying to Parliament for minimum wage legislation along the lines of the Spitalfields Acts. Their Bill was rejected and they turned to strike action. Though successful in the short term, the gains were lost in the depression of 1811 when the rise in the price of provisions made the situation worse than ever, and in 1812 there were outbreaks of both food riots and machine-breaking. The long-term problem of the weavers was the introduction of the power loom, but for technological reasons this was not widely adopted until the 1820s. More immediately, the problem of the weavers was an overstocked trade and a vulnerability to cyclical depression, and whether the weavers turned to politics in large numbers at this early stage is a matter of controversy. Historians such as Duncan Bythell think not, though others have been prepared to see in the events of 1811 and 1812 signs that political radicalism was already rooted in the industrial scene.[20]

In Yorkshire the situation was slightly different. Here the croppers in the woollen industry were skilled workers whose role at the finishing stage of production put them in a good position to regulate the pace of work and the volume of output as a whole. The introduction of the gig-mill (used to raise the nap) and the shearing frame threatened them on both counts and was bitterly resented. Gig-mills had been prohibited as early as the reign of Edward VI, and there was a struggle in the early nineteenth century to secure the enforcement of this legislation similar to that which took place over the apprenticeship clauses of the Statute of Artificers. In 1802 there were riots in the West Country over the use of gig-mills, and in the same year the croppers employed by Benjamin Gott of Leeds struck against the employment of two over-age apprentices. But in 1806 the response of Parliament to an appeal for the enforcement of the ban on gig-mills was to repeal the legislation. Gig-mills now began to spread rapidly, along with the new shearing frames. These latter had been invented in 1787 but only with the expiry of the patent on them did local blacksmiths and founders begin to manufacture them and make them readily available. The croppers organised secretly to destroy them, and their endeavours culminated in the celebrated attack on William Cartwright's mill at Rawfolds, and the murder of William Horsfall of Ottiwells Mill, Marsden in 1812.[21]

Only an imaginative reconstruction of events can penetrate the secrecy of this Luddism and assess the degree to which it had a political content, but there are sufficient indications to suggest that political reform, industrial sabotage and revolutionary conspiracy should not be viewed in total isolation from one another.[22] In 1811 petitions were got up in Lancashire to the Prince Regent and to Parliament for the relief of the distress, and in October a printed address was circulated in Manchester which attributed the failure of these petitions to the want of political power on the part of the petitioners. This was an important step forward, and the author was probably John Knight, a small manufacturer who had been involved in sending a congratulatory address to Burdett on his stand against Parliament the previous year. A committee was formed to ask the Borough Reeve to call a Town Meeting, but nothing further seems to have come of this in Manchester. In Bolton, however, a Town Meeting did petition Parliament in support of peace and reform, but with no result. The failure of this petitioning, along with the depression which made striking hopeless, is the background to the events of 1812 when secret committees were formed in Stockport, Manchester and Bolton, oaths were sworn, and plans formulated for concerted attacks on power-loom factories. In March 1812 a group of Manchester loyalists called a Town Meeting to support the Prince Regent's unpopular decision to continue with the same ministers when he entered upon his full powers as Regent. Opposition among reformers was widespread. The lead was taken by a middle-class

Unitarian, Ottiwell Wood, but John Buckley, a prominent member of the Manchester trades secret committee, was also consulted, and a large attendance at the meeting was threatened. The Town Meeting was to have been held on 8 April in the Exchange, but on the pretext that the staircase was not strong enough for the throng of people the loyalists abandoned their idea. Nevertheless a crowd of some 3000 gathered and the locked Exchange was stormed by a riotous mob. The ghost of the 'Church and King' riots of the 1790s had at last been laid.[23] These events were then followed by food rioting in Manchester, and machine-breaking in Stockport, Middleton and Westhoughton. There seems little doubt as to the role of the secret committees in this violence. On 11 June a meeting of reformers in Manchester was raided by the police and thirty-eight men were arrested on a charge of administering an illegal oath. They were tried at the August Assizes and acquitted when the prosecution failed to connect the reformers with the oath taking of the underground organisation. The fact remains, though, that the oath had been widely administered in Lancashire in the spring and summer of 1812, that the dividing line between parliamentary reform and the secret underground was a thin one easily crossed, and that some people, including some of those tried, did cross it. Moreover, the oath taken seems to have involved for some more than the Luddite oath of secrecy not to divulge the identity of machine-breakers; it also seems to have encompassed those who wanted reform and were not prepared to stop at petitioning to get it.[24]

The same can be said of Yorkshire, and there is evidence of some co-ordination of activity across the Pennines. Spies reported that the secret oath being sworn in 1812 was of a revolutionary nature, and the wording of one oath, based on that of the United Irishmen, was the same as that quoted at the trial of Despard. Some of the leaders, like John Baines of Halifax, were old Jacobins; others, such as Craven Cookson, William Thompson, and Stephen Kitchenman of Barnsley were to put their revolutionary ideas into practice at Grange Moor in the rising of 1820. George Mellor, who led the attack on Rawfolds Mill and was convicted of the murder of Horsfall, was a radical and while awaiting trial in York Castle he collected signatures for a petition on parliamentary reform.[25] The evidence of spies, though, does not warrant the historian putting all this together to prove that there was in 1811-12, any more than in 1802-3, a broadly-based, nationwide conspiracy afoot to obtain change by subversion — though it does not warrant the rejection of such an hypothesis either. What the evidence does support, though, is the conclusion that there was some kind of underground revolutionary tradition, that there was within Luddism a strand of political subversion; and that trade and political organisations should not be artificially separated in any historical reconstruction of events. What the spies did not do, because they were not paid to do so, was to put all this within the broader context of constitutional radicalism which, as in the 1790s, set the prevailing tone in all but years of severe hardship and depair. What is more remarkable than the presence of an underground revolutionary tradition, linking 1802 to 1812 and 1818-20, is the survival of an open and predominantly peaceful tradition of reformism which contrived to keep within the law, despite the efforts of magistrates to confuse it with the genuinely revolutionary alternative.

The name which symbolises this continuity is that of Major Cartwright, brother of the inventor of the steam loom, whose independent devotion to the cause of reform from the 1770s until his death in his eighty-fourth year in 1824, was a tribute to his stamina and courage.[26] By reform, however, he meant political reform in a very eighteenth-century sense, and he was blind to the new forces thrown up by the industrial revolution. He did not speak out against the Combination Acts, and his experiences with his brother's invention left him a bitter opponent of the Luddites.[27] Reform was for him, as for Wyvill, an urgently needed alternative to revolution, and his career strengthened both the reality and the myth of the constitutionality of the British reform movement. Unlike Wyvill, though, he wanted universal suffrage and this made him a ready figurehead for the popular movement. In 1805 he began to write for Cobbett's *Political Register*, he gave his support to Burdett and Paull at the 1806 general election, and himself stood unsuccessfully for Boston in both 1806 and 1807. His dream was to unite Whigs like Whitbread with radicals like Burdett, though neither went so far as supporting Cartwright's call for universal suffrage. This was partly achieved in 1811 with the formation of the Society (later Union) of the Friends of Parliamentary Reform, which advocated annual Parliaments and taxpayer suffrage, and the Hampden Club, started in London in April 1812 with a similarly moderate programme — indeed so moderate that Cartwright withdrew for a time.[28]

Cartwright was prepared to co-operate with the moderates, though he sometimes grew impatient with them, but he was also looking for other bases of support. In August 1812 he travelled to Manchester to celebrate the acquittal of the reformers there, and whilst in the North he visited other towns and conceived the idea of undertaking more such provincial tours. In October 1812 a branch of his Union was established in Halifax, and early in 1813 he toured the West Country, the Midlands and the North, distributing petitions for reform. Halifax and district produced 17,000 signatures, and Manchester 30,000. He was even arrested for a time in Huddersfield, which led him to petition for the security to petition. Cartwright was not a popular leader, though, and he and the working men of the North were suspicious of each other.[28] One thing he did communicate to them was the example of organisation, and Hampden Clubs were to be taken up with great enthusiasm by reformers in the provinces after the war.

The years of the Napoleonic wars were therefore not sterile so far as the reform movement was concerned. Despite the repressive legislation with which the eighteenth century ended, organisations had been created and a tradition had been preserved. Men like Francis Place and John Cartwright were still active in the cause; William Cobbett had been won over; and new men, like Henry Hunt and Thomas Attwood, had been introduced. Furthermore, to the artisan Jacobins of the 1790s had been added a new element of industrial workers threatened by machinery, and the extension of capitalistic control over their organisation and control of work. These men were learning from the Jacobins and from the moderate reformers not merely to look to Parliament for the redress of grievances, but to demand the reform of Parliament itself. When the abnormal circumstances associated with the long war were over, the agitation for reform, which had been mounting since 1811, burst out into a new period of vigorous growth — and encountered renewed repression.

Chapter 7

POST-WAR DISCONTENTS, 1815-20

> The war had been undertaken to put down opinion considered to
> be dangerous to the existence of venerable institutions. When
> peace was restored, opinion averse to established abuses again
> began to manifest itself.[1]

So Archibald Prentice, a Manchester middle-class radical journalist,
observed from the vantage point of the mid-nineteenth century. Less
sedately, Samuel Bamford, a Middleton weaver-radical, recalled
how 'whilst the laurels were yet cool on the brows of our victorious
soldiers . . . the elements of convulsion were at work among the
masses of our labouring populations'.[2] Both men were agreed that
the Corn Bill of 1815, which proposed to prohibit the importation of
foreign wheat until the domestic price had reached 80 shillings a
quarter, was the immediate cause of unrest. In itself the Corn Bill
was defensible: much marginal land had been enclosed during the
war to meet the demands of the British food market, and the expense
and low profitability of such lands could be justified only by high
prices. Protection could not suddenly be withdrawn especially
when, with the withdrawal of the Property Tax in 1816, the land
bore the heaviest burden of direct taxation. Yet to reformers, the
Corn Bill represented legislation by the vested interest of land in
Parliament for its own selfish protection, at the expense of other
sections of the community.

A middle-class radical like Prentice was inclined to emphasise the
extent to which this common grievance against landlords linked
manufacturers and the popular leaders in their opposition. To some
extent this was certainly the case — and any study of radicalism which
does not recognise the possibility of shared interests among reformers is likely to mis-state the situation — but the popular protest
was not simply a shadow of that expressed by middle-class radicals,
and on some issues the antagonisms between the emerging middle
and working classes of the industrial districts were as great as — and
sometimes greater than — the bonds of common interest.

The Corn Law was passed in 1815 amid widespread rioting in

London and the provinces. In the capital the mob which had produced civil disorder in the Gordon Riots of 1780 and in the Burdett Riots of 1810 was again to the fore, with cries of 'Burdett for Ever' echoing the 'Wilkes and Liberty' of half a century earlier, even though Burdett was actually in favour of the Corn Bill. The high price of bread, which was easily attributable to the new law, produced widespread sporadic rioting throughout the rest of 1815 and 1816. There was a notable resurgence of Luddism in the Midlands, culminating in an attack on Heathcoat and Boden's lace factory at Loughborough on 28 June 1816 when fifty-three frames worth £6000 were smashed. In East Anglia disturbances broke out in May centred on Littleport and Downham Market, as protesters demonstrated against the high price of provisions, the low level of wages, and the threat to winter employment from threshing machines.[3] 'The fact is, they are people in *want*,' wrote William Cobbett. 'They are people who have nothing to lose, except their lives; and of these they think little, seeing that they have so little enjoyment of them.'[4]

Such riots were not unusual, and in the agricultural districts were to flare up again in 1830, but popular protest was undergoing a subtle change in the early nineteenth century. The food riots of the immediate post-war period were among the last of their kind. Strikes were replacing collective bargaining by riot, and organised political protest was taking the place of local demonstrations in favour of the just price.[5] This uneven transition can be attributed to the changing structure of the economy, the emergence of urban industrial centres, and the breaking down of the 'face-to-face' society in which earlier forms of protest had been effective. But such developments occurred only gradually and cannot bear the full weight of explanation. Alongside these social changes a new political education was taking place in which the press played an important part.

This was true among manufacturers as well as among workmen. Edward Baines at the *Leeds Mercury* was turning the minds of West Riding capitalists from commercial grievances to political remedies, and in Lancashire a similar function was shortly to be performed by the *Manchester Guardian*, founded on 5 May 1821. Its editor, John Taylor, was accused in 1818 of inciting the mob at the Exchange Riots of 1812; he in turn called his Tory accuser 'a slanderer, a liar and a scoundrel'; Taylor was then sued for libel but acquitted, an event widely celebrated by the Manchester radicals.[6] But men like Baines and Taylor were reformers rather than radicals in the popular sense;

they were liberals, and very cautious about the development of popular radicalism. Baines championed 'temperate discussion and repeated petitions', not the oratory of Henry Hunt, and when Edward Baines junior began to use the paper to propagate the doctrines of sound political economy he was fostering an ideology unacceptable to the defenders of working-class opinion.[7] The *Mercury* and the *Guardian* symbolised the development of a brand of provincial radicalism which was to witness success in the Reform Act of 1832, the Municipal Corporations Act of 1835 and the repeal of the Corn Law in 1846; but they also symbolised, no less than the Tories, a body of opinion hostile to the interests of the lower orders. By fostering a middle-class consciousness they were also helping indirectly to foster a working-class political consciousness.

Independent of this awakening of political determination among the manufacturers, the reform movement was also stirring on the more popular level. The tradition of the plebeian radicals had been sustained by 'Old Jacks' throughout the war years, but a new turning point appeared to come with Cobbett's decision in November 1816 to issue his *Political Register* on an open sheet at 2d as well as in the more normal folded newspaper form, which cost 1s 0½d, and was liable to pay the 4d Newspaper Stamp.[8] Cobbett was always inclined to emphasise his own importance (a failing common to many radical leaders), but the testimony of Samuel Bamford is worth noting at length. Writing of 1816, he recalled:

> At this time the writings of William Cobbett suddenly became of great authority; they were read on nearly every cottage hearth in the manufacturing districts of South Lancashire, in those of Leicester, Derby, and Nottingham; also in many of the Scottish manufacturing towns. Their influence was speedily visible. He directed his readers to the true cause of their sufferings — misgovernment; and to its proper corrective — parliamentary reform . . . Instead of riots and destruction of property, Hampden clubs were now established in many of our large towns, and the villages and districts around them. Cobbett's books were printed in cheap form; the labourers read them, and henceforward became deliberate and systematic in their proceedings.[9]

Passing over Bamford's failure to mention the West Riding in this encomium, one can verify its general sense by such casual references as that dropped by the future radical publisher, James Watson, that his mother was 'in the habit of reading Cobbett's *Register*' in Malton.[10] The circulation of the paper increased from around 1-2 thousand to around 40,000 for the first issue of the cheap edition. Working men were encouraged to act as hawkers of the paper, and to make a living out of it.[11] Cobbett's decision to publish the 2d sheet was prompted by his learning of threats made to the licensees of some of the public houses which took the paper. By issuing a cheap edition he hoped that working men would be encouraged to club together to buy copies for themselves (and to save the expense involved in going to the public house). Moreover, a copy of the *Register* in the home would be available for re-reading throughout the week — wives might look at it, and children might read it; so the whole family might obtain a political education: 'Many a father will thus, I hope, be induced to spend his evenings at home in instructing his children in the history of their misery, and in warning them into acts of patriotism'.[12] Though obviously not every — nor even a majority — of working men were instantly prompted to emulate this radical domestic scene, some clearly were. These became the leaders of opinion in their communities, and were at the heart of that revolution of the mind which generated support for the unstamped press of the early 1830s, and for the triumphs of the Chartists' *Northern Star*.

The Hampden Clubs to which Bamford referred were the fruit of Major Cartwright's provincial lecture campaigns, but they soon took on a life of their own, independent of the London Hampden Club which remained more favourable to household than to universal suffrage. In the provinces delegates and missionaries were sent out to stimulate local Hampden Clubs, which were in effect reading and discussion societies for working men, and on 1 January 1817 a delegate meeting was held at Middleton of twenty-one Lancashire clubs. They resolved to concentrate their reform efforts on annual Parliaments and universal suffrage, in the belief that the rest — reform of the House of Lords, the Church, factory conditions and the Corn Laws — would naturally follow.[13] Local petitions were got up, and a national delegate conference was organised by the London Hampden Club which, by presenting itself as a meeting of individuals preparing to petition Parliament, was able to circumvent the ban imposed on such organisations by the Seditious Societies Act of 1799. Both Cobbett and Hunt were present at the meeting, despite their being great rivals, but Burdett was not and Cartwright took the

Chair. The moderates, including Cobbett, wanted household suffrage, but Hunt and the men of Lancashire carried the day for universal suffrage. When Parliament met at the end of January, Hunt persuaded Lord Cochrane to present the bundles of petitions prepared by Major Cartwright and containing, it was said, 500,000 signatures.[14]

The reform movement at this time was divided, broadly speaking, into three groups. At the top came the parliamentary radicals such as Burdett and Cochrane; next came the constitutional radicals like Cartwright, Cobbett and Hunt; and at the base came the popular radicals whose activities straddled the fine dividing line between the legal and the illegal. The provincial Hampden Clubs and men like Bamford occupied this twilight area.[15] Hunt came closest to them, while Cobbett condemned the Clubs, despite the popularity of his *Policital Register* with them, and put his faith in mass meetings; but these, no less than the Clubs, were subject to the influence of extremists.

Whilst in London in January 1817, Samuel Bamford encountered such extremists, whose 'bad schemes' the delegates subsequently carried back with them to the not so innocent provinces.[16] Chief among these conspirators in London were the followers of Thomas Spence, a former poor Newcastle schoolmaster who, rejecting the possibility of a reform of Parliament, advocated the expropriation of the 'robber barons' of 1066, and the abolition of private ownership in land. He lived in London from 1792, where he gathered a following among London tavern audiences. After his death his leadership was assumed by Thomas Evans, who organised a Society of Spencean Philanthropists on the model of the London Corresponding Society, with divisions in various public houses. Other leading members included Evans' son (who, with his father, remained truest to the theoretical teachings of Spence), Charles Neesom, Robert Wedderburn, Allen Davenport, 'Dr' James Watson and his son, Camille Desmoulins, Thomas Preston, and Arthur Thistlewood, (who was rumoured to have taken part in the Despard conspiracy of 1802). Certainly his ideas, and those of Preston and the younger Watson, ran in the same vein. In 1816, when Hunt was trying to make a name for himself as the popular champion of reform against the claims of Burdett and Cobbett, the Spenceans were attracted to him, and he agreed to chair a meeting for them in Spa Fields, London. Hunt stipulated, though, that reference to land reform was to be dropped, and this demand split the group. The elder Watson agreed to Hunt's request, and Hunt's mastery of the meeting was such that the opposing Thistlewood group was unable to exploit the situation to its own advantage. At a further meeting on 2 December the younger Watson and Thistlewood arrived first, and after addressing the crowd the younger Watson led a contingent of several hundreds to Smithfield; gun shops were looted on the way. Eventually order was restored, but not before Thistlewood had become convinced that this insurrectionary strategy could succeed.[17]

This strategy, and the Spa Fields riot, divided not only the Spenceans but also the whole radical movement, for while Hunt was content to work with the Spenceans, Cobbett certainly was not. Matters were made worse by further rioting at the opening of Parliament on 28 January when someone threw a stone (or fired an airgun) at the state coach. This was sufficient to prompt ministers to introduce new repressive legislation. Habeas corpus was suspended on 3 March, and on 29 March a Bill was passed which restricted public meetings and publications. Radicals could now again be imprisoned without trial and William Cobbett, seeing himself a ready victim, decided to visit America (where he remained until 1819), leaving the field clear for Hunt and the more revolutionary elements.

Hunt's great popularity in London was matched by his appeal to the men of Lancashire where the plight of the weavers made the situation ripe for unrest. Three of their delegates at the Hampden Club meeting in January 1817, William Benbow, Joseph Mitchell and Samuel Bamford, had identified themselves with the Huntites and had met with the Spenceans. 'Mitchell and Benbow had cultivated a rather close acquaintance with these men,' recalled Bamford. On returning to Lancashire, Benbow helped organise a hunger march of Lancashire weavers, who were to petition the Prince Regent on their desperate situation. Mitchell stayed behind in the capital, where he was introduced to Charles Pendrill who had been involved in the Despard conspiracy, and he introduced him to a man known as 'William Oliver', who was to betray all their plans to the government.[18]

The weavers' march to London was probably intended to be no more than that, but any such march could easily turn into something much more serious. As thousands of people gathered in St Peter's Fields, Manchester, on 10 March, to see off the men with their blankets around them and carrying their inadequate provisions for the journey, the Riot Act was read. About three hundred 'Blanke-teers' set off for Ardwick Green, where others joined them, but most of the contingent was turned back by the yeomanry at Stockport, some of the leaders already having been arrested at the start.[19] This particular expression of discontent may have been peaceful in inten-tion, but this was certainly not true of other incidents which took place in the spring and early summer of 1817. It may be significant that the suspension of habeas corpus came not with the Spa Fields riot but with increasing signs of unrest in the industrial districts where Luddism had been strongest, and Bamford has left a graphic account of the way in which the reformers were scattered as the authorities began to use their extra powers. Spies began to infiltrate those flimsy organisations which were necessary if the scattered weaving communities were to co-ordinate their activities. A plot was hatched, possibly by *agents provocateurs*, to commit the Lanca-shire radicals to a march on Manchester, partly to free those arrested at the 'Blanket Meeting' in St Peter's Fields on 10 March; the signal to start would be a great fire which would make 'a Moscow of Manchester'.[20] On this occasion nothing happened, but the plotting continued and on 29 March a secret group of conspirators was arrested at Ardwick Green.[21] The discovery of these plots, in which Bamford had wisely refused to become involved, was made the pretext for the arrest of the leading reformers in the area. Bamford recalled how

> Personal liberty not being now secure from one hour to another, many of the leading reformers were induced to quit their homes, and seek concealment where they could obtain it. Those who could muster a few pounds, or who had friends to give them a frugal welcome, or who had trades with which they could travel, disappeared like swallows at the close of summer, no one knew whither.[22]

The organisers of the Blanket March, including Benbow, were already in gaol in London. The Hampden Clubs were smashed. Peaceful reform was pushed back to where it had been in the late 1790s:

> Our society, thus hopeless, became divided and dismayed; hundreds slunk home to their looms, nor dared to come out, save like owls at nightfall, when they would perhaps steal through by-paths behind hedges, or down some clough, to hear the news

at the next cottage . . . open meetings being thus suspended, secret ones ensued.[23]

Here was ready material for a rising. That it did not come in Lancashire, and that elsewhere it failed, was not for want of wishing, but for want of effective organisation, free from the infiltration of spies.

Meanwhile, as Bamford cautiously put it, Joseph Mitchell 'moved in a sphere of his own, the extent of which no man knew save himself '.[24] He was in fact engaged on a provincial tour in the company of Oliver, whose credentials were guaranteed by Mitchell. Delegate meetings were attended, and faithfully reported to the Home Office by Oliver. A rising was planned for 26 May, later changed to 9 June.[25] One of the most active of the delegates was Thomas Bacon of Pentrich, a member of the Nottingham committee. He was a veteran Jacobin, and had attended the Hampden Club meeting in January. On 5 May, the same day that Mitchell was arrested in Huddersfield, Bacon was at a delegate meeting at Wakefield, attended also by Jeremiah Brandreth and Oliver. Bacon was also in touch with Bamford and the Lancashire reformers, travelling the country as a yarn salesman, which gave him innocent entry into the weaving communities.[26] Though Bamford's evidence is subject to the criticism that it was written long after the event, it nevertheless provides useful support for the view that there was a widespread conspiracy at this time, and that Oliver, although a spy, did not create it for his own purposes.

Actual risings took place in June in only two places — the Holme Valley, near Huddersfield, and Pentrich, near Nottingham. After Mitchell's arrest, Oliver concentrated on these two districts, both of which had been hot-beds of Luddism. Each district was probably aware of the other's plans, with George Weightman of Pentrich as well as Bacon a familiar figure in Yorkshire. On 6 June ten Yorkshire delegates, who had been brought together by Oliver, were arrested at a secret meeting at Thornhill Lees, near Dewsbury. The arrests were a mistake, the work of an over-zealous magistrate, and probably panicked several hundred cloth workers (including many croppers) in the Holme Valley to commence a premature march on Huddersfield on 8 June. They were halted at Folly Hall, just short of the town, and though shots were fired no one was killed.[27] The same day Brandreth was making final plans at Pentrich, and on 9 June he led his famous but fruitless march on Nottingham.[28] The authorities were ready for the rebels, thanks to their spies, but on 13 June Edward Baines at the *Leeds Mercury* received a letter which prompted him to look closer at the part played by Oliver in the Thornhill Lees meeting. Immediately he published in his paper a thorough exposure of Oliver and his methods: the consequences were momentous.[29]

The revelation of the spy system established the *Mercury* as 'the accepted leader of the English provincial press'.[30] More importantly it shocked a wide spectrum of respectable liberal opinion, and caused a general revulsion against the government which, though it did not save the lives of Brandreth and the Pentrich leaders, did probably account for the acquittal of the Folly Hall insurgents. It also led to a re-assessment of the reform issue by both working-class and middle-class radicals. As Edward Thompson has cogently observed:

> A rising *without* Oliver would have panicked the middle class to the side of the administration. A rising *with* Oliver threw Whigs and middle-class reformers on to the alert. For three years the crucial political contests centred upon the defence of civil liberties, and the rights of the Press, where the middle class itself was most sensitive . . . From 1817 until Chartist times, the central working-class tradition was that which exploited every means of agitation and protest short of active insurrectionary preparation.[31]

Suspicious of spies and chastened by the events of early 1817, most reformers now followed Bamford's resolve to avoid strangers and secret meetings.[32] Peaceful intentions were fortified by a good harvest and an improvement in the economic situation in the autumn of 1817, followed by the restoration of habeas corpus and the release of political prisoners early the following year. The open reform movement was now resumed and was further stimulated by a general election.

The released prisoners without delay immersed themselves once more in the agitation for reform; while in Parliament itself reform again seemed to be stirring. The death of the Prince Regent's only child in November 1817 prompted ministers to arrange financial inducements to encourage the other royal princes to marry. The terms reached were rejected by the Commons. At the same time Sir Samuel Romilly, having attacked the suspension of habeas corpus, was bringing damaging revelations about the cruelty of British slave–owners in the West Indies to the notice of the House; while Henry Brougham obtained a Bill setting up the Charity Commissioners, and a Committee to look into popular education. 'Corruption' was under attack at last.[33]

As in 1806–7, the symbolic centre of politics in 1818 was Westminster. Here Francis Place had persuaded Jeremy Bentham and Sir Francis Burdett to make a pact, one consequence of which was that on 2 June 1818 Burdett spoke in the House in favour of universal suffrage. He doubtless had the forthcoming election in mind, but neither he nor Bentham was prepared for the Whigs deciding to put Romilly up against him at Westminster. In the event, Romilly came top of the poll with Burdett second. The other radical, Douglas Kinnaird, withdrew. Westminster had returned to its Foxite tradition, but before the year was out Romilly had committed suicide and preparations were afoot for a by–election. In the manoeuvrings to find a candidate acceptable to the Whigs, all the divisions among the radicals were revealed – the Huntites, the Burdettites, the Benthamites, and the Westminster Committee of Place. Finally J C Hobhouse was put forward, which satisfied neither extreme. The Whigs ran George Lamb, who drew the popular support of John Gale Jones and Henry Hunt; Burdett supported Hobhouse: and Cartwright offered himself for the radicals. Lamb was easily elected, and the lesson to be learned was that, however powerful the organised radicalism of the Westminster Committee might be, 'the common people's support was not enough'. Hobhouse, however, managed to get himself committed to Newgate for breach of privilege, and he and Burdett were successful at the election which followed the king's death in 1820.[34]

The dealings of radicals and Whigs in Westminster, both in and out of Parliament, were not of great significance for the provinces. The non–electors were powerless to influence the result of any parliamentary election, and could hope for change only by sustained pressure from without or by a subversive *coup* leading to a general rising. In the circumstances of 1818 the latter was not entertained by the majority. Instead groups of working men began meeting for discussion and mutual education in organisations modelled on those adopted by the Methodists with societies, classes, class leaders and penny subscriptions. The first of these 'Political Protestants' was formed at Hull in July 1818 for the purpose of sincerely protesting against the mockery of our indispensable right to a real representation; and to use every means in our power, which are just and lawful, to rescue the House of Commons from the all-devouring influence of the Borough Merchants, and to restore it to the people, agreeable to Magna Carta, and the spirit of the Constitution.[35]

This Hull plan was welcomed by supporters of the former Hampden Clubs and was encouraged by the radical press, but the ambiguities present in the Hampden Clubs were repeated when the Reverend Joseph Harrison of Stockport started a Political Union alongside the local Political Protestants to pursue a more politically active role.[36] Societies of Political Protestants and, more especially, Political Unions, spread rapidly to the Midlands, the West Country, and the North-East as well as to the rest of Lancashire and Yorkshire. At a delegate meeting held at Hunslet on 7 June 1819, James Mann, who had been one of those arrested at Thornhill Lees two years earlier, told the assembly 'that Unions on the principles of Radical Reform are found in almost every part of England; and without Radical Reform our country will be ruined'.[37]

In London, the Spenceans continued on their own revolutionary way. The Thistlewood group set about plotting a rising in September, and then in October, 1817 planned to establish a Committee of Public Safety and to implement Spence's land scheme. In February 1818 they were plotting to assassinate the Home Secretary, Lord Sidmouth, together with other ministers.[38] The followers of the elder Watson, meanwhile, moved closer to Henry Hunt, and when Thistlewood was imprisoned for a year in May 1818 after challenging Lord Sidmouth to a duel, the Watsonites felt free to work for a more widely-based revolution. Through Hunt they continued to have some influence in Lancashire where they followed the mass-meeting strategy of 1816. The Stockport Political Union fell under their influence, and they were responsible for creating a London Political Union in April 1819.[39] With the release of Thistlewood the following month, renewed plans were made for a rising in London, while mass meetings were held in the country. On 14 July 1819, the anniversary of the fall of the Bastille, Hunt chaired a meeting in Smithfield which Watson and Thistlewood intended to lead to revolution, but as in 1816 Hunt retained control and the meeting passed off with few incidents. Though Hunt was not a

Spencean, or a revolutionary in their sense, it is difficult to believe that he was unaware of their true intentions.[40]

Hunt was next invited to address a meeting in Manchester on 9 August. He was threatened with arrest if he appeared, and so called a massive protest meeting of reformers from all over Lancashire, which was to take place in St Peter's Fields, Manchester on 16 August. It is unlikely that the Spenceans were hoping to exploit this meeting to their own advantage, since their strategy was for the rising to start in London, and in any case Hunt's record suggests he could have kept control of the meeting, but the authorities proved themselves incapable of distinguishing the subversive from the constitutional. Those who came to the meeting had been drilling on the moors, but their processions with their banners and their bands were more like a Sunday School outing than a military parade, with women and children as well as men in the throng. But when Hunt appeared to take the Chair, supported on the platform by veterans like John Knight, the yeomanry cavalry advancing through the crowd to arrest him, panicked, and began slashing their way through with their sabres. Regular troops were called (who knew how to use the flats of their swords) to restore order, by which time eleven people had been killed and over 600 wounded.[41] This was the notorious 'Peterloo' massacre which, more than any other single event in the period 1815-32, helped feed the hostility of working-class reformers to the government and the social class from which the yeomanry was recruited. The massacre was indeed a tremendous propaganda victory for the extremists, though the fact that it pro-duced no rising indicates the impotence of the Spenceans. News of the massacre was carried back to the communities of Lancashire by eye witnesses, and the press conveyed the scene to those in more distant parts.[42] Though Whigs rallied to the defence of the reformers and attacked the government, a new steel entered into the resolve of working men who felt they could trust no one but their own class.

This is not to say that all the industrialists of Manchester were hostile to reform in 1819, or that some were not outraged by the conduct of the authorities at Peterloo. A significant number — many of them Unitarians and leading citizens — shared the anger of the working-class reformers. Men like Joseph Brotherton, a Sweden-borgian (who was to become the first MP for Salford in 1832), Thomas and Richard Potter (both later mayors of Manchester), J E Taylor (first editor of the *Manchester Guardian*), and Archibald Pren-

tice, formed a nucleus of middle-class reformers who differed from
the Huntites more over means than over ends. They joined with the
popular reformers in exposing the malpractices of Joseph Nadin, the
Deputy Constable of Manchester, and they established a strong
reformist tradition in the town which was to last until mid-
century.[43] But even in 1819 their tone and attitude towards the
popular radicals set the two groups apart. Though when the
working-class *Manchester Observer* closed its pages in 1821 it commended the new *Guardian* to its readers, suspicion between the two
groups remained.[44] 'Middle-class and working-class Radical agitations were often parallel in Manchester', writes Donald Read, 'but
they were never allied.'[45]

The Peterloo massacre was a national event, not only because it
occurred at one of a series of nationwide reform meetings, but also
because by 1819 the radical press had given a greater coherence to the
reform movement than would have been possible through the Political Unions alone. The public meeting and the press — an amalgam
of a Hunt and a Cobbett — were of more importance than the Clubs
favoured by Major Cartwright in establishing a radical presence in
the country. When Cobbett fled to America in the spring of 1817, he
left behind him an example which others were quick to follow. Chief
among these was Thomas Jonathan Wooler (1785(6) -1853), whose
Black Dwarf had the support of Major Cartwright and lasted from
1817 until its patron's death in 1824. Wooler threw his influence
behind the Hampden Clubs and the constitutional agitation for
reform. More extreme was William T Sherwin (b 1799), who at the
age of seventeen came to London after being dismissed from the
keepership of the Southwell Bridewell for his interest in the ideas of
Thomas Paine. After failing with a paper called the *Republican* in
February 1817, he commenced in April a much more successful
Weekly Political Register, which resembled Cobbett's paper in title
only and which has been described by Joel Wiener as 'one of the
formative radical journals in early nineteenth-century Britain'.[46]
Sherwin was a keen supporter of Hunt, whose attempt to offer
himself at Westminster in 1818 he wholeheartedly supported, and he
was open to Spencean influence without actually adopting Thistlewood's political theories.[47] The latter were expressed, however, in
Thomas Davison's *Medusa*, which ran from February 1819 for a
year. Finally the Benthamite and Place group supported the *Gorgon*
(1818–19), edited by John Wade, who in 1819 began to expose

'corruption' more systematically with his *Black Book*. Among more respectable reformers, the Burdettites had the *Independent Whig*, while Leigh Hunt's *Examiner* supported both Burdett and Brougham.[48] The more popular of these papers followed Cobbett in either ignoring or circumventing the Stamp Duty and selling at a price which commended themselves to the working classes. The government was prepared to use the laws against seditious and blasphemous libels to suppress them. Convictions were not easy to secure, though, as juries proved themselves to be unreliable. In 1817 Wooler was twice tried for seditious libel: on the first occasion the jury was divided, and on the second he was acquitted. William Hone was charged with blasphemous libel in the same year for his political parodies on the *Book of Common Prayer*. At three celebrated trials in December 1817 he was acquitted by a jury before whom he made the prosecution a laughing stock.[49]

Through the cheap popular press in these years after 1815, the ideas of the old Jacobins were given new life for the next generation. Sherwin played an important part in this, and in 1819 his short biography of Paine was the first attempt to reinstate the radical hero since his death in 1809. The Jacobin tradition had, of course, been kept alive by individuals such as John Gale Jones and John Thelwall, and by stalwart publishers like Daniel Isaac Eaton who, as an old man, suffered a pillorying in 1812; but the post-war years threw up an important new convert in Richard Carlile.[50] As a tinsmith who had come to London from his native Ashburton in Devon, Carlile was drawn into metropolitan radical politics in 1816. He attended political meetings, read Paine's *Rights of Man* and in 1817, when short of work, borrowed money from his employer and began to hawk the *Black Dwarf* in the streets. In April 1817 he commenced a partnership with Sherwin, who introduced him to the trade of printing and publishing. In August he pirated Hone's parodies, and was imprisoned until Hone's acquittal at the end of the year. During this time of enforced leisure he studied Paine's *Age of Reason* and became dedicated to the task of propagating Paine's views. Together he and Sherwin republished Paine's works and other freethought and radical classics of the eighteenth century, and a charge of blasphemous libel was laid against Carlile by the Society for the Suppression of Vice, the moral reformation organisation associated with Wilberforce and the Evangelicals. In August 1819 Carlile was present with Hunt on the platform at Peterloo, and wrote a graphic account of it the following week for *Sherwin's Weekly Political Register* under the heading 'Horrid Massacre at Manchester'.[51] About this time Sherwin withdrew from the business, and the following week Carlile continued their periodical under its original title of *Republican*. With one break, this was to be his banner until 1826. The response of the government to Carlile's inflammatory account of Peterloo was to charge him with seditious libel, but on reflection they preferred to let the earlier blasphemy charges go ahead instead. In this they were wise, for Carlile did not have the wit of Hone and the jury had no hesitation in convicting him at his trial in October 1819. He was sent to Dorchester gaol where he remained until 1825.[52]

The Spenceans had meanwhile taken new heart from the reaction to the Peterloo massacre. A series of public protest meetings was held in various parts of the country as the news united all classes of reformers in opposition to the government. This was a situation the extremists could exploit, and a new Political Union was set up in Manchester, in rivalry to the Huntite Union, to organise simultaneous meetings. Hunt now broke with the Spenceans, though this did not save him from a 2½-year gaol sentence in March 1820.[53] By December 1819 the Thistlewood group in London had decided that, like Despard in 1802, they must act to give a lead to the provinces, but their plot to assassinate the Cabinet at a dinner in Cato Street in February 1820 was uncovered by a spy named Edwards, and the conspirators were arrested. Four leaders, including Thistlewood, were executed on 1 May, and five others were transported.[54] As with the Despard conspiracy it is impossible to say whether there were any provincial connections, or whether the plotters simply hoped that their *coup* would spark off a rising in the country. The provocation was certainly there, not least with the passing of the Six Acts which came into force at the beginning of 1820. These Acts gave greater powers to magistrates to search for arms and to restrict public meetings; one, the Blasphemous and Seditious Libels Act, was specifically aimed at the radical press, and another was designed to close all the loopholes through which radical publishers had followed Cobbett since 1816. Henceforth all periodical publications were deemed to be newspapers and subject to the 4d stamp merely by virtue of their being cheap (under 6d).[55] With public meetings and cheap publications thus limited, the revolutionary *coup* had renewed appeal as the only means to secure reform.

There was certainly unrest in the country, and it could have been connected with the extremist activity in London. Delegates were active in both trade and political matters. Union societies had been spread to Glasgow in 1819 by an English radical, Joseph Brayshaw, and a delegate central committee was set up in the Glasgow area to organise mass meetings. Peterloo slogans were rapidly adopted by the Scots reformers after August. By December the government was nervous about events in both Manchester and Glasgow, and in February a number of Scottish reformers were arrested. Brayshaw was again touring the area in March, and a strike called from 1 April was surprisingly successful and caught the authorities off-guard. On 5 April, as the strike was collapsing, a small contingent of radicals from Strathaven marched on Glasgow, but dispersed when no further support was forthcoming. A force of about twenty-five men had meanwhile set out from Glasgow for Stirlingshire; they were caught by troops at Bonnymuir and fought a rearguard action before succumbing to arrest.[56] A week earlier, on 31 March, there had been an attempt at a rising near Huddersfield, which came to nothing, but on 11 April there was a more serious march from Barnsley to Grange Moor. The affair ended when lack of support from elsewhere and rumours of spies caused the Barnsley men to flee, but it is noteworthy that some of these men had been involved in the plotting of 1812.[57] Despite further rumours of a co-ordinated rising, this was to be the final attempt. With the leaders in gaol or in exile, their confidence sapped by spies and their forces scattered, the reformers of 1820 were in no position to challenge the forces of law and order. Moreover, all but a tiny minority lacked the will. Despite the tone set by Peterloo, the mainstream of reform since 1817 had been for open organisation in which spies were powerless, and for constitutional reform. As R J White has written, 'It was a case of conversion to Cartwright and Cobbett'.[58]

Chapter 8

THE FORMATIVE DECADE

Between the marchings and plottings of the spring of 1820 and the agricultural riots and reform demonstrations of the early 1830s, the political temperature in Britain was generally low. The economy was beginning to recover from the distorting effects of the long war, harvests were as a rule good until the later 1820s, and the economic basis of unrest was thereby undermined. The decade was, in Edward Thompson's phrase, 'a mildly prosperous plateau of social peace'.[1] But to regard the 1820s as some kind of hiatus would be misleading. On the one hand these years did see economic distress for some sections of the population, notably agricultural labourers especially in the southern counties, and textile workers who everywhere were being subjected to both the increasing control of capitalism and technological innovation. On the other hand it is to this period that the historian can trace the early development of many of those ideas and institutions which were to become central to radicalism and reform in the 1830s and 1840s. The force behind the agitation for the Reform Bill in 1832, and the subsequent reactions to the Reform Act, can only be understood against the background of events in the 1820s.

The decade opened with the unusual spectacle of radicals and Whigs vying with each other in defence of the queen. On 29 January 1820 (the anniversary of Paine's birthday), George III died and the Prince Regent became king. In June his estranged wife, Caroline of Brunswick, returned to England to claim her position as queen. The result was what the affair's most recent historian has called 'the last of the old-style metropolitan agitations in which London gave the lead to the rest of the country'.[2] The queen had for some years provided the Whigs with the traditional Hanoverian opposition court, and the determination of George IV to exclude her was — however much she deserved it — too good an opportuniy to miss. Henry Brougham and Thomas Denman (who had defended the Pentrich rebels) became her legal advisers; Alderman Wood (who had led the City support for Burdett in the 1810 crisis) made the queen's cause his own; Major Cartwright chaired a meeting to celebrate her birthday; and Wooler's *Black Dwarf* joined in the exploitation of the issue by the ministry's opponents. Above all Cobbett, who had also supported the queen in an earlier attempt to use her in the cause of reform in 1813, now came to her aid and urged her to rely on public opinion.

Throughout the summer the affair was kept on the boil. The *Black Dwarf* looked forward to a victory which would match that of the contemporary revolutionaries in Naples, and William Benbow expected the queen to 'bring down the corrupt Conspirators against the Peace, Honour and Life of the Innocent [a reference to Peterloo].[3] The political cartoonist made the most of the ministry's embarrassment. William Hone followed up the success of *The Political House that Jack Built*, published earlier in 1820 with illustrations by George Cruikshank, with a further series of satirical pamphlets. The radical press may have been set back by the Six Acts, but the pamphleteers and broadsheet writers proved irrepressible in the queen's cause. Public opinion and the threat of civil unrest caused the ministers to abandon their Penalties Bill against the queen after it had passed its Third Reading in the Commons by only nine votes. The lesson was not lost on the Whigs a decade later. But in January 1821 the queen accepted a pension of £50,000 and her support began to fall. When locked out of the coronation, the popular demonstration on her behalf was less vociferous than expected, though her death a few months later saw a slight resurgence. Her funeral procession in August was diverted through the city by popular force, and when two men were killed by the accompanying troops their funeral became the occasion for a demonstration organised by Dr Watson, John Gale Jones, John Gast and other leading London radicals. The Queen Caroline affair temporarily united Whigs and popular radicals, but in a negative rather than positive sense. It also exploited both radical and royalist prejudices among the populace. The victory was short-lived and ambiguous in its implications for the future.[4]

Over the next few years the artisans of London nurtured in their clubs a tradition of radicalism which was independent of City and Whig leadership. In Parliament the Whigs found the cause of reform too difficult for sustained commitment. In 1819, after the general election the previous year had highlighted the usual abuses in the system and the need for reform, Lord John Russell brought to the attention of the Commons the notoriously corrupt boroughs of

Penryn and Grampound. His call for piecemeal reform was, surprisingly, supported on both sides of the House, but there agreement ended. In 1821 Russell moved a Bill to transfer Grampound's two seats to Leeds, but the problem of devising an appropriate borough franchise was too great, and finally two extra seats were given to Yorkshire instead.[5] The experience of this effort helped convince the Whigs that there was little hope of a significant measure of reform by the piecemeal approach, but it was not until 1827, with the deaths of Liverpool and Canning, that opinion began to shift significantly within Parliament, when the realignment of political groupings in the Commons led to renewal of support for a serious reform of the electoral system.

Meanwhile the attempt of radicals to elect their own 'Legislative Attorneys' in 1819, to serve the place of non-existent MPs for such places as Birmingham and Manchester, was declared illegal and came to nothing. Sir Charles Wolsey, who was 'elected' for Birmingham, was imprisoned for sedition shortly afterwards. In Manchester the meeting on 16 August was intended by some (but not Hunt) to be Hunt's electoral meeting, hence the attempt to arrest him and the consequent massacre.[6] In 1822 Russell moved in Parliament for a general measure of reform which received an encouraging level of support. The following year he repeated the exercise, backed by petitions from county meetings, but his opponents remained in the majority. Thereafter he gave up even the show of demanding reform until 1827 when he unsuccessfully moved for the transfer of seats from Penryn and East Retford to Manchester and Birmingham respectively.[7]

In such circumstances the efforts of the popular radicals were doomed to impotence, but this is not to say that the determination created by Peterloo and the popular fervour stirred up by the Queen Caroline affair immediately died down. Organisations soon began to appear under the guise of relief funds for prisoners. In London Wooler helped mobilise a Liberal Alliance, which played an active part in the agitation on behalf of the queen.[8] In the North, some Union Societies survived, and in 1821 Hunt tried to reorganise them from gaol into a Great Northern Political Union, with support from Cartwright, Wooler and the *Black Dwarf*. By January 1822 there were eighteen branches in the northern textile districts, organised, like the Political Protestants, on class lines with a 1d subscription. By July the Union had spread to the Midlands, and when Hunt was released in October 1822 his organisation seemed to be thriving. But in 1824 Wooler was lamenting how public support for reform had fallen away.[9] The achievement of these years was nevertheless great, for even if a mass movement for reform had not been sustained, dedicated and organised groups of radicals had been banded together. Together they learned forms of organisation and self-expression and received a political education through the radical press which stood them in good stead in the years to come.

In the summer of 1819 Hunt began to disentangle himself from the extremists. Then, in the vacuum left by the execution of Thistlewood, Richard Carlile emerged to rally groups of republicans from his cell in Dorchester gaol. Typical of the local men he inspired was Joseph Brayshaw, whose Scottish lecture tours in 1820 were alleged to have been behind the unrest there. He was a committed and doctrinaire radical who, after Peterloo, espoused the full Paineite programme of reform in Church and State; but he was not a revolutionary of the Thistlewood type, and played an ambiguous part in the risings of 1820.[10] After the defeats of the spring he, like Carlile, was ready to advance revolution through the educational renewal of the people.

Passionate radicalism blended easily into a moral and religious crusade. Brayshaw himself was a member of the sect of Freethinking Christians.[11] A Spencean, Robert Wedderburn, opened a chapel in Soho where he and Allen Davenport preached anti-Christian sermons.[12] Both men were also connected with Carlile who after 1825 was himself drawn into the radical sectarianism of London in the company of the Reverend Robert Taylor.[13] By the early 1830s radicalism in London co-existed with sectarian religion in a series of overlapping circles centred on John 'Zion' Ward, the Rotunda radicals (Carlile, Taylor, Eliza Sharples and John Gale Jones), Robert Owen, James 'Shepherd' Smith, and Edward Irving.[14] A similar sort of thing can be noticed in the provinces. After Peterloo the schismatic Swedenborgians known as Bible Christians expanded rapidly in Manchester, with James Scholefield (later a prominent Chartist) organising a Union Sunday School in Hulme and in 1823 opening a radical chapel in Ancoats.[15] In the same year a young protégé of the Swedenborgians, Rowland Detrosier, was given the pulpit of Mount Brinksway Chapel, near Stockport, under the patronage of Joseph Brotherton. Detrosier was influenced by some of Carlile's Stockport disciples, but lost his use of the chapel when he allowed

Carlile to speak there.[16] In nearby Ashton–under–Lyne a branch of the Southcottians gathered to await the Second Coming of Christ. Their New Jerusalem lay on James Smith's path from Presbyterianism to Owenism.[17] This rich and fervent sectarian aspect to radicalism was no exotic freak. Though Carlile was a difficult man and increasingly isolated from other leaders after 1825, the contribution which he made both to the ideas and the organisation of radicalism in the 1820s were of central importance.

Carlile was sentenced in October 1819 to two years in prison and a fine of £1000. Resolved to be a martyr rather than pay, he remained in prison until unconditionally released in November 1825. His contribution to radicalism during these gaol years was twofold. First, through his publishing he drew others into his struggle in both London and the provinces, encouraging a network of publishers and distributors of radical literature who would go to gaol rather than obey the law. Secondly, he stimulated local radicals to form themselves into educational or 'Zetetic' societies.[18]

During the reform agitation of 1819 there were about seventy-five prosecutions for blasphemous and seditious libels, over half of which occurred outside London, and a proclamation against 'wicked and seditious writings' was issued even before Peterloo. In Manchester, James Wroe of the *Manchester Observer* was suspected of circulating an account of the events of 16 August to which he applied the sobriquet 'Peter-loo'. His family and workmen were hounded by the law, and finally he was committed on the nominal charge of selling *Sherwin's Weekly Political Register*, and imprisoned for a year. The cost of the trial forced him to close the *Observer*. In Macclesfield, where a serious riot took place on the night of 16 August, a Stockport hatter and radical newsagent, Joseph Swann, was sentenced to two years for seditious conspiracy, two years for blasphemous libel, and six months for seditious libel, to run consecutively. This was the most extreme example of what occurred in a number of provincial towns in the autumn of 1819, with Carlile's publications in many cases being cited in the indictments. Under the harsher laws of Scotland, Gilbert MacLeod, editor of the *Spirit of the Union*, was transported to New South Wales for five years for allegedly seditious remarks in his paper.[19] The names of men like James Mann of Leeds and Joseph Russell of Birmingham, who became associated together in the press struggle of 1819–24, read like a roll call of prominent local radicals of the first half of the nineteenth century. An insight into this local scene can be gained through the recollections of one of the most celebrated of future radicals to receive his baptism of fire in these years, James Watson. He remembered how by chance he went to a meeting of the Radical Reformers in Leeds in the autumn of 1818 (he probably meant 1819), and found a group of men reading the *Black Dwarf*, *Cobbett's Weekly Political Register* and the *Republican*. Among their numbers were Joseph Brayshaw, Joseph Harley, Robert Byerley, Humphrey Boyle 'and a number of other friends [actively engaged] in collecting subscriptions for Mr Carlile, spreading the liberal and freethinking literature, and, by meetings and discussions, endeavouring to obtain the right of free discussion'.[20] Two of their number, Boyle and Watson, were shortly to go to gaol themselves.

To avoid the Stamp Duty in 1820, Carlile put up the price of the *Republican* to sixpence but this was the only concession he was prepared to make. His wife Jane and his sister Mary Ann struggled to keep the business going in 1820, and during the course of 1821 both were sent to join him in prison. In October 1820 Carlile issued an appeal for volunteers to keep his shop open and to challenge the prosecutions, which were initiated principally by either the Society for the Suppression of Vice (the 'Vice Society') or the newly-formed Constitutional Association (the 'Bridge-Street Gang').[21] The system of volunteers appears to have been managed by a London committee led by Thomas Evans and John Gale Jones, who guaranteed a steady stream of volunteer-victims from the provinces, beginning with Joseph Rhodes from Manchester, William Vamplew Holmes from Sheffield, Susannah Wright from Nottingham, and Humphrey Boyle and James Watson from Leeds.[22] Gradually the war of attrition was won. The number of prosecutions fell and, after a brief revival in 1824 when eleven arrests occurred in Carlile's shop between 7 and 31 May at the instigation of the Home Office, the attempt to silence the radical press solely by the laws of libel was abandoned.[23] The prosecutions had been counter-productive for they were very much identified with the Tories and brought to the victims the support of Whigs and middle-class reformers. The most notorious case illustrating this came in Manchester where David Ridgeway was prosecuted at the Lancaster Assizes in 1822 at the instigation of the Constitutional Association. The case was taken up by Richard Potter and the Manchester middle-class radicals who engaged Henry Brougham for the defence. The case was in fact put off and never came to trial, but what it revealed of the Constitutional Association's methods was enough to discredit it.[24] In this way the government eventually was brought to give in to the combined pressure of liberal reforming opinion and direct confrontation with the law. By November 1825, when Carlile was released, only three publishers still remained in gaol. A significant moral victory had been won for although in the short term success meant an end to public interest, in the longer term the 'war of the unstamped' of the early 1830s was to be built on the foundations of the earlier campaign led by Carlile.

The *Republican* was not published during 1821, but on resuming it in 1822 Carlile printed reports which showed the extent to which his local support had been building up since October 1820. His birthday on 9 December, and Paine's on 29 January, were excellent excuses for disloyal toasts and dinners at which clubs and discussion societies could be formed or revived. One such society, the Edinburgh Free-thinkers' Zetetic Society, served as a model for many others, with its commitment to the politics of the French Revolution and to the philosophy of the Enlightenment. The society dated back to the spring of 1820 when it had been formed 'for the purpose of discussing literary, philosophical and theological subjects'. At Whitsuntide they took the Cordiners' Hall where they began to collect together a library, and in December they adopted the name 'Zetetic' under the leadership of two grocers, James and Robert Affleck.[25] The idea of zetetic mutual improvement societies spread. A London society was formed in May 1822, and over the next few months others appeared in Bolton, Sheffield, Ashton, Salford and Glasgow. Other groups simply called themselves 'Friends of Free Discussion', and these met in Bath, Bethnal Green, Birmingham, Carlisle, Leeds, Liverpool, Manchester, Nottingham and Stockport. The last illustrates the links between these societies and those of 1817-20, for the leader, William Perry, had been active since the days of the local Hampden Club.[26] In Ashton in 1822 four supporters of Carlile were charged with sedition for hanging a black flag from the Union Rooms with the words 'Murder! August 16th, 1819'.[27] Prosecution was unusual in England though as the activities of the societies were not against the law, but in Scotland on 17 November 1822 the Sheriff and police entered the Edinburgh Zetetic Society, interrupted a meeting of about 150 people, arrested the chairman and the Affleck brothers, and seized the library. James Affleck was subsequently charged with publishing blasphemous works, including the *Theolo-gical Works of Paine*. He pleaded guilty and under Scots law was lucky to receive only three months in prison.[28] The blow temporarily closed both the Edinburgh and Glasgow Societies, but they were functioning again in 1824.

The Zetetics were the heirs to the Paineite Jacobin tradition, and like the Jacobins they provided the cutting-edge of artisan radicalism. But they were overwhelmingly recruited from the artisan and small-shopkeeper class, and their intellectual approach scarcely fitted them to speak to the economic needs of the new industrial working class which was in the making. Their language was that of abstract political rights. Carlile's programme was 'Britain a republic upon the base of a completely representative system of government, with the abolition of kingcraft and priestcraft'.[29] He rejected an article by Allen Davenport on 'Agrarian Equality' on the grounds that his readers would not be interested.[30] The Zetetics did not even speak for the whole of popular radicalism, for they were rivals of that other gaol-creation, Hunt's Great Northern Political Union, which Carlile dismissed as 'a cheat that picks the pocket and corrupts the mind' because it seemed prepared for compromise.[31] Carlile was not above erecting his own definition of Paineite radicalism which he then used as the standard by which to measure and condemn all other radicals. He was also an élitist, and this trait became increasingly obvious after his release from prison. When visiting Salford in 1828 (he lodged with James Wroe) he attended a discussion group at the 'Dog and Partridge' of which the landlord was John Gatrix who had been a faithful supporter over many years. 'I was not very much pleased with the character of the discussions that were carried on in the room,' he noted. Elijah Riddings, silk handloom weaver and poet, was urged to show

> a little correction in manners, a little more of the *fortiter in re, et suaviter in modo*, a little more softness, affability and complaisance of manner, with as much sternness and integrity of principle as he pleases.

What did impress Carlile, though, was the vitality of provincial radicalism in a place like Stockport, where he met Rowland Detrosier.[32]

After 1825 two new influences began to reshape Carlile's outlook: the first was the Reverend Robert Taylor, at whose

'Christian Evidence Society' lectures in London blasphemy rubbed cheeks with mysticism. The combination proved popular with men like John Gale Jones, and after Taylor's conviction for blasphemy in 1828 Carlile rallied to his support. Thereafter, on a provincial lecture tour in 1829 and the Blackfriars Rotunda in 1830-1, the two men worked closely together in the cause of reform, though their mystical-religious approach was viewed with suspicion by other leading radicals.[33] The other new influence on Carlile was Francis Place, whose moderate approach and connections with middle-class radicals had isolated him from many of the popular radicals in the 1820s. Carlile had two points of contact with Place and the Benthamites. First, Bentham was as hostile to religion as was Carlile, and in 1822 Carlile published Bentham's *Analysis of the Influence of Natural Religion on the Temporal Happiness of Mankind*.[34] Secondly, in 1825 Carlile was won over to the 'Malthusian' views on birth control held by Place and the young John Stuart Mill. Carlile printed birth control information in the *Republican* in 1825, published separately as *Every Woman's Book* in 1826.[35] The importance of this development is that it gave an impetus to Carlile's radical feminism, and it brought him to an acceptance of Malthusian political economy. The latter set Carlile even further apart from many other London radicals, including those who in the late 1820s were espousing the cause of socialism. The merits of Owenism were urged upon Carlile by correspondents to his periodical, the *Lion*, but he was not persuaded.[36] His legacy to the 1830s was to be a para-doxical one, with root-and-branch republicanism allied to social and economic individualism — a combination which was eventually to prepare even some of the most outspoken of heirs to the old Jacobins to hitch themselves to the extreme wing of the Liberal Party as it emerged in the 1850s.

The roots of socialist thinking are to be found more in the work experiences of artisans, domestic workers and factory hands than in periodicals and books, though such experiences did prepare a fertile soil for the writings of men like Thomas Hodgskin, William Thompson and Robert Owen. Economic as well as political matters were almost certainly discussed in the radical societies, but the most pervasive form of organisation among working people were the trade societies through which they attempted to control and regulate the conditions of labour. This is not to suggest a rigid division between political and trade matters, but it is true that economic affairs had more immediate relevance than politics, and a school of thought did develop among socialists which lay stress on the former rather than the latter.

The Combination Acts did not make trade combinations any more illegal than they already were under both statute and common law, but the Acts were more easily enforced and were resented as a symbol. They did not put a stop to trade organisations, which were an essential feature of artisan life providing a system of finding work through houses-of-call and offering friendly-society facilities for mutual protection in time of trouble. Trade associations also aimed to preserve the level of wages and the honour of the workman's skill through restrictions on access to the trade in question. In London especially this kind of labour organisation flourished. In so far as some of the trade societies' objects required political solutions they were political organisations, and in years of depression the membership often turned to political agitation, but this was not their primary purpose. In December 1818 John Gast, a shipwright and political radical, organised the 'Philanthropic Hercules' to bring all the London trades together to defend the skills, wages and respectability of the artisans of the metropolis.[37] His inspiration came partly from the very different environment of industrial Lancashire where, earlier the same year, a general union or 'Philanthropic Society' had been organised by the cotton spinners (including their future leader John Doherty). A federation of local spinners' unions existed from at least 1810, and in 1818 a strike was organised with support from as far afield as London and Scotland for the restoration of wages reduced in 1816. Some advances were won for a time, but by August 1818 the back of the union had been broken and the struggle collapsed amid violence and recriminations. The government had become alarmed at the Philanthropic Society's sinister network of secret committees and delegates, where noted radical agitators were seen to be active. Such was the background to the political agitation which gripped Lancashire in 1819.[38] Though neither the Philanthropic Society nor the Philanthropic Hercules survived long, they set an example for trades unions which was to be copied in the suceeding decades.

In 1814 Francis Place turned his mind to the problem of the Combination Acts, and in 1818 he and Bentham helped John Wade set up the *Gorgon* as a trade union newspaper. Over the next few years Place worked at building contacts both with artisan leaders and radical politicians such as Joseph Hume and J C Hobhouse. Petitions were presented in Parliament, and in 1824 a Committee of Inquiry was set up which, with careful management of witnesses by Place, was persuaded to support three Bills introduced by Hume in 1824. One of these not only repealed the Combination Acts of 1799 and 1800, but also removed the common law prohibition on combinations and conspiracies. The Bills were enacted before most MPs realised the significance of what had been done, but a series of strikes following the repeal led Parliament in 1825 to restore the common law on conspiracy, whilst legalising associations for the regulation of hours and wages. With this degree of legal protection trade unions could now come out into the open as legitimate forms of working-class organisation.[39]

The history of trade unions and of industrial disputes as such is beyond the scope of this book, except in so far as strikes and union objectives contributed to the development of radicalism. This was certainly the case with the cotton spinners, who in 1819 won the first measure of protective legislation for factory workers since the repeal of the apprenticeship clauses of the Statute of Artificers. The Act of that year, introduced by Sir Robert Peel the elder, and based on proposals put forward by Robert Owen in 1815, was a half-hearted measure to limit the hours of employment of 'free' child labour (as opposed to 'apprenticed' pauper-child labour which had been regulated by Peel's earlier Act in 1802). It nevertheless represented a restoration of the principle of interference by the state to protect labour, which the union aimed to turn into an opportunity to work for protection of adult male and female labour as well. In 1824 the spinners opposed the employment of women, but in this they were not being entirely altruistic for the spinners were under attack from cheap female labour and were reacting in a way traditional among skilled trades.[40] At the same time as Place and Hume were working to have trade unions legalised, Place and Hobhouse were pressing for further factory legislation to reduce the hours worked by children to eleven a day. Petitions were organised throughout the spinning towns of the Manchester and Glasgow areas, and when the subsequent Act proved as ineffective as its predecessor the spinners' leaders pressed for the prosecution of offending employers. In November 1828 Doherty called a meeting of spinners, attended also by Richard Potter and William Clegg of the middle-class reformers, which set up a Society for the Protection of Children Employed in Cotton Factories to secure the enforcement of the law prohibiting the employment of children under nine and restricting the hours of children under sixteen. Other radical factory masters, such as Joseph Brotherton, subsequently joined but most remained hostile. The Society, though independent, was closely identified with the spinners' union. Some prosecutions were brought but with little overall effect, and in 1830 the Lancashire movement merged with that begun in Yorkshire by Richard Oastler to secure a wider Factory Act for all branches of the textile industry.

The Lancashire movement of the 1820s was not a complete failure, though, for it had begun to rouse public opinion and had utilised a broad base of radical support. Not only had union leaders joined with reforming masters, but the power of the radical press had also been harnessed. In 1823 Cobbett published in his *Register* a letter to William Wilberforce denouncing the condition of the factory children and comparing it unfavourably with that of negro slaves — a comparison picked up later by others including Oastler as the campaign against slavery intensified. In 1828 Carlile published in the *Lion* a 'Memoir' of Robert Blincoe who had been a factory 'apprentice', written by John Brown of Bolton, a journalist who had actively supported the spinners in Lancashire. Oastler, Doherty, Owen and others were to build on these foundations in the 1830s.[41]

After the trade union legislation of 1824–5 the London committee of trades which Place and Gast had organised during the agitation was kept in existence and began to issue its own journal, the *Trades Newspaper*. The artisans rejected Place's suggestion that Edward Baines junior should be its editor, and appointed J C Robertson, editor of the *Mechanics' Magazine*, instead. Disgusted, Place withdrew his support.[42] The division of opinion was significant, for Place and Baines represented one view of political economy, and Robertson and the artisans quite another. Just as the 1820s saw an important development in political thinking with Carlile's re-establishment of Paineite republicanism, so the decade also saw an important new stage in economic thinking with the radical challenge to orthodox political economy.

The *Mechanics' Magazine* was started in 1823 by Robertson and Thomas Hodgskin, a retired naval officer and associate of Bentham and Place. The two editors were keen to establish in London a mechanics' institution on the model of that in Glasgow, and they approached Place for help. The latter easily secured the support of middle-class radicals like Bentham, Brougham and Burdett, but as a consequence the institution grew beyond what Robertson and Hodgskin had intended. Instead of being an educational club for mechanics it became a large and expensive society under the control of, and appealing to, wealthier classes. Nevertheless, it provided Hodgskin with a platform on which to expound his views on political economy. These were in opposition to the Ricardian theory, espoused by Place and the middle-class radicals, and were published in 1827 as *Popular Political Economy*. Two years earlier Hodgskin had published his most famous work, *Labour Defended against the Claims of Capital*, in which he argued that labour is the only source of value. The *Trades Newspaper* supported these views. In 1826, however, Robertson was imprisoned for debt and Place's influence with it was restored. Hodgskin broke with both the paper and the mechanics' institution, but his influence continued to grow amongst trade societies in both London and the provinces. By the later 1820s such 'labourist' ideas were common currency with mechanics and artisans, especially those threatened by the increasing control which capitalists and middlemen were exerting over their labour. Hodgskin's works, together with John Gray's *Lecture on Human Happiness* (1825) and William Thompson's *An Inquiry into the Principles of the Distribution of Wealth most Conducive to Happiness* (1824), were the most important contributions to the intellectual armoury of labour in the 1830s.[43]

It would be wrong, though, to imply that one 'school' of radical thought was emerging. Hodgskin and Thompson both attacked capitalism, but the former was an individualist and the latter a socialist. Carlile attacked the lack of political education at the mechanics' institution, but supported Place's economic views; Robertson supported the political but attacked the economic. Gray, like Attwood, was a monetary reformer opposed to gold; Cobbett followed Paine in attacking paper money. Radicalism contained many contradictions and paradoxes, which is probably why room was found among its ranks for Robert Owen.

Owen was a wealthy capitalist, Tory in politics and philanthropic in outlook like the elder Peel. His chief claim in the 1820s to be a reformer lay in his keen interest in three areas of social policy which were attracting a great deal of public attention — factory reform, poor law reform, and popular education. He was probably the first propagandist to use the phrase 'working classes', but he showed no awareness of the realities of class divisions and his theories assumed class conflict to be an irrational aberration from the rational harmony which united all society.[45] When Owen began to advocate his community schemes in 1817 he was condemned not only by orthodox political economists but also by radical journalists like Wooler and Cobbett.[46] Yet within a decade his ideas were becoming accepted among the working class.

In the 1820s artisans in London and Glasgow showed interest in his community schemes as outlined in his London Tavern speeches of 1817 and his *Report to the County of Lanark* of 1820. The Scottish interest led to the founding of the Orbiston community (1825-7), a leading member of which, Alexander Campbell, was already emerging as a radical in Glasgow. A joiner by trade, he supported Carlile, and was on the Glasgow committee formed to congratulate him on his release in 1825. After the failure of Orbiston Campbell involved himself in trade unionism, co-operation, radical journalism and the political reform movement.[47] In London the first group of artisans to catch hold of Owen's ideas was mainly of printers, led by a Scotsman, George Mudie. In 1821 they formed a Co-operative and Economical Society 'for improving the condition of the working classes during their continuance in their present employments'. Communal living was organised for twenty-one families in Spa Fields, but the scheme came to an end in 1823. One of their number who became a life-long Owenite was Henry Hetherington.

Owen had nothing to do with either the Orbiston or Spa Fields communities for they did not meet the full requirements of his own grand plan. In 1824 he went to America to organise a true community at New Harmony, Indiana, but his self-styled disciples persisted, for the idea of co-operation and communitarianism corresponded closely with the sense of independence and mutuality which characterised artisan life. In 1824 a further attempt was made in London with the eventual aim of forming a community. The co-operators were as much influenced by William Thompson as Robert Owen, though the latter gave them an impossible vision. In 1827 they started co-operative trading to raise funds for a community of artisans. James Watson and William Lovett were two of the early storekeepers. Their work was as much educative as economic, as they devoted themselves to co-operative propaganda, issuing a periodical, the *Co-operative Magazine*, and gathering together a library. A Union Exchange Society was also started in 1827 for the exchange of goods between members, thus eliminating the middleman and restoring to the artisans control over their own labour and giving them full payment for it. This idea was not new, and needed little theoretical justification. Nevertheless propaganda was important.[48]

In 1825 Dr William King of Brighton decided to emulate the London educational radicals and opened a mechanics' institute in Brighton. Enthusiasm flagged and it closed in 1828, but not before it had given birth to the Brighton Co-operative Benevolent Fund. In July 1827 this became a co-operative trading association to raise funds for a community. A variety of artisans was attracted, and Dr King was moved to begin to educate the working classes more widely in the principles and (especially) the practice of co-operation. His instrument was a monthly four-page leaflet, *The Co-operator*, issued between May 1828 and August 1830. Its impact was out of all proportion to its size. By 1830 King was able to claim that his paper had inspired over 300 societies in places as different as Birmingham, Halifax and Chester. 'To the benevolent author of *The Co-operator* the working classes are under lasting obligation, as from his pen they have received much valuable instruction; indeed his publication has become a sort of text-book to co-operators', acknowledged the *Co-operative Magazine* in March 1830.[49] The societies were well scattered across the country, but the textile districts of the North were particularly well represented as was London, which by May 1829 had at least fourteen societies.[50] The original London Co-operative Trading Association members started the British Association for the Promotion of Co-operative Knowledge to co-ordinate activities in London. Its leading propagandists included Lovett, Watson, Hetherington, John Cleave and William Carpenter – all soon to become involved in the struggle of the unstamped press. By the summer of 1831 there were over five hundred societies in touch with the BAPCK when the first of a series of six-monthly Co-operative Congresses was held in Manchester. None of this activity owed much to Owen, but when he returned from America in 1830 he threw himself wholeheartedly into it, seizing the opportunity to transform this eager manifestation of the co-operative spirit into the secular millennium.[51]

Despite the calm which dulled the political reform movement in the 1820s, therefore, reforming opinion in general was quietly seething. Republicans and co-operators, trade unionists and zetetics, factory reformers and popular educators were all in the field and were rapidly caught up in the reform crisis which broke in 1830. But the 1820s had one final lesson for reformers, and that was in the art of organisation. The petition was a traditional right, asserted by the supporters of Wilkes in the 1760s and 1770s; the 1780s had added the Association; from Methodism (and the London Corresponding Society) had come the small division or class meeting; from Cobbett and Carlile had come the press. But the characteristic expression of radicalism in the 1830s and 1840s, embracing all these other elements, was the mobilisation of public opinion at large through mass organisation. The models for this form of action were widely recognised at the time as being the anti-slavery campaign, and Daniel O'Connell's Catholic Association. The former had already achieved some success with the abolition of the slave trade in 1807, and was to triumph in 1833 with the abolition of slavery itself within the British Empire. With the emancipation of the Catholics in 1829, the latter achieved what had escaped both Pitt and the Whigs over the previous thirty years.

The abolition of the slave trade in 1807 had been followed by a period of uncertainty as people awaited its results, but the Congress of Vienna, with its promise to renew French slave-trading rights, stimulated a resurgence of abolition politics. Within a month 800 petitions had flowed into Parliament. The final number of signatories totalled 1½ million (from a population of 12 million). In the words of Whitbread, 'The country never has, and I fear, never will, express a feeling so general as they have done about the slave trade'.

In the post-war years the arguments about slavery were carried along by the wider debate about political reform. The early success of slave registration (a census) and the demographic proof it yielded that abolition had not dramatically improved the lot of the slaves, in conjunction with news of slave revolts, persuaded more and more people that slaves ought to be freed. Thus, from 1822, the humanitarians regrouped. They were now strengthened by new, younger leaders and by a new economic critique of slavery, but they returned to their well tried tactics. Thomas Clarkson's lecture tours in 1823 and 1824 stimulated more than 800 petitions and the formation of more than 200 local associations. Parliamentary candidates were forced to declare themselves on slavery. Indeed by the mid-1820s it was quite clear that support for slavery had become an electoral liability. Anti-slavery publications, led by the influential *Anti-Slavery Monthly Reporter* (1825-36), poured from the presses in their millions. Female anti-slavery associations grew in number and influence — incidentally giving women their first major role in modern British politics. Ever more newspapers and magazines were won over and lent their weight to black freedom. Vast crowds, of all social classes and both sexes, attended metropolitan and provincial meetings, their size limited solely by the physical capacity of the meeting place. Public opinion was aroused by an expertly co-ordinated campaign. Within a decade of Clarkson's renewed lecture tours the necessary legislation was carried to abolish slavery in the British Empire.

Throughout the campaign astute lobbying channelled public feeling about slavery within Parliament and government itself. It was clear by 1830 that black freedom would only be a matter of time. The Reform Act of 1832 made it imminent by undermining the old West India lobby, which was pro-slavery. It is significant that, using the language of the age, Parliament was compared to 'the steam engine which required only *the steam of public opinion*, strongly expressed, to enable it to annihilate Colonial Slavery at one majestic stroke'. When, on 1 August 1838, three-quarters of a million slaves were freed, the campaign which had secured their freedom was confirmed as the triumphant model to be copied by any other group intent on pursuing political change. If slavery could be ended, then what else might not be achieved by careful and assiduous campaigning?[52]

Even more rapidly successful in achieving its object was Daniel O'Connell's contemporaneous movement for Catholic Emancipation — the very word captures the same sense of freedom. O'Connell was a radical Irish Catholic lawyer of middle-class background. The agitation he led in the 1820s was a basically middle-class one, though supported by the peasantry through the agency of the Catholic Church. 'O'Connellite radicalism was . . . the equivalent of the "Manchester" middle-class radicalism of England,' Edward Norman has observed. 'It was based, as theirs was, in religious dissent.'[53] Catholic Emancipation became a live issue again in English politics in 1821 when a Bill was narrowly passed by the Commons, only to be rejected by the Lords. Lord Liverpool now made the issue an open one in Cabinet, and strong support was given over the next few years by the followers of Canning. In 1823 O'Connell founded the Catholic Association to mobilise Irish opinion in favour of repeal. The Catholic priesthood were *ex officio* members, including the bishops. The Association thus had a ready network of agents in every parish to stir opinion and to collect the penny a month Catholic Rent to finance the agitation. The government was alarmed, and in 1825 suspended the Association by name, but all O'Connell did was to rename it the New Catholic Association. In the same year Burdett introduced a Relief Bill, which also proposed the disfranchisement of the Irish forty-shilling free-holders, but this achieved little other than to demonstrate the shallowness of Burdett's radicalism. In 1826 at the general election the voters rejected their traditional support for their landlords and supported Protestant Emancipationists instead. Then, in 1828, following the resignation of the Canningites from Wellington's ministry and the appointment of the member for County Clare to the vacant Board of Trade, O'Connell took his chance by standing himself at the consequent by-election. The sitting member, Vesey Fitzgerald, was a Protestant Emancipationist, but O'Connell captured the seat. Faced with the options of Catholic Emancipation or civil war, the Duke of Wellington chose the former and persuaded the king.[54] The Catholic Association had demonstrated the power of a centrally-organised mass movement, peacefully intended but backed by the threat of force, to compel Parliament to change its mind on a basic constitutional issue, and to carry legislation to which the majority of members probably remained opposed. The model was quickly copied. Richard Carlile and Robert Taylor had their 'Infidel Rent' in 1829, and when O'Connell assisted Thomas Attwood's Birmingham Political Union in 1830 the Irish dimension to English radicalism was underlined.[55]

Chapter 9

THE GREAT BETRAYAL, 1830-7

The movement for reform rapidly gathered pace in the late 1820s, leading to a remarkable series of reforms in the period 1828-35 which affected the political, social and economic life of the nation. Yet the radicals were far from satisfied. Looking back on the period of reform they saw not success but frustration and failure. What had been hailed as reforms soon came to be seen as moderate measures aimed at the preservation and support of the existing state of affairs. This might suit the moderates but it left the radical reformers in an isolated and weak position.

The period of reform can be dated from 1827 when Lord Liverpool suffered a stroke and retired from public life. The broad-bottomed Tory administration which he had virtually inherited from William Pitt, and which since 1822 had contained ministers such as Robert Peel who were reformers of a sort, now began to disintegrate. The 'Protestant' Tories refused to serve under Canning, Liverpool's successor, who was dangerously sympathetic towards freeing trade as well as Catholic Emancipation. Whigs were brought into Canning's Cabinet, although the prime minister himself remained implacably opposed to parliamentary reform. His death in August 1827 left a political void in which his supporters found themselves moving away from other Tories and towards the Whigs. Goderich's brief ministry broke on these divisions, and in January 1828 the Duke of Wellington was brought in to re-unite the Tories. A month later Russell's motion for the repeal of the Test and Corporation Acts was carried in the hope of uniting Protestant opposition against any concessions to the Catholics, but in May Huskisson led the Canningites out of the Cabinet over the failure of the government to support legislation for the disfranchisement of both Penryn and East Retford with a transfer of seats to Manchester and Birmingham respectively. Then came Catholic Emancipation which convinced many Tories that the radicals were right to argue that the Commons no longer represented the country. The cause of parliamentary reform now received important and unforeseen support from Tories, angry at the betrayal of their Church, at the same time as radicalism was again stirring in the country in the face of renewed economic depression. The death of George IV in 1830 removed a further barrier to reform, and when Wellington again failed to rally the Tories after a general election in which reform had become an important issue, Grey was called upon by William IV to form the first predominantly Whig ministry since the 'Ministry of All the Talents' had fallen in 1807.[1]

The Whigs had rediscovered their commitment to reform, but even so when Thomas Attwood formed the Birmingham Political Union in January 1830 it was to the Tories that he turned for support. The founders of the Birmingham Political Union were almost exclusively High Tories protesting at the effects of the financial policy pursued by successive governments since Peel's Act of 1819 had restored the gold base to the currency. Finding little support among mainstream Tories and Whigs, they turned to the radicals and began to campaign for parliamentary reform. The BPU was to claim for itself an important part in the leadership of public opinion during the next three years, but it was in fact the product of the peculiar circumstances of Birmingham, where the existence of small workshops and comparatively easy social mobility fostered the alliance on which the Union was based.[2] Elsewhere it was to prove more difficult to secure co-operation between popular radicals demanding their natural rights and an end to economic distress, and mercantile and manufacturing interests seeking representation so as to secure desired reforms. In Leeds the Tories, who opposed political reform, ensured the sympathy of popular radicals with their support for factory reform against the Liberal-Whig manufacturers led by Edward Baines, while in both Manchester and London middle-class reformers and popular radicals remained mutually suspicious. London radicals were divided between Place's moderate Political Union, and the more extreme National Union of the Working Classes. The moderate reformers of Manchester wanted representation of their particular interests, and middle-class radicals like Archibald Prentice urged the repeal of the Corn Laws — a policy opposed both by most farmers (who were sympathetic to Attwood's currency proposals) and by many popular radicals who feared cheap bread would mean low wages.[3] Parliamentary reform finally triumphed in 1832 not because a united reform movement pressed for it but because different sections of society converged on the same point for different reasons at a time when a sympathetic government was in a position to respond.

The relationship between reform within Parliament and pressure from without has been much debated in recent years. The Whig view, propounded at the time by T B Macaulay (who fought and won a Leeds seat in 1832) was that the ministers made a judicious concession to the people in order to preserve the constitution by establishing it upon the firm base of property. The Reform Act marked in effect the acceptance of the new industrial urban interest by the old landed interest, in a joint effort to outflank the radicals. This interpretation was widely accepted at the time by both Whigs and radicals. Recent historians have begun to call it into question, seeing in the conservative nature of the Act good reason for emphasising the traditionalist basis of reform along 'country party' lines — making the executive subject to the legislature, and preserving the political power of the landed interest by limiting patronage boroughs, increasing the county representation, and dividing urban from rural constituencies. This line of thought is attractive, particularly as an explanation of the early stages of the reform crisis, and helps fix the measure in its true context which owed more to the tradition of Wyvill and the reformers of the 1780s than it did to the radicals of the rapidly emerging industrial centres of the early nineteenth century. But it is insufficient to explain the way the reform crisis developed in 1831 and 1832, during which time the Tories regrouped around Wellington and Peel, and anti-reformers controlled the House of Lords.[4]

Popular unrest appeared in three distinct forms in the early 1830s: agricultural riots, industrial disputes, and political radicalism. Only the latter is relevant to a consideration of the reform crisis, and this is significant for, had the economic grievances been harnessed in the cause of reform, the outcome might have been very different. The agricultural riots swept the southern and eastern counties in 1830 and 1831. A period of cripplingly low corn prices in the early and mid-1820s had been followed at the end of the decade by equally damaging high prices. Farmers were unable to pay their rents to their landlords, who sometimes had to remit them to keep their land tenanted, while taxes in the form of poor rates and tithes were resented as an additional burden. But above all the labourers suffered, and the last straw came in the south when threshing machinery was introduced on some farms, thus threatening winter employment. Machine-breaking and wage riots broke out in Kent, with some farmers sympathising as their neighbours' machines were wrecked. Waves of violence spread outwards along the southern counties as far as Cornwall and South Wales, and up the east coast to Lincolnshire and even parts of Yorkshire and the North. The methods used were the traditional ones of direct action — threatening letters, arson, machine-breaking and food riots in favour of the old 'moral economy' of the just price. The response of the government was also traditional — nineteen men hanged, 644 imprisoned, and 481 transported. If one could measure the seriousness of the threat by the intensity of the response then the greatest danger in the early 1830s came from the countryside, though it could be that the governing classes were most sensitive to unrest in their own backyards. Certainly the Canningite-Whig Home Secretary, Lord Melbourne, was no 'reformer' when dealing with agricultural rioters. Not even Cobbett, though, could turn this labourers' revolt into radicalism. 'Captain Swing' had far less in common with the political reformers than had his industrial equivalent, 'Ned Ludd'.[5]

The agricultural crisis peaked in 1830 before the reform crisis really broke. The industrial unrest, though building up from 1829, did not peak until 1833-4, after the crisis was over. There was some Luddism in 1830 and 1831 in Norwich, the West Country, Redditch, Glossop and Loughborough but nothing as serious as in 1811-12. What is really significant about the industrial protest of the early 1830s is the way in which it was channelled into relatively peaceful organisations — the factory movement, trade unionism and political unions.

Popular radicalism, such as had been nurtured in the 1820s, played a central part in the reform crisis of 1831-2, even though it had little influence on the final shaping of the Act. Without the radicals the middle-class reformers would have made little headway, and only in places like Birmingham could a strong middle-class movement emerge based on working-class support. The middle classes, for the most part, lacked both popular support and internal cohesion. Indeed it has been suggested that the 'middle class' enfranchised in 1832 was, for the most part, a myth. They were able to use their newspapers to create the image of a 'public opinion' in favour of reform, a fact clearly exemplified in Leeds where Edward Baines' *Leeds Mercury* played a central role.[6]

Before George IV was even buried, the *Mercury* was floating in an editorial the idea that Henry Brougham should be a candidate for Yorkshire in the forthcoming general election. Although he was already nominated for Knaresborough, he had no land in the county and was not an obvious candidate, but Leeds was determined to claim one of the county seats for itself. Brougham, as a moderate reformer and opponent of slavery, was a good choice in the circumstances, and the *Mercury* was successful in its efforts.[7] Baines and his son continued to play a similarly active part in the reform politics of the next two years as the *Mercury* both expressed and became Leeds' public opinion, willing to see the creation of peers to see the Bill through the Lords, and strongly urging the withholding of supplies to prevent the formation of an anti-reform ministry in May 1832.[8] But the opinion which Baines projected in the *Mercury* was not that of all leeds citizens, and his opposition to universal suffrage and equivocal position on factory reform lost him much of the support which his earlier exposure of 'Oliver the Spy' had won. When the Bainesite Holbeck Political Union had 200 members, the Leeds Radical Political Union had ten times that number.[9]

The middle-class myth was also fostered in London by Place, Mill and the Philosophic Radicals. They took the lead in May 1832, threatening revolution if the Duke of Wellington were to form an anti-reform Ministry and so permanently oust the Whigs. Whether this propaganda was entirely bluff will never be known for the occasion never arose to test it. A run on the banks was a real possibility, and more likely to be effective than any parallel working-class threat of a general strike or abstinence from excisable goods, but no middle-class reformers were likely to risk the threat of social revolution to which any attempt to resist the Duke might have led. It is perhaps significant that the Duke, who had yielded over the threat of civil war in his native Ireland in 1829, did not yield in May 1832. His failure to form a ministry was not because he feared the consequences in England but because Robert Peel was unwilling to join him to put through a conservative measure of reform. Pressure from without certainly helped Grey, and undoubtedly convinced the king of the need to promise to create peers and thus secure the acquiescence of the Lords, but there was always sufficient accord between the Whigs and the People for there never to have been any danger of reform turning into revolution. The BPU was organised both to agitate for reform and to preserve law and order.[10]

Grey formed his first ministry in November 1830, and Russell introduced a Reform Bill into the Commons in March 1831. A general election was then held to strengthen the reformers in the Commons, and here public opinion was able to play an important part, with both counties and 'open' boroughs overwhelmingly returning reformers to Parliament. A new Bill was then quickly passed through the Commons, but in October the Lords rejected it by forty-one votes. If twenty-one bishops had voted the other way the Bill would have been carried. As it was not, the country demonstrated its feeling. Rioting was particularly severe in Derby, Nottingham and Bristol where the authorities temporarily lost control of the situation. Russell then introduced a third Bill, relying on the king to create enough Whig peers to see it through the Lords. When in April 1832 the king refused, Grey resigned, precipitating the May crisis. The failure of the Duke of Wellington to form an alternative ministry led to the recall of the Whigs, and their third Bill became law in June 1832. Except in Scotland, where reform meant expanding the electorate from about 4500 to 65,000, thus giving that country a political life for the first time since the Union, the achievements of the legislation were modest. Some rotten boroughs were disfranchised, but not all. There was some redistribution of seats, but the populous areas were still under-represented. The extension of the vote to the £10 urban householder did not, in some parts of the country, enfranchise even all respectable middling folk, while it limited the franchise in former 'scot-and-lot' boroughs like Westminster and Preston. In the counties the 'Chandos' clause, enfranchising £50 tenants-at-will, actually increased the power of the landlords. 'Legitimate' influence and the 'politics of deference' emerged unscathed. The middle-class radicals were soon to find how little they had actually been given, and the popular radicals were immediately aware of a great betrayal.[11]

Popular radicalism had been increasing in extent and fervour since the election of 1830, with peaks of activity in October 1831 and May 1832. Political unions sprang up in many parts of the country, giving the popular radicals in some parts the chance to take over the reform agitation from the moderates. In Manchester on 12 October a crowd of 10,000 carried resolutions in favour of universal suffrage. In Bolton in November the moderates walked out, leaving the ground to the radicals. In Nottingham, where many working men already had the vote, the Political Union had difficulty attracting moderates, though it did come to symbolise radical opposition to the Whig

town council. In Leicester, the Political Union managed to draw
support from both moderates and radicals in opposition to the Tory
town council. Local background and circumstance is all important to
an understanding of how the reform movement developed. In
Nottingham, Cobbett was paid £69 by the Corporation to speak in
favour of reform, and his speech prompted the formation of the
Political Union in revulsion. In Manchester, where Cobbett stood as
a candidate in 1832, he was the hero of the radicals, attacking the
middle classes and being attacked in turn by them.[12]

The most potent centre of reform was London, not because the
number involved in political organisations was large but because the
London radicals were in the best position to make an immediate
impact on Parliament, their leaders were among the most experienced, and their newspapers had a national readership. The
actual membership of the main London organisations has been
estimated at no more than 20,000 (compared with the 15,000 of the
BPU). In both cases, however, the active membership appears to
have been much lower and the numbers attracted to mass meetings
much higher.[13] What one can see in the radicalism of 1830-2 is an
organised, independent working-class presence, sometimes working in co-operation with radicals from other classes, sometimes
standing alone in opposition to all. A tradition of agitation had
grown up since about 1815 which the middle-class campaign of the
early 1830s kindled, and which the modest measure of 1832 failed to
extinguish. The radicals expressed themselves not only in 'low
unions', which continued in existence after June 1832, but also in
trade societies and through their press. Had this radicalism become
fused with economic discontents, as it did briefly in Merthyr Tydfil
in 1831, then England might have experienced a revolution far
beyond what Place and Mill were threatening. As it was, neither the
Derby and Nottingham, nor even the Bristol riots approached either
the scale or the political significance of the Merthyr rising.[14]

The middle-class reformers of 1832 were concerned primarily
with the franchise, whereas the popular radicals were campaigning
for a whole series of interrelated reforms. Central to these was the
struggle for the legality of the unstamped press, for the cheap newspaper — as Cobbett and Carlile had demonstrated — was the
backbone of any serious and sustained radical activity. This had been
recognised by the ministry in 1819, but in 1830 the popular press
declared war against the 4d newspaper stamp and particularly

against that provision of 60 George III cap.9 which classified all cheap periodicals as newspapers. The 'war of the unstamped' was begun by the authorities themselves in July 1830 when the Stamp Commissioners suppressed John Doherty's *United Trades Co-operative Journal*. Then in October a London journalist, William Carpenter, began to issue a weekly series of separate, unstamped *Political Letters and Pamphlets* in the cause of reform and in blatant circumvention of the law. Prosecution ended the *Political Letters* in May 1831. Also in October 1830 Henry Hetherington adopted the same subterfuge of separate weekly publications for his *Penny Papers for the People, published by the Poor Man's Guardian*, but in July 1831, following Carpenter's trial, he began an openly illegal weekly periodical, *The Poor Man's Guardian: A weekly newspaper for the people, established contrary to "Law" to try the power of "Might" against "Right"*. The price was 1d and the maximum circulation reached was about 16,000 copies a week. The paper formed the spearhead of the campaign to change the law, though Hetherington also published other papers in the same cause. Like Carlile's *Republican* it also inspired imitators across the country, enlisted armies of volunteers willing to become 'victims' in the cause, raised 'Victim Funds', and gave its readers a powerful radical education by word and deed. Prosecution merely fed Hetherington and his agents with new resolve. The *Poor Man's Guardian* itself was born after Hetherington had been summonsed in June 1831 as publisher of Baden Lorymer's *Republican*. On that occasion he evaded arrest by undertaking a provincial lecture tour to encourage vendors of the unstamped, and was not arrested until September 1831 when he returned to London to visit his dying mother. Of such pathos was propaganda made. Hetherington served six months in prison and was sentenced to a further similar period in December 1832. From the September of that year the *Poor Man's Guardian* was edited by James O'Brien ('Bronterre'), an Irish radical lawyer who brought to the paper a sharp intellectual critique of capitalism which went beyond the staple anti-clerical radicalism of the day.[15]

Hundreds of vendors of the unstamped were arrested across the country. In London alone 737 vendors came before the police courts on 1092 charges. Around half the cases were against street vendors who were in the business more for profit than for ideals, but the rest were self-consciously agents of the unstamped and what it stood for. The bulk of them were men under thirty, some not out of their teens.

One such was George Julian Harney (b. 1817), employed as a shop-boy by Hetherington and twice imprisoned in 1834 and again in 1836 as he obtained his radical education in what he termed the 'radical school of the thirties'. Throughout the provinces there were over a hundred centres from which the unstamped was distributed, and in the major towns independent unstamped papers appeared. In Manchester, Doherty followed up the *United Trades Co-operative Journal* with the *Poor Man's Advocate;* in Glasgow were issued such radical papers as John Sharp's *Agitator;* and in Huddersfield Joshua Hobson produced the *Voice of the West Riding.*[16]

Hobson's experiences may serve as an example of the vitality of the unstamped and its links with provincial radicalism. Hobson (b.1810) was an apprenticed cabinet-maker and one time handloom weaver. In the autumn of 1830 he took an active part in the formation of the Huddersfield Political Union, and with it from the start was deeply involved in the factory movement. He was one of the six Huddersfield radicals who made the 'Fixby Hall Compact' with Richard Oastler in June 1831. In April 1833 the Political Union announced its intention of publishing its own paper, and in June appeared the *Voice of the West Riding*, a 1d unstamped devoted to radical reform. Hobson was both editor and publisher, and printed the paper on a wooden hand-press which he had built himself. In August he was sentenced to six months in prison after refusing to pay a £20 fine for publishing an unstamped newspaper. The *Voice* was kept going in his absence by William Rider of Leeds, and in total ran for fifty-three weeks. Its tone throughout was uncompromisingly militant, voicing the political and social grievances of the West Riding working class. Hobson then moved to Leeds, and in 1837 was selected to use his experience in the production of the *Northern Star.*[17]

In London and elsewhere there was a similarly close connection between the 'low' political unions and the unstamped.[18] Although the aims of the *Poor Man's Guardian* and the National Union of the Working Classes were not exactly the same — the former denouncing the Reform Act even before it was passed, while the latter grudgingly accepted it — there was a large overlap of personalities involved and in many ways the *PMG* was the mouthpiece of the NUWC radicals. Founded in May 1831 out of the remnants of the British Association for Promoting Co-operative Knowledge and the Metropolitan Political Union, the NUWC was led by Hetherington, Watson, Lovett, Cleave, Carpenter and Lee — all of them active in the unstamped. The *PMG*, however, differed sharply from the NUWC over the question of the repeal of the Act of Union, which it opposed. O'Brien in particular did not trust O'Connell. After the passing of the Reform Act in June 1832, Irish issues generally began to loom large against a background of Whig coercion and the tithe war. Struggles for control of the NUWC occurred between various factions of London radicalism led by Benbow (who collaborated with Carlile for a time) and Cleave (who was associated with the 'Owenite' group). Irish politicians, including Feargus O'Connor, began to gain some influence in 1833. By the end of the year the best of the Union was clearly over; radicalism was breaking into new forms; energies were again being put into trade union organisation. Throughout these changes it was the unstamped press which gave unity and coherence to diversity.[19]

Trade union developments in the early 1830s were based partly on the trade societies of the artisans and partly on the co-operative endeavours which had sprung up in the late 1820s. Co-operative production and distribution, coupled with an embryonic socialist theory which sought to eliminate the middleman, led naturally to the labour exchange experiment in which 'labour value' could be given a practical expression in the transfer of labour products. A Union Exchange Society had been started at the Red Lion Square headquarters of the London Co-operative Society in 1827, but this did not involve the use of labour notes. Two further such ventures were commenced in 1832. Then, in September 1832, the Owenite National Equitable Labour Exchange was opened in Gray's Inn Road (later in the Charlotte Street Institution) with a branch in the Blackfriars Rotunda where both Carlile and the NUWC held their meetings. Significantly the only provincial imitation of this came in Birmingham, where William Pare and other Owenites attracted the attention of Thomas Attwood and the currency reformers. An Exchange was opened there in July 1833. Though initially successful all these ventures had failed by early 1834. Their legacy in London was the United Trades Association, set up in March 1833 to run the Exchange on behalf of the trade societies. Co-operation passed into trades unionism.[20]

The principal journals of the Owenites at this time were the *Crisis*, started by Owen in London in April 1832, and the *Pioneer*, begun in Birmingham in September 1833 by James Morrison. The latter was the unofficial organ of the Builders' Union, formed in Birmingham in 1831 as an expression of the builders' resentment at the increasing control being exercised in the trade by capitalistic middlemen. Morrison and James Smith, who became editor of the *Crisis* in September 1833, gave Owenism a powerful voice in 1833–4. Both men were considerably more radical in their socialism than Owen, though both, unlike the *PMG*, stressed the economic rather than the political path to reform.

The movement towards general unionism gained strength in the early 1830s, beginning with the renewed efforts of the Lancashire cotton spinners. Under the leadership of John Doherty a National Association for the Protection of Labour was started in 1830, based on the spinners' union. In the same year he also started a Potters' Union in Staffordshire, while in Yorkshire unionism was again evident among the woollen and worsted workers after the set-back of their defeat at Bradford in 1826. In London the tailors were active and militant among the trade societies, but Owen had grand plans for them all. In the pages of the *Crisis* in October 1833 he announced the Grand National Moral Union of the Productive and Useful Classes. In February 1834 this was metamorphosed by trades delegates into the Grand National Consolidated Trades Union, with Morrison's *Pioneer* as its official organ. Aid was given to turn-outs at Derby and Worcester, with Derby becoming something of a trial of strength, but as the Union grew so too did the opposition of employers. The GNCTU was said to have had a million affiliated members within a few weeks, but the largest number of paid-up members was only 16,000, mostly from London. There was one isolated provincial lodge in Dorset, where six agricultural workers were sentenced to seven years' transportation for taking an illegal oath. Protests in support of these 'Tolpuddle Martyrs' followed swiftly throughout unions associated with the GNCTU – in Newcastle, Leeds, Huddersfield and Manchester, but chiefly in London where Owen now belatedly put himself at the head of the GNCTU. But Owen did not speak the language of class conflict, and was out of sympathy with the increasing bitterness being expressed by Morrison and Smith. The *Crisis* was closed by Owen in August. The GNCTU, already ruptured by the decision of the London tailors to strike on their own, collapsed in the face of the employers' use of 'the document' to break the united ranks of labour. Owen moved blithely on to form the British and Foreign Consolidated Association of Industry, Humanity and Knowledge. The trades fell back into sectionalism, and were soon to resume the political weapon in their contest with capitalism and exploitation.[21]

Just as the trade societies in London formed the basis of both Owenism and every other expression of organised labour in the metropolis, so in the provinces it was the factory movement which linked Owenites, radicals and trade unionists. Doherty's involvement in all three symbolises this unity, which was given organisational expression in 1833 in the National Regeneration Society, involving radical factory masters like John Fielden and leaders of organised labour like Doherty. As with the GNCTU, however, the broad aims of the Regeneration Society were gradually pushed aside amid the bitterness of industrial conflict. The agitation for shorter hours, though, survived, but it was the ten hours movement, rather than the Regeneration Society's demand for eight hours, which attracted the more widespread attention and support.[22]

Though the contribution of Lancashire to the ten hours movement must not be neglected — the factory system was more widespread in Lancashire, and experience of legislation and agitation was greater — it is the West Riding of Yorkshire which has attracted historians most, chiefly because of the colourful impact of Richard Oastler, the passionate ultra-Tory land steward from Fixby near Huddersfield. Indeed the ten hours movement is traditionally, if somewhat erroneously, dated from Oastler's first letter on 'Yorkshire Slavery', published in the *Leeds Mercury* on 16 October 1830. Oastler was drawn into the already existing working–class agitation the following June when six members of the Huddersfield Short Time Committee walked up the hill to Fixby Hall and persuaded him to take the lead. In Parliament Oastler's close friend, Michael Sadler, proposed his Ten Hours Bill on 16 March 1832. He was put off with a Select Committee which took horrifying evidence from the operatives during the summer. The ten hours campaign was therefore being waged at exactly the same time as the political unions were agitating the political reform issue. Nothing could more clearly illustrate the muddy waters of reform in the 1830s, with Tories, opposed to an extension of the franchise, joining with working–class radicals against the Dissenting liberal manufacturers who saw themselves as the champions of enlightenment and reform. The dilemma of the parties is illustrated by events in Leeds where Edward Baines' *Leeds Mercury* spoke the mind of the manufacturing class. Baines senior had been a friend of Oastler's father (they had visited Owen's New Lanark together in 1819) and he was not immediately hostile to Oastler's letter on the conditions of child employment in the Bradford worsted mills. But Oastler's tone was unfortunate. His reference to 'Yorkshire Slavery' was made in an attempt to harness the powerful anti-slavery feelings then current among Wesleyan manufacturers for the cause of the children in their employ. The manufacturers failed to see the parallel, and Oastler grew righteously indignant. Baines did not want to hand a propaganda victory over to his rival editor, Robert Perring of the Tory *Leeds Intelligencer*, but he could not afford to alienate his readers and his advertisers. Finally, on 19 March 1831, Baines junior cut Oastler's fourth letter; it appeared in full in the next issue of the *Intelligencer*.[23]

Oastler led the factory movement as speaker and organiser, but the Short Time Committees of working men played an indispensable part in the agitation as a whole. Throughout the spring of 1832 the textile districts were mobilised in response to Sadler's Select Committee, and at Easter 1832 there was a great 'pilgrimage' to York from all over the West Riding. Footsore and wet, "King Richard's" loyal subjects gathered. Perring came with them and gave a full and sympathetic report in his paper. Baines did not, but implied that many of the working men were drunk and that the whole affair was a Tory election gimmick. The following Saturday a crowd of operatives in Leeds marched through the streets bearing an effigy of Baines senior, which they solemnly burnt outside the *Mercury* office.[24] These demonstrators may have sung the National Anthem outside the *Intelligencer* office, but they were no more in the pocket of the Tories than of the Whigs. They had their own paper (until February 1833), the *Leeds Patriot;* their own leaders in men like James Mann, the radical bookseller; and their own organisation in the Radical Political Union which still championed universal suffrage although that was anathema to the otherwise friendly Perring.

The ambiguity of relationships is illustrated by Sadler's electoral fortunes under the new franchise. In the first Leeds election, in 1832, he contested a seat in the Tory and Radical interest against John Marshall junior, son of the great flax manufacturer, and T B Macaulay. Sadler came bottom of the poll with 44 per cent of the vote in the two-member constituency. When Macaulay retired at the end of 1833, the Leeds Tories dropped Sadler for a safer man, which did not prevent Baines from winning the vacant Leeds seat.[25] A by-election also occurred in Huddersfield, which Sadler fought for the Tories, but here not all radicals were willing to drop their own candidate, Captain Wood, who had previously fought and lost in a straight contest with a Whig. Only when Oastler fought Huddersfield, in a by-election and then in the general election of 1837, were the white-and-blue rosettes of radicalism and toryism pinned on the same chest. Oastler narrowly failed to win, chiefly because he refused to court the small Irish vote by compromising his hatred of Catholic Emancipation.[26] The same kind of political dealing was to be seen between Tories and radicals in Nottingham in 1841 and 1847 but this was exceptional.[27] What the Leeds experience in particular showed was that, however sympathetic Tories might be to the social problems of the working class, radicalism had to stand on its own and expect no favours from either party. And if Tory-Radicalism was something of a marriage of convenience in Yorkshire, it was not even that in Lancashire. The factory movement in Lancashire rested on the alliance forged by Doherty in the 1820s between radical factory masters and trade unionists. Their parliamentary champions were Charles Hindley (elected for Ashton), Joseph Brotherton (Salford) and John Fielden (Oldham), though in Joseph Rayner Stephens they did attract an Oastler-like popular champion in Ashton-under-Lyne.[28]

Sadler's Select Committee came to a premature end with the dissolution of the last unreformed Parliament in 1832. Out of the Commons after his defeat at Leeds, Sadler now handed responsibility for his Ten Hours Bill to Lord Ashley. The Select Committee's findings seemed to ensure success, but the manufacturing interest and opponents of legislative interference in economic matters steadied themselves with a Royal Commission with Edwin Chadwick as Secretary. Efficiently he produced a report leading to a Factory Act which accorded well with the ideas of the *Leeds Mercury* — a reduction in the hours of children under thirteen to eight per day, and of young persons under eighteen to twelve per day. The ten hours advocates had hoped that such a reduction in child labour would force a similar reduction in adult hours, and feared that eight hours would simply mean double-shifts and therefore sixteen hours for adults. In practice relays were operated and, despite the innovation of inspection, the Act proved difficult to enforce, though the twelve-hour limit on the labour of young persons tended to set the norm for adult labour. The ten hours campaigners had to fight until

1847 for their Bill, and the relay system was not effectively suppressed until 1853.[29]

The factory movement in the 1830s crossed not only political and social barriers, but also spanned a wide range of radical activity. Reports of popular meetings about political reform, the unstamped, trade unionism, and the short-time movement all read very similarly, with the same local names cropping up time and time again. In reality what the decade was witnessing was popular radicalism come of age. In every centre of the industrial districts of the North there were now experienced groups of working men demanding their natural and political rights in an independent fashion. One more movement was to summon up all their energies before the whole was plunged into the vortex of Chartism, and that was the anti-Poor Law agitation.

The Poor Law Amendment Act of 1834 was, like the Factory Act of 1833, based on the report of a Royal Commission dominated by political economists and Utilitarians with Edwin Chadwick as Secretary. As such it was certainly a radical measure, but not one of which the popular radicals approved. The Act was conceived primarily as a means of dealing with the agrarian crisis of the 1820s and early 1830s, which had erupted in the 'Swing' riots, and which made itself felt in high poor rates. The accuracy of the diagnosis offered by the Royal Commission is now much doubted, and the Act was greeted with opposition from the start.[30] Sporadic outbursts of violence met the assistant commissioners as they tried to impose the amended law in the South, but nothing like the sustained campaign of opposition which swept the North in 1837.

The opposition to the new Poor Law drew largely on the factory movement, with short-time committees becoming anti-Poor Law committees overnight. The movement displayed the same broad social base. Local gentry, like W B Ferrand of Bingley, resented the centralised bureaucracy which had usurped the position of traditional local government. Parishes were suspicious of losing some of their autonomy to the new Poor Law Unions. Working men feared the prospect of the new Union workhouse and the dreaded workhouse test which would cut off all outdoor relief to the able-bodied poor. Clergymen denounced the Malthusian division of families which was to occur in the new workhouses. Rational, cold, probably more efficient but certainly less humane, the amended Poor Law symbolised all that the popular radicals hated in the new order of society.[31] The Reform Act with its £10 urban franchise spelt out the political rejection of the working class. The Poor Law Amendment Act, coming on top of the failure of the Ten Hours Bill, underlined the social inferiority of those who had nothing to offer but their labour — and not even that as depression came in late 1836, the start of six years of almost unrelieved economic gloom.

Popular community protest greeted Alfred Power, assistant commissioner responsible for introducing the new law in the North. Whipped up by champions of the factory cause, like Matthew Fletcher of Bury, R J Richardson of Manchester, J R Stephens of Ashton, John Fielden of Todmorden, Lawrence Pitkethly of Huddersfield and Peter Bussey of Bradford, crowds in each centre of a proposed Union voiced their anger. Elections of Poor Law Guardians were thwarted when no candidates appeared, or dared to appear. Then Guardians were elected who were intent on preventing the implementation of the law. Boards were paralysed by the refusal of the Guardians to elect a secretary, until the rules were changed to permit the appointment of a secretary because he was also to be Registrar under the 1836 Registration Act. Gradually the total opposition to the law crumbled, and the framework of Unions and Guardians was introduced. Nevertheless important points were won. The Poor Law Commission realised that the workhouse test could not be enforced; outdoor relief remained the norm. In some Unions new workhouses were simply not built — the out-townships of Bradford, for example, refused to pay for a central workhouse and their Guardians paralysed the working of the Union until it was eventually split into two separate units. In practice little was changed under the new Poor Law in its early years. This drew the sting from the anti-Poor Law movement, which was defeated by its own success. By 1838 it had been swallowed up in the broader movement for universal suffrage, but for over a year the people had spoken back to the 'People' of 1832.[32]

To write of radicalism in the 1830s is especially difficult, for there were so many conflicting streams, not readily identifiable with class or party. The periodical and newspaper literature, especially the popular radicals' unstamped press, saw events in stark terms of Whig betrayal and, especially in the factory districts, of the inhumanity of bourgeois capitalism and political economy. This approach over-simplifies and confuses two important points: first, the extent to which these 'middle-class reformers' were themselves genuine radicals with something to offer the popular radicals; and secondly, the extent to which they too were disappointed (even betrayed) by the 1832 Act, and were prepared to join again with the popular radicals to demand further measures of reform.

Political reform in the period 1828–35 rested on three Acts of Parliament. The 1832 Reform Act created borough constituencies for many previously unrepresented (except as parts of counties) towns, and extended the franchise in many existing boroughs to the £10 householder. The Act repealing the Test and Corporation Acts in 1828 removed the slur of second-class citizenship from those Dissenters who increasingly made up the economic and social leadership of the industrial towns. And the Municipal Corporations Act of 1835 broke the oligarchies which had controlled local government for well over a century, and challenged unincorporated towns to press for incorporation. In Leicester, Liverpool and Leeds Dissenting Whigs and Liberals broke the Tory hold on power. In York it was the Whigs who were rooted out. In Birmingham and Manchester the campaign for incorporation was begun. That in Manchester is especially significant, for in it Richard Cobden took the lead. Success came in 1838 and Cobden was in the first group of aldermen. Working men saw no gain in this, and many joined Tories in opposing incorporation. 'The Whigs are at their dirty work again . . . no Middle-class Government . . . No Cotton-Lord Mayors', exclaimed one poster.[33] But this is precisely what the reforms of the 1830s meant. By the end of the decade middle-class Liberals were becoming entrenched as councillors, aldermen, magistrates and Poor Law Guardians. The economic and social masters of the working class had emerged also as their political masters.[34]

Seen from the national point of view, however, this was not quite the case. The cotton lords of Manchester and the Bainesocracy of Leeds, along with their equivalents in other industrial towns, were not masters at Westminster. Richard Cobden and Thomas Attwood were not satisfied by the outcome of 1832. Neither were the Philo-sophic Radicals happy. Despite radical innovations in government, introducing the principle of election into Poor Law and municipal government, experts into factory inspection, and non-parliamentary bureaucrats into Somerset House, the system of 'Old Corruption' remained virtually unchanged.[35] Though in the North, symbolised by Manchester, two strands of radicalism polarising around middle- and working-class positions were to remain distinct and even at times mutually hostile, elsewhere the picture could be different. In Birmingham the Political Union was revived in 1837 and shortly afterwards adopted the full platform of universal suffrage. In London the war of the unstamped was joined by such Philosophic Radicals as Place and Roebuck. The reduction of the newspaper stamp to 1d in 1836 may have been yet another Whig pseudo-reform to help the respectable press compete more effectively with the unstamped, but it also owed something to the efforts of middle-class radical educationalists; and though the reduction did not satisfy the popular radicals, it did make possible the enormous triumphs of the *Northern Star*.[36]

The radical politics of the next decade were to be born out of the conflicting trends of the 1830s. The scars of the 'Great Betrayal' ran deep. The positive side of class consciousness — ideology and organisation — which had been nurtured in the 1820s flourished in the 1830s. The negative side — conflict — was added in the 1830s, especially by the Poor Law Amendment Act. Yet Chartism was built not only on class consciousness and conflict, but on the compromises which it was still possible to work out with radicals such as Thomas Attwood and Francis Place. Whether Chartism could transcend the contradictions implicit in its origins was another matter.

Chapter 10

THE CHARTER AND NO SURRENDER

The failure of the radicals to secure what they regarded as a real measure of political reform led them to regroup in 1837 for another attack on the political establishment. The reformers of Birmingham revived the 'talismanic name of the Political Union' at a mass meeting on Newhall Hill on 19 June 1837, but the leaders of the Union at this stage had not yet emancipated themselves from the programme of moderate reform which they had espoused in the early 1830s as the means to obtaining currency reform.[1] More radical ideas were being canvassed in London where an American, Dr J. R. Black, had involved himself with Place, Lovett, Gast and other artisans in educational endeavours and the campaign against the newspaper stamp. In April 1836 Black founded the Association of Working Men to Procure a Cheap and Honest Press. With the reduction in the newspaper stamp to 1d, and the failure of the agitation for complete abolition, this was transformed in June into an educational society for working men, the London Working Men's Association. Members were attracted not only from the free press struggle but also from the Dorchester Labourers Committee, the former NUWC and local trade unions.

The LWMA became the single most important body in the transformation of 1830s radicalism into Chartism, but it was not the only one. Radical associations had been formed in various parts of the country, including Marylebone (then merely an urbanised parish beyond the northern edge of Westminster) where Feargus O'Connor staked his claim to a position in the leadership of English radicalism in September 1835. Provincial lecture tours by O'Connor in 1835 and again in 1836 further advanced his claim, and by the end of 1836 he had made himself a well known figure both in London and the North. Significantly he was prepared to work with James Bernard of the Cambridgeshire Tenant Farmers' Association, who founded the Central National Association in London (March–September 1837) on a Tory-Radical basis. The LWMA would have nothing to do with Bernard. Also in London, a group of Spenceans and Owenites started a more extreme East London Democratic Association, in which Charles Neesom, Allen Davenport and George Julian Harney were active advocates of a full Paineite programme of political reform.[2]

Although deepening economic distress in 1837 undoubtedly helped strengthen the call for a further measure of political reform, this alone cannot explain the rise of Chartism, for never before had radicalism commanded the mass audience which it was to reach in 1837–42. Each generation of political radicals from the days of Wilkes onwards had bequeathed to its successors both a programme and also groups of individuals firmly committed to it. Place was perhaps unusual in spanning the full half-century from the London Corresponding Society to Chartism, but many others, locally as well as nationally, had been active since 1815. For the bulk of the radicals of 1837–42, however, it was probably the Political Unions of 1830–2 which drew them into active politics, and it was the experience of Whig 'reform' between 1832 and 1837 which turned them into Chartists. Chartism was, first and foremost, a political reaction to political events, though undoubtedly the social dimension of such a political event as the Act of 1834 added new dimensions to the passions which infused their radicalism.[3]

No one realised this better than Feargus O'Connor as he associated the campaign for universal suffrage with the anti-Poor Law movement in 1837, thus antagonising the Tory supporters of the latter. At first even radicals like Matthew Fletcher of Bury were suspicious and thought the new movement a reactionary device to defeat the anti-Poor Law movement, but he and others were soon won over.[4] The great anti-Poor Law meeting at Hartshead Moor in the West Riding in May 1837 was not markedly different from that held in connection with the Charter in the same place in October the following year. The movement which became Chartism therefore existed before the name — not in Thomas Carlyle's sense that Chartism was the cry of the suffering poor,[5] but in the sense that radicalism and protest were forged in the minds of many people before the symbolic adoption of the Charter in 1838.

The Charter was nevertheless an important symbol, like Magna Carta or the Charter on which the liberties of the French were based after 1815. The six points encompassed the traditional radical programme of universal suffrage together with those reforms — the secret ballot, annual elections, the payment of members, the equali-

sation of electoral districts, and the abolition of the property qualification for members — which were necessary to undermine 'Old
Corruption' and make universal suffrage a reality. The actual points
of the Charter emerged from the LWMA during the autumn of 1836
and spring of 1837, though they had much earlier been in Major
Cartwright's programme of reform. In June 1837 a joint committee
of six Radical MPs (Daniel O'Connell, J A Roebuck, J T Leader,
Charles Hindley, W S Crawford and Colonel Perronet Thompson)
and six working men (Henry Hetherington, John Cleave, James
Watson, Richard Moore, William Lovett and Henry Vincent) was
formed to draft a full text of the Charter. The presence of the MPs on
the committee at this stage indicates both the close relationship
which could exist between radicals of various kinds, and the potential differences of opinion latent within Chartism on which the
alliance was to founder. O'Connell in particular, as an outspoken
opponent of trade unions, represented a brand of radicalism unacceptable (except in the narrowest political sense) to the representatives of working men. In fact the general reaction against all
radicalism in the 1830s swept three of the six members out of
Parliament in 1837, and the document known as the Charter was
drafted by Lovett with advice from Place. It was published in May
1838. Meanwhile the repeated failure of Attwood to interest the
government in his currency schemes helped propel the BPU
towards universal suffrage, and in May 1838 the Union published its
own National Petition for parliamentary reform. The Petition and
the Charter were brought together at mass meetings in Glasgow on
21 May and in Birmingham on 5 August. Chartism was now offi-
cially launched.[6]

In fact the popular movement was already well under way. Not
only was O'Connor active in the North, but also LWMA missionaries were busy on provincial lecture tours encouraging the
formation of local Working Men's Associations. Hetherington was
particularly well received — a mark of the esteem in which he was
held from the days of the war of the unstamped.[7] In the North a
group of radicals from Barnsley and Hull, led by a Swedenborgian
named William Hill, began collecting subscriptions to start their
own newspaper. O'Connor had the same idea and, at the great Poor
Law meeting on Hartshead Moor in May 1837, he approached
Joshua Hobson as a possible printer and publisher. O'Connor then
launched an appeal for funds and, incorporating Hill's project, raised

£690 in share capital with which to start the *Northern Star and Leeds General Advertiser* on 18 November 1837.[8] This was a stamped local newspaper with national coverage and appeal, costing 4½d. By January 1838 it was already selling 10,000 copies a week, more than the *Leeds Mercury* which had hitherto been the leading provincial weekly paper.[9]

The tactic of the Chartists was to gather signatures on behalf of the Charter in a massive national petition. This hallowed constitutional device, which the anti-slavery movement had so successfully exploited, was the means chosen by which to demonstrate the overwhelming weight of popular opinion in favour of the Charter. Signature-gathering was the principal local activity of working men's associations in late 1838 and early 1839. A National Convention was to meet in London to superintend the Petition and its presentation to Parliament, and the delegates were elected at mass meetings in London and the provinces in the autumn of 1838. At a great Lancashire meeting on Kersal Moor, Manchester, on 24 September 1838 J R Stephens made his celebrated 'knife and fork' speech in which he identified in his opinion the close link between the suffrage and the anti-Poor Law and factory movements.[10] The nation was now roused; the Northern Political Union was revived in Newcastle; Edinburgh and Glasgow were as active as the major towns in England. When the Convention met in London in February 1839 it could claim to be more representative than the Commons (despite the almost total absence of representatives from rural areas), with twenty delegates from northern England, eight from Scotland, seven each from London and from the West Country, and five from Birmingham forming the major contingents. They included veterans of earlier movements, like James Wroe of Manchester, Matthew Fletcher of Bury and William Rider of Leeds. The BPU dominated the Birmingham delegation, and the LWMA London.[11]

The year 1839 was a crucial one for Chartism. First of all the strategy of the petition was tested and found wanting. The first National Petition, with 1,280,000 signatures, was ready to be presented on 7 May, but the resignation of the government on the same day, followed by the 'Bedchamber Crisis', delayed matters until 12 July. The motion, proposed by Attwood and Fielden, that the Petition should be considered, was then defeated by 125 votes to 46. A few Radicals and Tories (like Disraeli) supported the motion, but there was never the remotest chance that the Chartists' painstakingly-gathered petition would even be looked at by Parliament.[12] Secondly, the events of these months showed up the divisions in the Chartist ranks. The Convention was by no means unanimous over its function or strategy. The BPU moderates soon left and the BPU itself faded out in April. Extremists wished to go beyond being a petitioning body to become an anti-Parliament, and called for 'ulterior measures' should the petition not be accepted. A motion to this effect was passed at a meeting of the London Democratic Association chaired by Harney as early as 28 February 1839 on the initiative of William Rider and Richard Marsden (a Preston handloom weaver).[13] By 'ulterior measures' they meant a National Holiday or month-long general strike as proposed by William Benbow in 1832, a run on the banks, exclusive dealing to put pressure on enfranchised shopkeepers, and abstinence from excisable goods such as tobacco, as well as physical force, but the latter was the more ready and realistic option for the rank and file of petitioners. As spring dragged on into summer their frustrations spilled over into violence. Rioting began in Llanidloes at the end of April and became an excuse for the arrest of local Chartist leaders. Feelings throughout Wales ran high, with an upsurge in rural anti-Poor Law violence in May — the 'Rebecca' riots — and Chartism took deep root in the industrial valleys of the south. Merthyr alone contributed 14,710 signatures to the petition.[14] On 7 May Henry Vincent, who had been the foremost national agitator in the West and south Wales, was arrested and this threw the Convention into a panic. They feared the new Tory government which Peel was trying to form was about to indulge in a new wave of old-style repression.[15] The Convention adjourned itself to Birmingham, but here too there was violence, and in May meetings in the Bull Ring were banned. Shortly after the Convention had reconvened in Birmingham, on 4 July, the Mayor called in a posse of London police to deal with the unrest, but this only aggravated the affair.[16] Lovett proposed a motion in the Convention which symbolised the breakdown in the alliance on which Chartism had been founded. In it he attacked the 'wanton, flagrant, and unjust outrage' that had been made on the people of Birmingham

> by a bloodthirsty and unconstitutional force from London, acting under the authority of men who, when out of office sanctioned and took part in the meetings of the people; and now, when they share in public plunder, seek to keep the people in social slavery

and political degradation.[17]

Lovett and John Collins were arrested for posting this motion in the streets. To make matters worse, the magistrate before whom they appeared was P H Muntz, a leading member of the defunct BPU.

Between the Llanidloes and Birmingham riots the delegates to the Convention had dispersed to rally the country in a series of mass meetings. Had there really been a widespread willingness to resort to force this might have been the best opportunity, for there was a governmental crisis at the centre and the forces of law and order were stretched to the limit. Even so, Colonel Charles Napier, the commander of the troops in the North (and himself a Wiltshire radical) was concerned not so much for the eventual outcome as to overawe the Chartists sufficiently to prevent any silly attempts at violence which would lead only to bloodshed and bitterness.[18] In fact, with the petition not yet rejected, most people were unwilling to contemplate serious violence, and his handling of the situation proved adequate.

After the rejection of the Petition the Convention proceeded to call a general strike in August and then, realising the lack of support in the country at large, went back on its decision. Discredited and reduced to a rump, the Convention disbanded itself in September. The worst violence came after this, as winter approached. Moves seem to have been made in south Wales and the North for a concerted rising. There was talk in Wales of an attempt to release Vincent from Monmouth gaol by force. In Yorkshire on 30 September delegates led by Peter Bussey of Bradford agreed on a simultaneous rising there. O'Connor condemned the idea and left for Ireland. Contacts were maintained between Wales and Bradford by Dr John Taylor, who had temporarily been arrested in the Birmingham rioting, and Charles Jones, who was wanted in connection with the Llanidloes riots. On 4 November three contingents of men, led by John Frost, Zephaniah Williams and William Jones, gathered in the night and marched on Newport. They were dispersed by about thirty troops in the Westgate Hotel.[19] What the exact purpose of this march was, and whether it was the intended rising, remains unclear. If a simultaneous rising in the North were intended then the men of Yorkshire were not ready, though in January 1840 there were incidents similar to those of 1820 in Sheffield, Dewsbury and Bradford.[20] As in the days of Luddism the idea of a conspiracy cannot by entirely dismissed, though as in earlier days a government spy appears to have

been the main instigator at Bradford. Though there was undoubtedly widespread unrest and the potential for violence, this
proved hard to turn into revolution. Half-hearted as it was, the
physical-force strategy alienated the more moderate radicals who
had helped Chartism in its earliest days, and played into the government's hands. Between June 1839 and June 1840 over 500 Chartists
were imprisoned, including most of the leaders. The forces of
Chartism were defeated and scattered on all fronts.

What is remarkable about Chartism is its resilience, for by 1842
the Chartists were ready with a new petition, and the whole cycle of
hope, frustration and violence was repeated with the same immediate consequences. But they did learn some things from 1839,
and one was the need for organisation. The Scottish Chartist movement had developed independently of that in England and Wales,
although close contacts were maintained through delegates and
meetings. Scotland did not have a Poor Law in the English sense, and
had not known the 1834 Act. Trade union radicalism was strong,
especially among the cotton spinners of Glasgow, five of whom had
been sentenced to transportation in 1837 in a case as important as that
of the Tolpuddle Martyrs. Early Glasgow Chartism was very much
based on the trades. But the economy of the west of Scotland was not
as depressed as that of northern England, for the great expansion of
shipbuilding on the Clyde was just beginning. The Govan yard was
laid down in 1840 at the same time as the first Glasgow railways were
being built. Though Scotland knew economic anguish and had its
violent side, moderate and even religious Chartism usually pre-
dominated. While England was still in disarray in August 1839 the
Scots were forming the Universal Suffrage Central Committee for
Scotland and starting a weekly newspaper, the *Chartist Circular*.[21]
Nearly a year later, on 20 July 1840, the English Chartists meeting in
Manchester set up the National Charter Association. Henceforward
Chartism was to have at its centre a nationally organised body which
attracted most, though not all, Chartists. Whereas the Convention
of 1839 had been elected at mass meetings, future Conventions were
to represent smaller numbers of committed members. By the end of
1841 the NCA had 282 localities with 13,000 members. By April
1842, when the next Convention met in London, 401 localities and
50,000 members were being claimed, the majority of the localities
being situated in the textile districts of the North and in London,
with others being scattered mainly along a line from Tyneside

through the Midlands to the West Country.[22]

As the leaders were released from gaol (Lovett in July 1840, O'Connor in August 1841), new plans were made for a Petition and a Convention. The latter assembled in London in April, and on 2 May the Petition, with 3,317,752 signatures, was presented to the Commons by T S Duncombe, the Radical MP for Finsbury. Once more the Petition was rejected, by 287 to 49 votes. During 1841 the economy had turned down severely, and early 1842 brought worse hardship to many areas than had been experienced in 1839 or in any other year of the early nineteenth century.[23] In such circumstances outbreaks of violence were widely expected, but the failure of the Petition once more added a political element to the bitterness. The economic and political aspects of the wave of strikes which swept the industrial districts in the summer of 1842 are very difficult to disentangle. Matters are made worse by the fact that the NCA executive was meeting in Manchester in the midst of the troubles in August 1842, to unveil a statue to Henry Hunt at James Scholefield's chapel on the anniversary of 'Peterloo'.

The industrial unrest began among the Staffordshire miners, following a reduction in wages, in July. By September the strikes had spread to fourteen English counties, Glamorgan, and eight Scottish counties.[24] Not all this activity can by any means be attributed to politics, but the strikes which affected the northern textile counties following the reduction of wages in Stalybridge did inspire local Chartists to try to harness feeling in the cause of the Charter. A mass meeting held on Mottram Moor on 7 August resolved to prolong the strike until the Charter became the law of the land. Within a few days about 50,000 workmen were idle in the Manchester area and a conference of Manchester trades delegates had endorsed the Charter. Radicalism seems to have taken greatest hold among the trades, with factory workers giving a more varied response. The technique of halting factories by drawing the plugs of the engine boilers gave the strikes their name — the 'Plug Plot', as gangs of strikers moved from town to town in Lancashire, Cheshire and over the hills into Yorkshire. Hunger protests, with women noted among the crowds,[25] and demonstrations against cuts in wages at a time of high food prices were probably more important than political considerations, and the Chartist leadership was caught by surprise. At first some members of the NCA executive, including Hill and Harney, condemned the turn-outs as an Anti-Corn Law

League plot (a view shared by the government); others eagerly supported the strikers; O'Connor fluctuated between the two positions. By 20 August the Manchester trades had recommended a return to work, and tension gradually eased. The Chartists had neither taken the lead nor kept out of the trouble, and the authorities were soon arresting them as agitators. Over 200 arrested from Staffordshire were either imprisoned or transported. Some of the fifty-nine, including O'Connor, who were tried at Lancaster were luckier for, having been convicted, their indictment was quashed on a technicality.[26] Still, enough had been done to end for some time all idea of the attainment of political reform by direct action. Firebrands like Thomas Cooper, who was gaoled for inciting riot in the Potteries, emerged from prison changed men and became stalwarts of 'moral force'.[27] Earnest revolutionaries like G J Harney had learned by 1846 that

> Notwithstanding all the talk in 1839 about "arming," the people did not arm, and they will not arm. . . . To attempt a "physical force" agitation at the present time would be productive of no good, but on the contrary of some evil — the evil of exciting suspicion against agitators.[28]

There was to be a resurgence of the old Chartism in 1848, against a familiar background of depression and encouraged by the outbreak of the European revolutions, but despite this much of the spirit and anguish of Chartism was over by 1842.

What is important is that so much survived. The mass movement may have fallen away but, stripped of the hunger politics and protest of the period 1837-42, a nucleus of political radicalism persisted. In towns of any size and in many smaller industrial villages organisation and activity could still be maintained at a level higher than that reached by earlier radical movements in all but exceptional years. The *Northern Star*, which had sold approaching 50,000 copies a week during the heady days of 1839, sold only 12,500 copies on average each week during 1842 and only half that number in the mid-1840s, but this was still an impressively large number for a stamped newspaper (costing 5d from November 1844), each copy of which was read by many subscribers.[29] Around individual sections of the NCA and the weekly *Northern Star* a vigorous local life was maintained in which was nurtured the radical tradition of Paine and his successors. Evidence from the autobiographical recollections of provincial participants like Ben Wilson of Halifax and Benjamin Brierley of Failsworth, points unequivocally to the contribution made by Chartism in these years to a continuously developing political awareness among ordinary working men and women.[30]

The extent to which Chartism did appeal to the rank and file of working folk has recently been illustrated by a study of those Chartists taken prisoner during 1839-41.[31] Only for a group such as this does the historian have sufficient data to spell out quantitatively the overwhelming subjective impression which other evidence conveys of the nature of the Chartist membership. The conclusion is that the Chartists were representative of the working populations of their home communities — in fact they were 'ordinary' working men. This is not of course to say that all such people became Chartists, though many may have signed the petition and come across a copy of the *Northern Star* or a Chartist tract. The minority who became Chartists were distinguished by their commitment to radicalism — 'the Chartists took their politics seriously'.[32] Any attempt to dismiss them as 'hunger politicians' only (though many undoubtedly knew hardship) is to do them a grave injustice and seriously to undervalue what their Chartism was and meant. As Disraeli put it in a sympathetic Tory-Radical speech on the Charter in July 1839, 'where there were economical causes for national movements they led to tumult, but seldom to organization'. Disraeli, however, went on to avow 'that this movement was not occasioned by any desire of political rights', for 'Political rights had so much of an abstract character, their consequence acted so slightly on the multitude, that he did not believe they could ever be the origin of any great popular movement'.[33] This interpretation, shared by such men as Thomas Carlyle, was an article of Tory creed. Though it may have applied to those who were brought in on the fringes in 1839, 1842 and again in 1848, it failed to recognise the importance of radicalism to the Chartist movement throughout its existence.

A further reinterpretation of Chartism which has gained force in recent years has concerned the role of Feargus O'Connor.[34] For many years he received a bad press, thanks largely to the evidence left by other Chartist leaders, most of whom quarrelled with him; the writings of the first Chartist historian, R G Gammage, who admired O'Brien not O'Connor; and the voluminous papers left by Francis Place.[35] O'Connor clearly did transform the artisan-radicalism of the LWMA into a mass movement which, by its very nature, was likely to alienate middle-class sympathisers. He thus cut across the strategy advocated by men like Place, Lovett and the 'moral force' constitutionalists, adopting the form if not the substance of violence. But in so doing he was able to take Chartism beyond the confines of respectable artisans to hungry handworkers who, since the days of Luddism, had existed half in and half outside the radical political movement. The strategy of mass action, as the Catholic Association had shown (in the days when O'Connor was an O'Connellite), needed more for success than petitioning and persuading alone. O'Connor in this sense made Chartism. His quarrels with other leaders, robbing the movement of intelligent and experienced leadership, were undoubtedly damaging, but he did not make Chartism into mere O'Connorism as his opponents claimed. Radicalism had always been riven by clashes of personality — Place against Burdett, Hunt against Cobbett, Carlile against Hetherington, to name but three. Leadership had always been highly personalised — the *Weekly Political Register* had been distinctively Cobbett's, the *Republican*, Carlile's, even the *Poor Man's Guardian*, Hetherington's. The *Northern Star*, although owned by O'Connor after he had bought out the shareholders with the early profits, was never a personal nor even a partisan paper, it was open to all views. In the early years it owed more to Hill, O'Brien and Hobson than to O'Connor. The editor during the later 1840s, G J Harney, admitted in 1846 that O'Connor 'never interferes with what I write in the paper nor does he know what I write until he sees the paper'.[36] Though Chartism is often said to have been let down by its leadership, in fact Chartism as a movement expressed considerable maturity in being able to exist apart from (even despite) its leaders.

Widespread and popular as Chartism was, however, it did not emcompass the total body of working-class opinion and reformist energies. Other reformers continued to offer different avenues by which to reach the promised land. As in the early 1830s one of the basic divisions was that between political radicals and the followers of Robert Owen.

Many Owenites were also Chartists, and thought political reform the essential precursor to socialism,[37] but for Owen and his more orthodox followers the reverse was true. The new moral world was to be created by the reorganisation of society upon socialist lines through the medium of 'communities of united interest'. To this end in May 1835 Owen set up the Association of All Classes of All

Nations, which in 1837 was transformed against Owen's better judgement by the local co-operators of Manchester and Salford into a democratically organised working-class body.[38] By means of missionaries, tracts and meetings in local Social Institutions or Halls of Science it was to prepare public opinion for the coming of the new order. A parallel body was set up to organise a community. Membership and influence grew in 1837-9 in harmony with the rapid spread of Chartism. With his reputation among co-operators, factory reformers and anti-Poor Law agitators, Owen was a popular figure in the textile districts of the North, where much of his support was concentrated. Experienced radicals like Alexander Campbell of Glasgow, William Pare of Birmingham (a founder of the BPU), Lawrence Pitkethly of Huddersfield, and Joshua Hobson of Leeds joined with the Manchester men — George Alexander Fleming (editor of their weekly *New Moral World* and last editor of the *Northern Star*), Lloyd Jones, James Rigby and Robert Cooper. Together they spread the message. By 1839 there were over fifty branches of what was not called the Universal Community Society of Rational Religionists, half of them in the textile North. Though never able to rival Chartism in size, by 1840 its progress was beginning to alarm certain Tory minds both inside and outside Parliament.[39] In the autumn of 1839 the Owenites began their proposed community, at Queenwood Farm in Hampshire. Though probably drawn from the better-off sort of working men, the Owenites found finance a problem, especially during the depression years, and the community dream began to slip out of reach of reality. Signing a petition for the Charter was a comparatively easy matter compared with building a new moral world. Nevertheless local groups survived the troubles at Queenwood and had much in common with NCA localities after 1842, with some overlap of membership and leadership, and even on occasions shared premises. With the failure of the Petition some Chartist-Owenites even began to take a renewed interest in the Queenwood Community, particularly after 1844 when the rank and file rejected the leadership of Owen and took the community over for the working class. Men like Hetherington, Hobson and his fellow Leeds Chartist, John Ardill, and Isaac Ironside of Sheffield now appeared as active Owenites. But with the failure of the Community in 1845 they and the local followers merged back into the general radical and co-operative scene.[40]

The appeal of the land to radicals was not, however, lost on

Feargus O'Connor who, in the early 1840s, was evolving his own ideas on the subject. O'Connor's Land Plan may seem one of the most inconsistent features of his long period of Chartist leadership. It certainly scarcely seems compatible with the idea of political radicalism. The fact is that no radicals were single-mindedly political in their strategy, and O'Connor as in so much else reflected the many-faceted nature of working-class aspirations. Like Cobbett he believed in the value of independence on the land. He also saw that a movement of population away from the urban labour market would force up wages.[41] Curiously he does not seem to have thought of the Land Plan as a means of creating forty-shilling freeholders and thereby voters. What his scheme did for Chartism was to give it a wider basis of support and a renewed appeal in the doldrum days of the mid-1840s. Though commended to Owenites by G A Fleming in 1845 as more practical than Owen's scheme,[42] its basis proved equally unsound and in the end the Land Plan only contributed to the general discredit which O'Connor was held to have brought on Chartism after 1848.[43]

Far more working men in the 1840s concentrated on their trade unions and sought improvement through the traditional methods of collective action and aid. Chartism was supported in the North by those whose trades had been destroyed by technological change or the reorganisation of work which devalued skill. Artisans everywhere were threatened by the latter. Where their trade societies were too weak to maintain a defence of skill the workers turned to politics. This applied to all in times of depression, but in normal years the trade union offered many radicals more tangible forms of relief and more immediate ways of absorbing their energies. The fluctuations in support are exemplified by events on the north-east coalfield. In 1839 some Tyneside pitmen had struck during the aborted National Holiday, only to be let down by the Convention and Chartists elswhere. In 1843, after the failure of the two Petitions, they resolved to request speakers to 'confine themselves as much as possible to the grievances that exist between us, the pitmen, and our masters'. Only after the failure of the great coal strike of 1844 were the miners inclined to swing back to Chartism, attracted by the Land Plan.[44] WP Roberts, solicitor to the miners' union, acted in the same capacity for the Land Company. O'Connor himself saw the importance of attracting the support of the trade societies, and was aware of their importance in London Chartism. The *Northern Star* was moved to

London in November 1844 and assumed the subtitle '*and National Trades Journal*'. This was occasioned not only by the miners' strike, but also by the general unrest among unionists caused by a proposed change for the worse in the Master and Servant Law. T S Duncombe led the parliamentary opposition to the proposal, and at Easter 1845 became president of a new National Association of United Trades for the Protection of Labour.[45] The *Northern Star* took a keen interest. Undoubtedly following the prevailing wind in the mid-1840s, O'Connor did much to preserve close contact between the unionists and the Chartists and to maintain the links between radicalism and other avenues to reform.

The depression which swept Europe following the agricultural crisis of 1846 gave the Chartists their final chance. As thrones toppled across Europe in 1848, unrest grew at home and Harney became excited in the *Northern Star* as to the possibilities of the situation.[46] A new Petition was gathered with, it was said, nearly 6 million signatures. The reality was nearer a third that number, but this nevertheless still represented an impressive revival of former support. A Convention again met, and arranged for a mass meeting on Kennington Common in south London prior to the Petition being escorted *en masse* to Westminster. What happened at that meeting on 10 April 1848 is well known[47] — London was protected by thousands of special constables, with regular troops held in reserve; the bridges across the Thames were held; and the meeting was persuaded to disperse peaceably after O'Connor had been made aware of the alternative. The Petition was carried to Parliament in three cabs. As the tension subsided London began to laugh at the 'fiasco', and historians have often laughed since. When the Petition was brought before the Commons by O'Connor (he had been elected MP for Nottingham in 1847) and the inflated size of the number of petitioners was questioned, he mismanaged the whole thing and lost his temper.[48] That was the end of the People's Charter.

It was not, however, the end of Chartism, for the relief felt by its opponents was misplaced. Indeed, it has been suggested that the ridicule poured on the Chartists was a deliberate attempt to discredit a still-potent force.[49] As in 1839 and 1842 the failure of the Petition was followed by unrest of a political and economic nature. What is different and important about 1848 is that, although disturbances occurred in the provinces — most seriously in Glasgow, Manchester and Bradford — London was at the centre. London had been slow to

gain momentum in the Chartist movement, and the overall weak-
ness of the metropolis in 1839 had been crucial at a time when the
movement in the provinces was at its height. But London had had
very little in the way of factory and anti-Poor Law movements to
give an initial impetus to a national radical campaign. Radicalism in
London was rooted in the trade societies in their many and scattered
clubs. Gradually, however, especially after the formation of the NCA,
London Chartism gained ground. Provincial Chartism declined
from 1839; London Chartism rose from 1839.[50] The failure of the
two to synchronise was an important reason for the ineffectiveness
of the Chartists' campaign.

There were disturbances in London throughout the spring of
1848, beginning on 6 March when a meeting to demand the repeal of
the income tax was taken over by G W M Reynolds, a radical
journalist. Three days of mob violence followed. This fore-
shadowed the events of May and June. In May there were nightly
gatherings on Clerkenwell Green, followed by processions through
the streets. On 29 May about 16,000 working men, some of them
with pikes, marched through London and approached the West End.
In June activities centred on Bethnal Green, and on 4 June there was a
violent clash with the police. A further meeting was arranged for
Whit Monday, 12 June, but by this time the authorities were sufficiently alarmed to take strong measures to break the meeting up.
Thereafter militant London Chartism was driven underground as
police raids produced numerous arrests.[51] One man arrested after 4
June was Ernest Jones, fast emerging as the most coherent strategist
of latter-day Chartism.[52] A national rising was planned for 15
August, but everywhere the police were able to deal with what had
now become very much a minority activity.[53]

What was also new about the events of 1848 was the involvement
of Irish extremists. This touches on an old theme, current in the
1790s, with Irishmen anxious to achieve their own liberties by
working with and within English radical organisations. But hitherto
they had shown little interest in Chartism, despite the part played by
individual Irishmen at both the local and national level.[54] The main
reason for this lack of co-ordination between English and Irish
radicals was Daniel O'Connell, and the rivalry between O'Connell
and O'Connor. The Irish in Britain remained largely loyal to
O'Connell's Repeal movement which, like the earlier Catholic
Association in Ireland itself, utilised the power of the priests to keep

the movement loyal to O'Connell. Chartism was a tool of the godless English. But after O'Connell's death in 1847 the Irish Repeal movement began to change, though not initially in its attitude to Chartism. Slowly, however, some Irish Confederates began to see merit in O'Connor's dream of a united movement to secure repeal of the Act of Union. First John Mitchel and then, after February 1848, Smith O'Brien were prepared to work alongside the Chartists. But in May the pattern of 1798 was repeated. An Irish rising was suppressed, Smith O'Brien was arrested, Mitchel was transported for fourteen years. The Chartist-Confederate alliance fell into disarray before a wave of arrests in England. Just for a moment the Irish dimension gave a glimmer of reality to the government's fears about Chartism, but animosity between the English and the Irish precluded any longer-term co-operation: their political and religious cultures were poles apart.[55]

The involvement of O'Connell's Irish in anti-Chartist activity, despite the fact that O'Connel himself had been one of the original six MPs who put their names to the Charter, points to a further important division in the radicalism of the period, for O'Connell stood for a kind of radicalism which was for many an alternative to the Chartism of O'Connor. O'Connell was more than just an Irish patriot — he was also a middle-class Radical, very much at home in the world of Cobden and Bright, and a close supporter of Political Economy, the amended Poor Law and the movement to abolish the Corn Laws. Though the first two items in this 'Manchester School' programme were scarcely popular with working men, the last did gain a great deal of support.

The Anti-Corn Law League, which grew out of the Manchester Anti-Corn Law Association into a national body in March 1839, was in many respects the middle-class equivalent of Chartism, but with some notable and significant differences. Richard Cobden's explanation of the nature of the League, given in 1842, is well known:

> I do not deny that the working classes generally have attended our lectures and signed our petitions; but I will admit, that so far as the fervour and efficiency of our agitation has gone, it has eminently been a middle-class agitation. We have carried it on by those means by which the middle class usually carries on its movements. We have had our meetings of dissenting ministers; we have obtained the co-operation of the ladies; we have resorted to tea parties, and taken those pacific means for carrying out our

views, which mark us rather as a middle-class set of agitators.
. . . We are no political body; we have refused to be bought by
the Tories; we have kept aloof from the Whigs; and we will not
join partnership with either Radicals or Chartists, but we will
hold out our hand ready to give it to all who are willing to
advocate the total and immediate repeal of the corn and provision
laws.[56]

This description is accurate, but the reasoning is deceptive.
Cobden's claim was that the ACLL had been forced into being
middle-class by the activities of Chartist agitators and that the
League was not itself a political body; both these statements were
half-truths. The League did wish to appeal to the working classes,
both to get up a broadly-based agitation for repeal and to avoid the
appearance of representing merely a sectional interest. And it did
attract considerable working-class support, though it failed to capitalise on the widespread (though not universal) opposition to the
'bread tax' among the working classes. Nevertheless the perception
that the League was middle-class was not just the consequence of the
work of agitators. Cobden may have had wider ideals, but many of
the rank and file of manufacturers who contributed to funds did not.
The narrow self-interest of a manufacturing class provided the fuel
for Cobden's idealistic flame.[57] Secondly, Cobden may have chosen
to present the League's agitation as a question of commerce and not
of politics, but he and the other leading members of the League were
committed Radicals looking for a cause. Cobden's slogan had been
'Incorporate your Borough' and Bright's had been anti-Church
Rate. In 1837 Cobden considered taking up the ballot as a rallying
cry, but in 1838 chose the Corn Laws instead.[58] 'By 1839 the Corn
Laws stood out as the visible legislative symbol of the predominance
of the landed interest, and this symbolic importance made them an
attractive focus for Radical attacks,' explains Norman McCord.[59] In
the tradition of Ricardian Political Economy, the ACLL saw the
great divide in society as lying between the landlords and the people.
Chartist thinkers offered the alternative diagnosis of the great divide
between capital and labour. The one view claimed the support of all
radicals for the League. The other divided them into Leaguers and
Chartists, each fostering the class consciousness of the other.

Many working-class radicals favoured the repeal of the Corn
Laws. In Sheffield a Mechanics' Anti-Bread Tax Association was in

existence before 1832, and leading figures in the movement such as Ebenezer Elliott were also active in early Chartism.[60] But the events of 1839 bitterly divided those who were channelling anti-Corn Law protest towards the League, and those who supported the Charter. In London the moderate *Charter* newspaper addressed an open letter to the men of Sheffield:

> Our object in addressing you is to expose the wickedness and craft of those who renouncing all principle (except a bad one), are endeavouring to persuade you to sacrifice your principles on the altar of expediency, by leaving the people to join a party comprised of avaricious, grasping, money-mongers, great capitalists, and rich manufacturers.[61]

Even those Chartists who favoured repeal of the Corn Laws thought the League misguided in its aims, if nothing worse. The moderate Scottish *Chartist Circular* asked in September 1839:

> When will the Corn-Law repealers direct their efforts into the right channel; when will they condescend to look about and ascertain how the incubus of which they complain can be got rid of? Do they still possess ignorance and infatuation enough to expect to succeed with a landowner's parliament? Cannot they see by this time that the Chartists were right, perfectly right, and are so now, in urging that *the first thing to be done is to alter the constitution of the House of Commons.*[62]

The difference here resolved itself into a matter of strategy. Chartism was a political movement with economic objectives — a Ten Hours Bill, reform of the 1834 Poor Law, repeal of the Corn Laws. The League, for its leaders, was an economic movement to secure a political end — the weakening of the landed power which still dominated Parliament. Cobden adhered firmly to the latter policy and in 1846 was proved right in so far as one reason why Peel repealed the Corn Laws was to protect the landed classes from what he saw to be a needless attack. Where Cobden was wrong was in believing that this would be a Radical victory. After 1846 there was still much to be done, and in the 1850s and 1860s both ex-Leaguers and ex-Chartists moved into a compromise position.[63]

Conflict between the League and the Chartists was fiercest between 1839 and 1842 and was based on two attitudes among the Chartists. First, there were those Chartists such as O'Brien who favoured repeal but thought that, without the protection of a demo-cratically elected Parliament, any reduction in taxation would simply lead to a reduction in wages; this suspicion was not entirely ill-founded.[64] Secondly, there were protectionist Chartists, includ-ing O'Connor, who saw agriculture as the basis of national strength and security, and a strong home market as the best guarantee of industrial prosperity.[65] This view was shared by the Oastlerites and many Tory Radicals. The actual physical conflict between Leaguers and Chartists was by no means one-sided, with O'Connell's strong arm Irish doing sturdy work for the League, even breaking up a lecture by O'Connor on the repeal of the Act of Union in Man-chester in March 1842.[66] Nor did the League's hands appear clean of more widespread civil unrest. In the summer of 1842 some members, including Bright, were suggesting turning out the fac-tories to precipitate a crisis. The fact that the Stalybridge owners whose wage reductions preceded the Plug Riots were members of the League added circumstantial evidence to the belief that the League was behind the rioting, (though this now seems unlikely).[67] After 1842, the League changed its strategy and the worst conflict was over.

Despite such clashes and mutual hostility between Leaguers and Chartists, the leaders of the ACLL remained political radicals and had much sympathy for a further extension of the suffrage. What they disliked was not radicalism but Chartism, with all that that implied by way of bluster, violence, instability and class hatred. The middle-class radicals were capable of working towards an alliance with moderates like William Lovett, and there were men of good will on both sides in the 1840s who tried to agree upon, and work for, a common cause. Founders of the League, such as Thomas Potter, George Wilson, J B Smith and Archibald Prentice were all political reformers. Smith, the League's president, even proposed a toast to the memory of the victims of 'Peterloo' at a banquet in January 1840.[68] In every town there were some such men willing to work for reform, some of long-standing, others recent converts out of principle or expediency. In Leeds Samuel Smiles of the *Leeds Times* represented a more radical wing of middle-class opinion than did Baines of the *Mercury*, and W P Byles of the *Bradford Observer* followed his line.[69] In Leicester the Biggses, master manufacturers and political bosses, offered a 'rather diminuitive olive branch' to the Chartists, which they declined.[70] In London Francis Place continued his dedicated quest for a broadly-based, sensible, radical reform movement, and in Birmingham Joseph Parkes, a Philosophic Radical, and Joseph Sturge, a Quaker reformer, attempted to create a political equivalent of the ACLL. Sturge was a veteran campaigner, though originally less radical than Thomas Attwood. He had been a leading opponent of slavery in the early 1830s, and a founder of the British and Foreign Anti-Slavery Society in 1839. He had also attended the Manchester anti-Corn Law conference in 1838 out of which the ACLL had developed. He was one of the first aldermen on Birmingham Town Council, and chaired the committee to investigate police brutality at the Bull Ring Riots in 1839 — as a pacifist he entered a dissenting Note to the Report which overall exonerated the police. His motivation in adopting a political programme of 'complete suffrage' lay partly in an optimistic faith in the masses and partly in a realistic fear of their revolutionary potential.[71] To this extent the emergence of a new middle-class reform movement represented a victory for the Chartists.

The theme of the 'Reconciliation between the middle and labouring classes' was developed in a series of articles in Edward Miall's newly-formed *Nonconformist* in 1841, and Sturge took up the matter with urgency. About the same time in Leeds the moderates of Samuel Smiles' Leeds Parliamentary Reform Association were attempting a similar sort of move. The timing was partly determined by the need for a united radical front in the 1841 General Election.[72] O'Connor rejected the overture, and advised support for Tory candidates to defeat the Whigs.[73] In November 1841 Sturge attended an Anti-Corn Law conference in Manchester at which he gained support for his ideas on complete suffrage, and his Complete Suffrage Union was formed in Birmingham in January 1842. The move proved premature. At a conference in April the CSU was forced to adopt all six points of the Charter. Later that same month the House of Commons rejected the CSU's own petition by 226 votes to 67, showing it to be as impotent as that of the Chartists rejected by a similar margin a few days later. Then came the turbulent summer of 1842. Finally in December the Lovettites unexpectedly supported the O'Connorites in defence of the name of the Charter, and the attempt to unite the middle- and working-class agitations came to an end.[74] Those Chartists like Henry Vincent who favoured the CSU now moved over to it completely.[75]

But all was not lost. Moderate radicals had pledged themselves to an extension of — even complete — suffrage, and Chartists were beginning to modify their views. When Sturge contested a by-election at Nottingham in 1842, he found O'Connor had abandoned the politics of 1841 and now supported him against the Tory. In 1844, after his celebrated debate with Cobden at Northampton, O'Connor even began to praise his opponent, and by January 1846 the *Northern Star* was positively rapturous about Peel's conversion to repeal.[76] After the final repulse of 1848 the way was at last clear for the old guard of radicals — Place, Hume, Lovett, Hetherington — again to form an alliance. In 1849, on the anniversary of Paine's birthday (29 January) Place called a meeting in London which led to the formation of the National Parliamentary and Financial Reform Association, under the presidency of Sir Joshua Walmsley, the Radical M P for Leicester. In this body, middle-class reformers united with moderate Chartists behind Joseph Hume's 'Little Charter' of household suffrage, the ballot, triennial Parliaments, and a more equal distribution of seats.[77] It did not instantly appeal to all Chartists, but unlike previous efforts to heal the divisions of a decade this and its successors had extensive appeal. In principle, the division between household suffragists and manhood suffragists continued (and was present in the distinction between the Reform Union and the Reform League in 1866-7), but in practice the barriers were being broken down and the suspicions of class-hatred removed. A significant editorial appeared in the *Northern Star* in the dying months of Harney's control. Celebrating the twelfth anniversary of the foundation of the paper, it said of the NPFRA:

> The middle and working classes have joined hands, without reserve or dissimulation. The one party says they cannot go further at present — the other, that they will accompany them as far as they go, but they do not mean to stop there. The ancient and honoured motto is not even in abeyance. We still exclaim, "The Charter and no Surrender!" but, taught by dear-bought past experience, we have varied the mode of operation by which it is to be attained.[78]

The first, tentative steps had been taken in a new stage of the history of radicalism and reform which, in the late 1850s, were to lead towards popular Gladstonian Liberalism.

CONCLUSION

In following the complex and meandering course of radicalism from the days of Wilkes and the American Revolution, to those of Chartism and the Anti-Corn Law League, many aspects of the subject have been neglected, as if backwaters, while the mainstream radical tradition has been pursued with Whig-like energy. If one moves from Major Cartwright's *Take Your Choice* of 1776 to the People's Charter, finally rejected in 1848, then some kind of tradition can legitimately be discerned, even though the same years contain major discontinuities. One cannot with equal confidence proceed from the American Declaration of Independence of 1776 to the Manifesto of the German Communist Party of 1848, first published in English in G J Harney's *Red Republican* in 1850.[1] Harney himself went back to Marat and Robespierre, not Lafayette. Nevertheless the tradition of native British radicalism is real enough, with links forged by men who survived to join successive organisations, and by a literature which ensured the transmission of ideas and the accumulation of a body of radical thinking which each generation could savour and to which it could add new insights. Much changed between 1760 and 1848, not least the structure of the economy and the outlook of governments, but Thomas Hardy's radical artisans of the 1790s were still recognisable among the supporters of Chartism in the 1840s. What had changed among them was their self-perception. Class had emerged to help them define and articulate their hopes and fears.

The relationship between political and economic activity has been frequently touched upon in this book. Because trade unionists drew their members largely from among the unfranchised, and because trade unions were often hampered in their operation by legislation, the connection between trade unionism and politics was a close one. This is not to assert that the majority of strikes, or that most Luddite activity, was political in nature. Many problems and relationships were conceived of in local terms, and local and immediate solutions were sought. If this is often true of that section of the working class who had trades to protect, it is even more often true of those below them. The London coal-heavers who cried 'Wilkes and Liberty' in the 1760s had much in common with the costers described by Mayhew in the 1840s, 'who were keen Chartists without understanding anything about the six points'.[2] Yet both knew a little, or were told a little by their leaders, and they appreciated and took part in the street theatre which was an essential part of radical agitations. Luddites who smashed machinery also wanted their skills protected by the enforcement of legislation. Factory operatives and pitmen wanted new protective legislation. The poor wanted the repeal of the hated Bastille Act of 1834. Politics could not be kept out.

Yet men did not live for politics alone. The totality of experience should be understood to give radicalism its proper context. The activities available should be viewed as a series of overlapping circles like an Olympic symbol: work, wages and conditions; leisure, education, religion and drink; politics, radicalism and conservatism. An individual might occupy all positions at once, or over time, or some but not all. All combinations occurred, though institutions within each set might try to exclude external influences for a variety of reasons. Churches banned political activism because this was not seen as their business, but that did not remove all church and chapel attenders from the ranks of radicalism. Chartists tried to exclude religion as divisive, without robbing individual Chartists of religious ideas and preferences. Trade unions often turned their backs on both religious and political involvement, without denying to their members an active role in both.

Too much attention should not be paid to the pronouncements of the Wesleyan Conference, eager to pledge its loyalty to the House of Hanover (all those Brunswick Chapels) and to secure the legality of its itinerant ministry and indoor meetings.[3] There is sufficient evidence to suggest that the people did not always do as their preachers told them — and preachers such as J R Stephens and Joseph Barker did not always do what their Connexions told them, either.[4] Plenty of past and present chapel members were active radicals, and the churches could only hope to discipline those who held official positions from which they could be removed.

The major debate about the contribution of Methodism to radicalism, however, is not about how many Luddites, trade union leaders and Chartists were, or had been, Methodists,[5] but about the impact which Methodism made on the shape and nature of radicalism as a whole. Elie Halévy took up this theme in 1906 when he followed Weber in postulating the power of religious ideas to modify the course of social change.[6] The 'Halévy thesis' — crudely, that Methodism saved Britain from revolution — has been central to discussions about religion and radicalism ever since, but with Edward Thompson's contribution in 1963 the terms of the debate have been redefined. In an ironically entitled chapter, 'The Transforming Power of the Cross' he sought to explain the acceptance of Methodist discipline as 'the chiliasm of despair':

> After 1795 the poor had once again entered into the Valley of Humiliation. But they entered it unwillingly, with many backward looks; and whenever hope revived, religious revivalism was set aside, only to reappear with renewed fervour upon the ruins of the political messianism which had been overthrown. In this sense, the great Methodist recruitment between 1790 and 1830 may be seen as the Chilasm of despair.[7]

Thompson admits, 'This is not the customary reading of the period', though he supports it with an impressive array of circumstantial evidence, relating particularly to the aftermath of Luddite activity. Some historians have been able to corroborate this thesis from their own researches; others have not.[8] The growth of the Bible Christian sect in Manchester after Peterloo, partly at the expense of Methodism, might be of significance here.[9] Overall the relationship between religious ideas and social action has not been conclusively established, and Thompson's understanding of the Methodist experience has been called into question.[10] Religious views and radicalism could spring from the same source and be held at the same time, being not alternative but complementary expressions of the same spirit.[11]

That Methodism made some important positive contributions to radicalism is nevertheless agreed. It often expressed the class consciousness of a community (particularly a village community) against the established symbols of squire and parson. It provided experience in organisation and leadership. And it contributed to that disciplining of protest, of which radicalism itself was a part, by which inchoate, unstable and violent outbursts were directed into effective, constitutional channels.[12]

In the late eighteenth century, Old Dissent made a clearer direct contribution to radicalism. The demand for Civil and Religious Liberties went hand in hand, yet many Dissenters became reluctant to involve themselves too deeply in the events of the 1790s and were repelled by the taint of Jacobinism. The years between 1792 and 1815 saw 'an uninterrupted decline of the revolutionary spirit among the sects,' wrote Halévy. 'It is safe to say that the advocates of revolution were the exception among the Baptists and Independents.'[13] Only the Presbyterians maintained some of their seventeenth-century republicanism, but they were in decline and their theological viewpoint (Unitarian) kept them outside the Toleration Act until 1813.

Despite this lukewarmness outside the ranks of Unitarian Presbyterianism — the sect of Price and Priestley — Dissent can still be identified with reform in the nineteenth century, for the obverse of the union of Church and State was that of dissent in religion and politics. Not all reformers were Dissenters by any means, but all (or practically all), Dissenters were Whigs, liberals or radicals. The middle-class reform campaigns of the 1820s onwards were marked by their Dissenting characteristics, as Richard Cobden (an Anglican) noted of the Anti-Corn Law League. Tithes, church rates, education and disestablishment were all issues calling forth Dissenting fervour in religio-political campaigns. For its part the Church of England was identified with conservatism and the landed interest, and not without cause. Religious divisions thus gained political expression, and vice versa.[14]

In the eyes of many popular radicals, not only was the Established Church regarded as an extension of the aristocracy, but Dissent (including Methodism) was identified with the middle classes. Opposition to organised religion, extreme sectarianism, or downright freethought became the characteristics of extreme radicalism. At the heart of the radical tradition was the duality established by Thomas Paine in his *Rights of Man* and *Age of Reason*. Carlile, the Spenceans, the Owenites (and, on another level, the Benthamites) were all hostile to traditional religion, and this hostility was an integral part of their radicalism.[15]

This may have been true of the most extreme forms of popular radicalism, but it would be a mistake to imply that religion therefore played little part in the progress of reform — far from it. Religious beliefs could inspire reformism as well as conservatism, sometimes with surprising consequences. The Evangelicals were reformers of the Established Church and in the wider world. Wilberforce, for example, supported Romilly in Parliament over prison reform, and in 1812 spoke in favour of Burdett's motion to abolish flogging in the British army. The Evangelical attempt to have bull-baiting suppressed, however, led the ex-Pittite, William Windham, successfully to oppose such a 'Methodist-Jacobin conspiracy to make the lower classes serious, gloomy, critical, and discontented' and produced the remarkable cry of 'Windham and Liberty'.[16]

The most effective contribution of the Evangelicals to reform was their agitation against the slave trade and slavery. Anglicans, Quakers and Methodists all played prominent parts in this most successful of agitations. Despite the trend in recent years to emphasise the economic rather than the religious reasons for abolition, the historiography has now moved back in favour of 'the politics of conscience'.[17] Other reform movements were similarly motivated, with Anglicans taking the lead in the Factory Movement, and Dissenters in the anti-Corn Law agitation. All religious groups, in the pursuit of sectarian advantage, contributed greatly to the expansion of popular education. To examine all these aspects in detail would take another book. It is sufficient to suggest that, despite widespread popular apathy to organised religion, and explicit radical hositility, religion played a central part in the lives of many who took the lead in the reform movements of the late eighteenth and early nineteenth centuries.[8]

The religious dimension to secular affairs is probably one of the most unfamiliar aspects of the period under consideration. The reverse is true of another important theme, that of the role of women, about which the present generation is more self-conscious than its predecessors. In this book we have concentrated on the part played by men in radical movements, with only passing reference to women, for this is how most contemporaries saw matters. Women do, nevertheless, occasionally emerge through the male-dominated evidence. As might be expected, middle-class women were more prominent than working-class women as reformers — they had more leisure and greater education than their counterparts in the working classes where the forces which limited male articulateness pressed even more heavily on the female.[19] But the social roles of middle-class women were also more clearly defined, which imposed stricter limits on the kind of reform activities in which they might participate. Campaigns channelled through the agency of churches and chapels were given a legitimacy which made them especially suitable for female participation and even leadership.

The anti-slavery movement is a prime example of this, with women's groups actively spreading propaganda and petitioning on behalf of the poor blacks overseas[20] — an extension of the world of missionary teas, collections and lectures which supplied nineteenth-century middle-class families with philanthropically useful leisure. This is not to belittle their efforts in reforming public opinion in the face of vested economic and political interests. There were limits, though, beyond which they were not permitted to go. At the Anti-Slavery Convention organised by Joseph Sturge in 1840, certain American societies sent women delegates. Sturge and a majority of those present refused to accept them — a decision which gave an important impetus to the women's movement in the United States.[21] Women were useful — as adjuncts to men. This was true of all middle-class agitations, including the Anti-Corn Law League. Movements got up for a specific purpose knew better than to alienate support by challenging accepted notions about the proper place and status of women.

This idealistic view of women, which was rapidly gaining ground in the nineteenth century, had its uses in the cause of reform. The poor had their own reasons for hating the Poor Law and for wanting a restriction on the working hours of women in factories, but propaganda which exploited middle-class sensibilities about the sacredness of the family and the proper place of women undoubtedly helped win additional support.

This sense of hierarchy, which was such a pronounced feature of middle-class culture in the Victorian period, was present also within the working class itself. Women were certainly active with their menfolk in radical agitations, and enjoyed a certain amount of auto-nomy in areas where the cotton textile industry had given them a measure of economic independence,[22] but overall their role can be compared to that of the womenfolk at a village cricket match. Their place was in the pavillion making the teas, and washing the whites afterwards. Seldom were they permitted to field a team of their own. The London Working Men's Association (no room for female artisans) originally championed *universal* suffrage, but they soon reverted to *manhood* suffrage as more expedient, whilst still referring to universal suffrage in their minutes and propaganda.[23] Certainly there were female radical groups. Female Reform Societies were formed in 1818 and 1819 in the textile districts of Lancashire, where

Samuel Bamford noted their active participation in radical meet-ings.[24] Visiting Manchester in the early 1840s, Leon Faucher similarly commented, 'The women have their clubs as well as the men, and claim enjoyment with the same privileges as those with whom they share the fatigues of labour'.[25] Chartism had its Female Political Unions, women factory workers were prominent among the rioting turn-outs of 1842, and about 8 per cent of the signatures on the 1848 Petition were identified as those of women.[26] While in gaol in 1840, R J Richardson wrote a pamphlet championing the political rights of women.[27]

The most explicit theoretical acceptance of women in a reform movement, though, came with the Owenites, who totally rejected the conventional attitude towards the role and status of women in society. Some indeed, following Owen, rejected conventional mar-riage itself.[28] Like many utopian thinkers, Owen saw the family as the bastion of conservatism and a socially disuniting hindrance to the coming of his new moral world.[29] The irony is that, in practice, Owenism appealed to women by strengthening the family. The social life at the Halls of Science was designed to attract women, catering for all the family and offering women complete equality with men in the organisation and running of local branch life. At the Queenwood Community the attempt to wean members away from their nuclear families proved very unpopular.[30]

Individual women played important parts in the socialism of the 1820s, 1830s and 1840s. Mary Wollstonecraft had dominated female radicalism in the 1790s with her *Vindication of the Rights of Women*, but in the 1820s Francis Wright and Anna Wheeler took her radica-lism a stage further. Wright spent her fortune on a community for freed slaves in America, espoused freethought, wore 'rational dress' and in company with Robert Dale Owen took up the cause of American labour. She shocked respectable opinion on both sides of the Atlantic for thirty years.[31] Anna Wheeler was a close friend of William Thompson, himself a champion of women. She later gave her support to James Smith and became a keen exponent of the French socialism of Charles Fourier.[32] The Owenites missionaries of the post-1837 period included two outstanding women, Margaret Chappellsmith and Emma Martin.[35] James Morrison's wife, Frances, was also important as a lecturer and author of *The Influence of the Present Marriage System*, a typically Owenite attack on what was seen as, in effect, a system of legalised prostitution.[34]

The role of women in Owenism can partly be related to the prominent part they traditionally played in millenarian religious movements. In the late eighteenth century at least three sects were formed in Britain under the inspiration of women — the Buchanites, the Shakers and the Southcottians.[35] Owen's communitarianism was influenced by Shaker experience, and James Smith was a South-cottian before he was a socialist. His feminism can partly be attributed to the Southcottian 'Doctrine of the Woman' which identified Man with the Fall, and Woman with Salvation.[36]

This radical sectarianism spilled over also into the world of Richard Carlile, especially after he had attracted the support of Eliza Sharples in 1829. In her first discourse at the Rotunda in February 1832 she announced:

> Yes, I will set before my sex the example of asserting an equality for them with their present lords and masters, and strive to teach all, yes, *all*, that the undue submission, which constitutes slavery, is honourable to none; while the mutual submission, which leads to mutual good, is to all alike dignified and honourable.[37]

She was still advocating the Rights of Woman in 1850 — 'Men will ever rise or fall to the level of the other sex'.[38] Carlile's response to his new admirer was almost, but not quite, as warm:

> I do not like the doctrine of women keeping at home, and minding the house and the family. It is as much the proper business of the man as the woman; and the woman, who is so confined, is not the proper companion of the public useful man.[39]

This just about sums up the position of women in the radical movement: emancipated or to be emancipated, she was still thought of as the 'proper companion of the public useful man'.

The final theme which warrants some further examination is the relationship between radicalism and class. In the shorthand of verbal expression a positive connection is often implied, by ourselves and others, between the emergence of radicalism and the formation of a class consciousness. Edward Thompson has argued that class and consciousness are discovered through struggle and organisation.[40] In *The Making of the English Working Class* that struggle and organisation is decidedly political. Thus the development and extension of Jacobin radicalism is in fact, and by definition, made central to the formation of the working class. Before 1963 Asa Briggs was already arguing for the instrumental roles played by Chartism in the development of working-class consciousness and by the Anti-Corn Law League in the making of a middle-class consciousness.[41] Radicalism as a set of ideas emerged independently of class, but part of the story of the years between 1760 and 1848 is of the emergence of class as a political force and of the way in which radicalism was divided and appropriated as an ideology by both working and middle classes.

Middle-class radicalism was defined by Political Economy. Following Ricardo, propagandists fashioned this as a tool with which to attack the legitimacy of landed and aristocratic dominance; and following Malthus, by which to undermine the self-respect of the poor. Neo-Ricardian socialists offered an alternative view of rent, wages and profits, from which they derived their labour theory of value. Traditionalists fought a long rearguard action against the unwanted radicalism of Chadwick, Southwood Smith and Nassau Senior. Ideological and class confrontation is all too evident in the periodicals of the decades after 1815.[42]

Yet radicalism was always something less as well as something more than class consciousness. Class was based on economic divisions between capital and labour as well as on political ideology. The economic structure of Britain was changing, unevenly but universally, between the days of Wilkes and the days of the Chartists. Not only was the factory system spreading — giving Engels his classic ingredient for class formation — but more importantly capital was increasing its control of labour outside the factories and in industries unaffected by factories. Apprenticeship, control of time, monopoly of skill were all under attack. This was the making of class, and it was among the artisans that radicalism struck its deepest roots. Radicalism had something to say to those whose economic and social position was uncertain, who were losing hope of becoming masters, but who had not yet been reduced to the ranks of a proletariat.

Middle-class radicalism is more complex, but bears some of the same features. Professional men in days when the professions were only just emerging, and journalists when theirs was scarcely an honourable calling, furnished one set of radical critics. They were hardly an intelligentsia such as fortified the middle-class radicalism of Europe. They owed little to the English universities, though something to the Scottish. But they were in a sense an uneasy group of men.[44] The same was true of the manufacturers. Earlier groups of wealthy men, rich from the West or East Indies, had been easily absorbed into the ruling class of the eighteenth century, but the new manufacturers were not in the same league. Few of the new capitalists could aspire to the wealth and ambitions of Robert Peel the elder. Most could not afford to buy themselves into the existing political system. They were only too well aware that the next depression might rob them of all they had.[45] Their radicalism was not always born of confidence in their new order. More often they were fighting to avoid the ruin being heaped upon them by a government apparently careless of their interests.

Radicalism was, therefore, not so much the language of a self-conscious class as the protest of men caught on the crevasses which were opening up in early industrial society. At a time when economic divisions were giving reality to class, radicalism curiously provided a language which was capable of transcending such divisions. Though the men who demanded a reformed political system had different and conflicting economic hopes of reform, their immediate programmes of action had much in common. Only in moments of crisis, such as the betrayal of 1832, were they set apart.

Starting from the point of view of class, one can easily show how radicalism contributed to class formation without implying that all working men were working-class radicals, or that all capitalists were middle-class radicals. But starting from the point of view of radicalism, one can less easily see correspondences between it and a single class consciousness. Radicalism as a concept and as a practical programme was born before class and owed its origins to no social group. Country squires and provincial shopkeepers could all find it speaking to their condition.[46] Even when democratised in the 1790s, its claims were comprehensive, not exclusive, and these remained its predominant characteristics. The years of conflict should be seen as exceptions; collaboration was the norm. Those historians who concentrate on class formation in the 1830s and 1840s have difficulty explaining the emergence of popular Radical-Liberalism in the 1850s. The establishment of 'middle-class hegemony' and the arrival of 'a viable class society' are only part of the answer, underestimating as they do the persistence of working-class autonomy and industrial conflict.[47] These undoubtedly important developments need to be set in a context in which a broadly-based radicalism was the norm. What has to be explained is the exception which reached its climax in Chartism, and the way in which normality was restored. Francis Place is a key figure in this interpretation, for he defies categorisation by belonging to all categories.

By concentrating on means rather than ends, and on politics rather than economics, the radicals were often able to avoid divisive issues. Despite the division in the 1840s between Manchester School radicals and Chartists, the two sides continued to speak a common political language. With the failure of both groups to secure a significant measure of political change the way was clear again, not for class to be abolished in the Owenite sense, but for class to be set aside as irrelevant to the narrower purposes of radicalism. Only when radical politics were replaced by labour politics, infused with socialist analyses, at the end of the nineteenth century was the broad back of radicalism finally broken.[48]

The question remains as to how popular this radicalism was. Were the radicals mere grasshoppers under a fern Were they merely intellectuals whose abstract theorising was lost on the practical sense of the common people? Did they appeal only to artisans, and not to the labouring masses? As a rule the answer to all these questions is yes, but only up to a point. Burke's disparaging reference to grasshoppers was intended to belittle the radicals of the 1790s; it would certainly do less than justice if applied to the radicals of the 1840s. One major development of the period is the steady expansion of radicalism's catchment. With an extension of basic literacy, and an educational system which gave no recognition to intellectual merit, an abstract system of ideas such as radicalism could find adherents in every class of men. Writing of the hierarchy of costermongers in London in the 1840s, Henry Mayhew observed how 'those leading men are all Chartists, and being industrious and not unprosperous persons, their pecuniary and intellectual superiority cause them to be regarded as oracles'.[49] These were the sort of men who could be drawn into radicalism and who could then mediate it to those around them. In a crisis, political or economic, this latent radicalism could then gain momentary expression on the streets. One such Chartist costermonger told Mayhew

The costers think that working men know best, and so they have confidence in us. I like to make men discontented, and I will make them discontented while the present system continues, because it's all for the middle and the moneyed classes, and nothing, in the way of rights, for the poor. People fancy when all's quiet that all's stagnating. Propagandism is going on for all that. It's when all's quiet that the seed's a growing. Republicans and Socialists are pressing their doctrines.[50]

He had probably been reading GJ Harney of Ernest Jones.

Unfortunately for the radicals, they were able to press their doctrines only during crises. The poor could not afford to sustain a prolonged struggle, and could easily be distracted from it. The radicals were most successful in those parts of the country where, in smaller communities, they could develop traditions of organisation and self-identity — community rather than class consciousness. That is why so much of the radical story draws evidence from the industrial villages and small towns of the textile districts of the North.[51] In these communities also lies the paradox of radicalism with radical factory masters, symbols of economic exploitation, articulating a political creed which embodied the hopes of radical working men.[52]

What had the radicals achieved by way of political reform in the years between 1760 and 1848? At first glance very little appears to their credit. The points of the radical programme, most clearly summed up in the People's Charter, were nowhere near being accepted by the political nation. That measure of reform which had been won in 1832 owed more to the conservative 'country' outlook of the gentry than to radical ideology. Yet much had been achieved. Popular politics were created in the two generations between Wilkes and the Chartists. If not the outward forms then at least the preconditions of democracy were established by 1848. The possibility of a widespread involvement by ordinary people in political debate was an unlikely nightmare in 1760; it was an established reality in 1848. The irrational nature of the electoral system was hallowed by custom in the late eighteenth century and to suggest change was to be thought revolutionary. After 1832 the structure of politics was recognised as an artefact, the product of human will and subject to change by a further act of human will. The instruments of change had been forged: mass petitioning, national organisation, the press and widespread literacy. A door (or a Pandora's box) had been opened. Despite the sense of failure in 1848 among radicals of all hues, the mid-Victorian era was to see the Golden Age of radicalism as a political force both inside and outside the walls of a Parliament increasingly open to the pressures of public opinion.

NOTES

Introduction

1   E P Thompson, *The Making of the English Working Class*, (London, 1963).
2   R S Neale, *Bath, 1680-1850: A Social History* (London, 1981).
3   M I Thomis, *Politics and Society in Nottingham, 1785-1835*, (Oxford, 1969), pp. 77-99; see also his *The Luddites: Machine Breaking in Regency England*, (Newton Abbott, 1970), pp. 41-70. For criticism of Thomis, see F K Donnelly, 'Ideology and early English working-class history: Edward Thompson and his critics', *Social History*, 2 (May 1976), pp. 219-38.
4   N McCord, 'Tyneside discontents and Peterloo', *Northern History*, II (1967), pp. 91-111; also *Strikes*, (Oxford, 1980), pp. 18-41. The extent to which radicalism could infuse industrial protest was dependent in part on the economic history and structure of each area and industry — a point recognised by John Foster in his comparison of Oldham, South Shields and Northampton, *Class Struggle and the Industrial Revolution*, (London, 1974). The textile areas of Lancashire and (to a lesser extent) Yorkshire experienced more rapid social change in the early nineteenth century than did Tyneside.

Chapter 1 Wilkes, America and After

1   J H Plumb, 'Political Man', in J L Clifford (ed.), *Man Versus Society in Eighteenth-Century Britain*, (Cambridge, 1968), pp. 1-21; L Namier, *The Structure of Politics at the Accession of George III*, (second edition, London and New York, 1957).
2   J H Plumb, op.cit., pp. 7-8; J Cannon, *Parliamentary Reform 1640-1832*, (Cambridge, 1973), pp. 41-2.
3   C Robbins, *The Eighteenth Century Commonwealthman*, (Cambridge, Mass., 1959); B and C Hill, 'Catherine Macaulay and the Seventeenth Century', *Welsh History Review*, III no 4 (Dec. 1967), pp. 381-402; Q R D Skinner, 'The Principles and Practice of Opposition: The Case of Bolingbroke versus Walpole', in N McKendrick (ed.), *Historical Perspectives*, (London, 1974), pp. 93-128; H T Dickinson, *Liberty and Property. Political Ideology in Eighteenth-Century Britain*, (London, 1979), pp. 163-92.

4   B Bailyn, *The Ideological Origins of the American Revolution* (Cambridge, Mass., 1973).

5   F Venturi, *Utopia and Reform in the Enlightenment*, (Cambridge, 1971), pp. 47-94.

6   H Butterfield, *George III, Lord North and the People, 1779-80*, (London, 1949), p. 183; see also, H T Dickinson, op. cit., pp. 197-205.

7   N Rogers, 'Resistance to Oligarchy. The City Opposition to Walpole and his Successors, 1725-47', in J Stevenson (ed.), *London in the Age of Reform*, (London, 1977), pp. 1-29; and L Sutherland, 'The City of London and the Opposition to Government, 1768-1774', reprinted in J Stevenson, op. cit., pp.30-54. For William Beckford, see J O Baylen and N J Gossman (eds.), *Biographical Dictionary of Modern British Radicals, vol. 1: 1770-1830*, (Hassocks and Atlantic Highlands, N J), 1979.

8   J H Plumb, op. cit., pp. 10-11; J Cannon, op. cit., pp. 47-9; N Rogers, op. cit., p.11; J Money, 'Taverns, Coffee Houses and Clubs: Local Politics and Popular Articulacy in the Birmingham Area, in the Age of the American Revolution', *Historical Journal* XIV (1971), pp. 15-47.

9   The most detailed treatment of the Wilkes affairs is in G Rudé, *Wilkes and Liberty*, (Oxford, 1962); see also J Cannon, op. cit., pp. 47-71.

10 Quoted in J Cannon, op. cit., pp. 58-9.

11 J Brewer, 'English Radicalism in the Age of George III', in J G A Pocock (ed.), *Three British Revolutions: 1641, 1688, 1776*, (Princeton, 1980), pp. 323-67.

12 J Brewer, *Party Ideology and Popular Politics at the Accession of George III*, (Cambridge, 1976), pp. 163-200; G Rudé, op. cit., pp. 61-2, 108-13.

13 J Brewer, op. cit., p. 179.

14 G Rudé, op. cit., p. 187.

15 T M Parssinen, 'Association, convention and anti-parliament in British radical politics, 1771-1848', *English Historical Review*, LXXXVIII (1973), pp.504-33.

16 See R R Palmer, *The Age of the Democratic Revolution*, vol.1; *The Challenge*, (Princeton, 1959; reprinted 1969), pp. 143-4.

17 I R Christie, *Crisis of Empire*, (London, 1966), p. 45.

18 quoted in J Brewer, op. cit., p. 211.

19 For details of the American Revolution and English radicals, see C Bonwick, *English radicals and the American Revolution*, (Chapel Hill, 1977).

20 G Rudé, op. cit., p.149; P Langford, 'London and the American Revolution', pp. 56-7 in J Stevenson (ed.), *London in the Age of Reform*, pp. 55-78.

21 Quoted in M Beloff (ed.), *The Debate on the American Revolution*, (London, 1949), p. 146.

22 ibid., p. 156.

23 Quoted by P Langford, op. cit., p.58.

24 ibid., pp. 66-7.

25 I R Christie, op.cit., pp. 85-6.

26 G S Veitch, *The Genesis of Parliamentary Reform*, (London, 1913;

reprinted 1965), pp. 44–6.

27   E C Black, *The Association* (Cambridge, Mass., 1963), p.28; C Robbins, *The Eighteenth-Century Commonwealthman*, ch. 9.

28   ibid., pp. 366–7.

29   G S Veitch, op. cot., p.49.

30   J Brewer, op. cit., p.215.

31   I R Christie, 'The Yorkshire Association 1780–1784', p.261, in *Myth and Reality in late Eighteenth Century British Politics*, (London, 1970), pp. 261–83.

32   ibid., pp. 261–2.

33   *First Address to the Public from the SCI*, April 1780, C Wyvill (ed.), *Political Papers*, 6 vols, (York, 1804), II, p. 465. (Hereafter, *Wyvill's Papers*.)

34   F D Cartwright (ed.), *Life and Correspondence of Major Cartwright*, 2 vols, (London 1826), I, p. 134.

35   *First Address*, p. 465.

36   *Declaration of Rights and Second Address*, *Wyvill's Papers*, II, p. 471.

37   SCI minutes, 1780–1782, TS. 11. 1133. (PRO).

38   For a list of provincial members see James Walvin, *English Democratic Societies and Popular Radicalism, 1791-1800*, D Phil., University of York, 1969, Appendix G.

39   E C Black, op. cit., p. 204; SCI minutes, 17 December 1784, TS 11.961.3507.

40   G S Veitch, op. cit., pp. 101–2.

Chapter 2 Early Progress 1783-91

1   J Walvin, *Black and White. The Negro and English Society, 1555-1945*, (London, 1973), ch.7.

2   Granville Sharp, Diary, 19 March 1783, *Sharp Papers*, Hardwick Court.

3   P Hoare, *The Life of Granville Sharp*, (London 1820), p. 241.

4   Memorial of Henry Smeathman, 17 May 1783, TS 631.1304.

5   P Hoare, op. cit., p. 260.

6   *Sharp Papers*, Cupboard 6. Drawer 13.

7   Minutes of the Committee for the relief of the Black Poor, T. 630.1000–T. 647.1572.

8   J Walvin, op. cit., ch.9.

9   Thomas Clarkson, *The History of the Rise, Progress and Accomplishment of the Abolition of the African slave trade . . .*, 2 vols, (London, 1808), I, ch.6.

10   ibid., p. 276.

11   S Drescher, 'Capitalism and Abolition', p. 167, in R Anstey and P E H Hair (eds.), *Liverpool, the Slave Trade and Abolition*, (Liverpool, 1976), pp. 167–95.

12   T Clarkson, op. cit., I, p. 415; *Manchester Directory*, 2 vols, (Manchester, 1788), II, p. 152. (Manchester Central Library).

13   Quoted in D Read, *The English Provinces*, (London, 1964), p. 41.

14 ibid.
15 R Anstey, *The Atlantic Slave Trade and British Abolition, 1760-1810*. (London, 1975), p. 257.
16 ibid., pp. 261-2.
17 *Gentleman's Magazine*, (1788), pp. 610-11, 613, 794-9, 800.
18 *Annual Register*, (1788), p. 133.
19 Minutes of the Abolition Society, 1790-1819, vol. III, 20 July 1790, Add. MSS. 21,256.
20 Petition, 24 January 1788, *City of York Housebook*, 1780-92, vol. XV, York City Archives.
21 *Diary of William Dyers, 1744-1801*, 30 January 1788, (Bristol Central Library).
22 T Clarkson, op. cit., I, p.505.
23 J Ehrman, *The Younger Pitt*, vol. I (London, 1969), p.392.
24 ibid., p.393.
25 House of Commons, 9 May 1789, *Cobbett's Parliamentary History* XXVII, col. 495.
26 ibid., col. 501.
27 ibid., col. 649.
28 R Anstey, op. cit., pp.269-70; Ehrman, op. cit., pp.392-4.
29 ibid., p. 396.
30 ibid., p.397.
31 R Anstey, op.cit., pp. 271-2.
32 ibid., p. 273.
33 G S Veitch, *The Genesis of Parliamentary Reform*, p. 104.
34 *An Abstract History and Proceedings of the Revolution Society*, (London, 1789), p.14.
35 G S Veitch, op. cit., p. 106.
36 F D Cartwright (ed.), *Life and Correspondence of Major Cartwright*, I, p.178.
37 H Ben-Israel, *English Historians and the French Revolution*, (Cambridge, 1968), pp. 6-7.
38 Quoted in G S Veitch, op. cit., pp. 111-12.
39 *The Correspondence of the Revolution Society*, (London, 1792), p. 18.
40 ibid., p. 3.
41 *Vindication of the Revolution Society*, (London, 1792), pp. 15-16.
42 *Correspondence*; Veitch cites 30-40, op. cit., p.130, n.2.
43 G S Veitch, op. cit., p.125.
44 *Abstract History*, p.9.
45 C B Cone, *Burke and the Nature of Politics; The Age of the French Revolution*, (Lexington, Kentucky), 1964, p.306; *Correspondence of Edmund Burke*, 10 vols, (Cambridge, 1958-78), vol. VI, A Cobban and R A Smith (eds), p.xiii. See also P A Brown, *The French Revolution in English History*, (London 1918; reprinted 1965), p.157; E C Black, op. cit., p.213.
46 London, Manchester, Cambridge, St Neots — *SCI*, 5 May 1791, 14 September 1791, TS. 11.960.3506(1).
47 P A Brown, op. cit., ch. 4; E Burke, *Reflections on the Revolution in*

France, C C O'Brien (ed.), (London, 1969), p.16.
48 *Correspondence of Edmund Burke*, VI, p.71.
49 O'Brien, op. cit., p.4.
50 Cone, op. cit., pp.301-11; *Correspondence of Edmund Burke*, *VI* pp. xii-xiv.
51 Burke, op. cit., p.91.
52 26 March, 1790, TS.11.960.3507.
53 ibid., January-August 1791.
54 4 December 1787, TS. 11.961.3507.
55 Thomas Paine, *Rights of Man*, H Collins, (ed.), (London, 1969), p. 30.
56 3 June 1791, TS.11.961.3507.
57 23 March 1791, TS.11.956.3510(1).
58 M D Conway, *The Life of Thomas Paine*, 2 vols, (New York, 1892), I, p.305; A O Aldridge, *Man of Reason*, (London, 1960), p.145.
59 J Woodforde, *The Diary of a Country Parson*, 5 vols, (London, 1927), III, p.285.
60 Aldridge, op. cit., p.151.
61 Veitch, op. cit., pp. 181-3.
62 W Walker, *History of Sheffield*, (1833), p.58; *Local Register for Sheffield*, (1830), p. 68; Black, op. cit., pp. 98, 248.
63 'To the Printer of Aris's Birmingham Gazette', H.O.42.19; *The Memoirs of the Rev Dr Joseph Priestley, written by himself*, (Birmingham, 1810), p.86.
64 Bayley to Home Office, 19 July 1791, H.O.42.19.
65 ibid., Letters from Dundas, 18-19 July 1791; from Leicester, 23 July 1791.

Chapter 3 The Rise of Popular Radicalism, 1791-3

1 Thomas Walker, *A Review of some of the Political Events which have occurred in Manchester during the last five years*, (London, 1794), pp. 13-16, 17.
2 Thomas Cooper to Tooke, 18 August 1791, TS.11.951.3495.
3 *Principles of the Warwickshire Constitutional Society*, H.O.42.19; and, *Rules and Regulations of the Manchester Constitutional Society*, 14 October 1791, (Manchester Central Library).
4 G S Veitch, *The Genesis of Parliamentary Reform*, p.44, n.1; *Wyvill's Papers*, I, pp.135-7; Letters to SCI, TS.960.3506(1).
5 I H Lloyd, *The Cutlery Trades*, (London, 1913), pp.235-40; S and B Webb, *History of Trade Unionism*, (London 1894; new impression 1956), p.39; W White, *History of Sheffield*, (Sheffield, 1837), p.58; *Local Register for Sheffield*, p.68.
6 *Report of the Committee of Secrecy*, (London, 1794), Appendix D, p.44.
7 Sheffield to LCS, 19 March 1792, TS.11.965.3510(A).
8 19 December 1791, 'Address', in *Wyvill's Papers*, II, p.576; for a dif-

ferent view of radical politics in Sheffield see J L Baxter and F K Donnelly, 'The revolutionary "underground" in the West Riding — myth or reality?', *Past and Present*, 64 (August 1974).

9   Sheffield to SCI, January 1792, TS.11.952.3496(1); Tooke to Sheffield, 2 March 1792, TS.11.951.3495.

10   *The Memoirs of Thomas Hardy*, (London, 1832), pp. 13, 102; *R v Tooke*, 1794, TS.11.958.3504; LCS Minute Book, 1792-4, Add. MSS. 27, 812,f.2.

11   On membership figures, see A Goodwin, *The Friends of Liberty*, (London, 1979), p.514; E P Thompson, *The Making of the English Working Class*, pp.152-4.

12   Hardy to Bryant, 8 March 1792, Add. MSS.27.811.,f.5; Add. MSS.27,814,f.36.

13   LCS letters, TS.11.959.3505(1); LCS circular, 15 November 1793, TS.11.966.3510B.

14   Capt Munro, 13 November 1792, TS.11.959.3505(1); Wickham to Nepean, 8 May 1794, TS.11.965.3510 A.

15   29 October 1792, TS.11.959.3505(1).

16   *LCS Address*, 2 April 1792.

17   Quoted in A O Aldridge, *Man of Reason*, p.161.

18   Miller to SCI, 4 July 1792, TS.11.951.3495.

19   Gales to SCI, 11 July 1792; Philips to SCI, 12 July 1792, TS.11.952.3496(1).

20   Letter from Newcastle, 17 December 1792, TS.11.954.3498.

21   These and similar comments can be found in the John Reeves papers, Add. MSS. 16,922,f.81;16,923,f.149;16,924,f.126;16,925,f.21.

22   Add.MSS.16,921,f.44.

23   Add.MSS.16.920,f.14.

24   Add. MSS. 16.920,f.14; 16,921.ff. 100-17; 16,927,f.41; 16,925.ff.120-1.

25   A O Aldridge, op. cit., pp.162-3; Goodwin, op. cit., pp.207; 215.

26   SCI meeting, 28 June, 1792, TS. 11. 962.3508.

27   Quoted in A O Aldridge, op. cit., pp. 162-3.

28   Norwich Revolution Society to LCS, 16 October 1792, TS.11.965.3510.A.

29   Cozens to Hardy, 20 November 1792, TS.11.958.3503.

30   For the origins of provincial societies see Albert Goodwin, op. cit., ch.5. See also *Trial of Thomas Hardy*, 4 vols, (London, 1794), III, p.102; *Manchester Herald*, 1 September 1792; *Manchester Mercury*, 23 October 1792.

31   *A Reply to Mr Burke's Invective*, (1792), pp.85-6.

32   G S Veitch, op. cit., p.190.

33   C B Cone, *Burke and the Nature of Politics*, pp.373,385.

34   SCI resolution, 11 May 1792, TS.11.962.3508.

35   Editor of the *Patriot* to LCS, 15 October 1792, TS.11.965.3510.A.

36   *LCS Address*, 29 November 1792.

37   *Hardy Memoirs*, pp. 20-1, 42; *Annual Register*, 'Chronicle,' Appendix, pp.70-2.

38   G S Veitch, op. cit., pp. 225-6.

39   Subscriptions, 30 November 1792, TS.11.952.3496(1); G S Veitch, op.

cit., pp.227-30.

40 On the wider government policy of suppression see C Emsley, 'An aspect of Pitt's "Terror": prosecutions for sedition during the 1790s', *Social History*, VI (1981), pp.155-84.

41 H Furber, *Henry Dundas*, (London, 1931), pp. 78-9.

42 Pitt to Dundas, 15, 19, November 1791, *Pitt Papers*, (William L Clement Library, University of Michegan, Ann Arbor).

43 *Proceedings of the Association for the Preservation of Liberty and Property against Republicans and Levellers*, 28 November 1792, pp. 1-8 (hereafter APLP); E C Black, *The Association*, pp. 232, 236-7, and letters in *Pitt Papers*.

44 See, *Politics for November 1792-August 1793*, (hereafter Reeves Collection), Manchester Central Library; Pitt to Dundas, 25 November 1792, *Pitt Papers*.

45 Thomas Walker, op.cit., pp. 41-3, 66; *Minute Book*, Association for Preserving Constitutional Order . . . (Chetham's Library, Manchester); A Goodwin, op. cit., ch.7.

46 Add.MSS. 16,920,ff.125-6.

47 12 December 1792, Reeves Collection.

48 Quoted in A O Aldridge, op. cit., p.73.

49 *Manchester Chronicle*, June, January, March 1793.

50 Thomas Walker, op. cit., p.127.

51 APLP, *Papers*, p.vii.

Chapter 4 English Jacobins

1 Quoted in A O Aldridge, *Man of Reason*, pp. 165-6.

2 *Annual Register*, (1792), p.85; Stockport to LCS, 27 September 1792, TS.11.965.3510A.

3 James Burgh, *Political Disquisitions*, 3 vols, (London, 1775), III, pp.428-9; C. Robbins, *Eighteenth-Century Commonwealthman*, pp. 365-70; E C Black, *The Association*, p.30.

4 W M Roach, 'Reform Movements in Scotland. 1815-1822', Ph.D., University of Glasgow, 1970, pp.5-11; H W Meikle, *Scotland and the French Revolution*, (Glasgow, 1912; new ed., London, 1969), ch.5.

5 Quoted in ibid., p.94.

6 ibid, p.110.

7 Add.MSS. 27,813,f.43; *Annual Register*, (1793), pp. 148-59.

8 Norwich to LCS, 23 June 1793, TS.11.956.3501(1).

9 Joseph Gerald, *A Convention the only means of saving us from ruin . . .*, (London, 1793), pp. 112-13.

10 Lord Cockburn, *Examination of the Trials for Sedition in Scotland*, 2 vols, (Edinburgh, 1888), I,pp.144-84; H W Meikle, op.cit., pp.114.ff.

11 A Goodwin, *The Friends of Liberty*, ch.8.

12 *Report of the Committee of Secrecy*, 1794, pp.42-3.
13 ibid.
14 Lord Cockburn, op.cit., II, p.40; H W Meikle, op.cit., pp.144-5.
15 LCS General Meeting, 24 January 1794, TS.11.960.3506(1).
16 Letter to Margarot, 2 January 1794, TS.11.966.3510B.
17 *LCS; Address to the Nation*, 8 July 1793; Add. MSS.27,813,f.45,50;*War* by 'Sidney', (Manchester, 10 December 1793).
18 *Place Collection*, XXXVII, p.38, (British Library); Letter from Sheffield, 24 April 1793, TS.11.956.3501(1); W T Laprade, *England in the French Revolution*, (Baltimore, 1909), p.113, n.8; *Report of the Committee of Secrecy*, 1794, Appendix E, pp.90-1.
19 *General Meeting of the LCS*, 14 April 1794; TS.11.954.3498; Add MSS. 27,813, ff.74-5.
20 Spies' reports, Reeves, 24 April 1794, TS.11.965.3510A; Metcalfe, 2 April 1794, TS.11.956.3510A.
21 Reeves' report, 29 April 1794, TS.11.965.3510A.
22 Thelwall, *Speech to the LCS*, 26 October 1795, p.10; *The Rights of Nature*, (1796), p.20; Letters, 13 February 1794, TS.11.959.3505(1); see also Mrs Thelwall, *The Life of John Thelwall*, (London, 1837), pp.115 ff.
23 Letter to Nepean, 30 March 1794, TS.11.959.3505(1).
24 Sir Joseph Banks, (enclosure) 22 April 1794, TS.11.959.3505(1).
25 *Politics for the People*, VI No.12 (1794), p.69.
26 ibid., Part II, No.1, p.5.
27 *Memoirs of Thomas Spence*, (Newcastle, 1826); E P Thompson, *The Making of the English Working Class*, pp.160-2.
28 A Aspinall, *Politics and the Press, c.1780-1850*, (London, 1949).
29 ibid., pp.152-3.
30 Letters to 'M. Chapeaurouge', TS. 11. 965.3510A.
31 Letter, 11 March 1794, TS.11.3510A; Letters to Nepean and Dundas, April-May 1794, ibid; Privy Council Examinations, TS.11.957. 3502(2).
32 Quoted in G S Veitch, *The Genesis of Parliamentary Reform*, p.306.
33 Quoted in F O'Gorman, *The Whig Party and the French Revolution*, (London, 1967), p.140; List of Committee members in House of Commons, 15 May 1794, *Cobbett's Parliamentary History*, XXXI, cols 474-5.
34 ibid., cols 475-97; G S Veitch, op. cit., pp.306-7.
35 List of persons charged, PC.1. 3536A; E P Thompson, op. cit., pp.132-3. But see also C Emsley, 'An aspect of Pitt's "Terror"', op.cit.
36 PC examinations of Tooke, Joyce, PC.1.22.A36(a); TS.11.963.3509; C Cestre, *John Thelwall*, (London, 1906),pp.91-2.
37 Examination of Spence, 23 May 1794, PC.1.22.A.36(a).
38 *Report of the Committee of Secrecy*, 1794,pp.54-5.
39 *The Times*, 27 June 1794.
40 *York Chronicle*, 16 May 1794.
41 Groves' Reports, May-June 1794, TS.11.965.3510A.
42 *Report of the Committee of Constitution of the LCS*, 1794; *Report of the*

Sub-Committee of Westminster, 1780.

43 Groves, 4 September 1794, TS.11.965.3510A.
44 H Twiss, *The Public Life and Private Life of Lord Eldon*, 3 vols, (London 1884), I, p.283.
45 See papers on jury selection in K.33.6.2-3. (PRO).
46 H Twiss, op.cit., I, pp.244-53; Lord John Campbell, *Lives of the Lord Chancellors*, 10 vols, (London, 1868), V, p.484; *Trial of Thomas Hardy*, 4 vols, (London, 1794), III.
47 Lord Mayor, 6 November 1794, TS.11.966.3510 B; H Twiss, op.cit., I,pp.268-9.
48 Lord Mayor, 6 November 1794, TS.11.966.3510 B.
49 H Twiss, op.cit., I, p.272.
50 ibid., pp.278-80; G S Veitch, op.cit., p.315.
51 *The trial of John Horne Tooke*, (1794), p.148.
52 *Place Memoirs*, Add.MSS. 35,142,f.236.
53 C Emsley, *British Society and the French Wars, 1793-1815*, (London, 1979), ch.3, part I; E P Thompson, op.cit., pp.65-6.
54 *Place Collection*, XXXVII, p.120; E P Thompson, op.cit., pp.141-5.
55 John Thewall, *Speech*, 26 October 1795, pp.7-8; *The Tribune*, 14 March 1795, p.35; *Morning Chronicle*, 16 October 1795.
56 E P Thompson, op.cit., pp.140-1; *Account of the Proceedings at St George's Field*, 29 June 1795; Add.MSS.35.143,f.14.
57 Perth to LCS, 19 October 1795, Add. MSS.27.815, f.5.
58 *Annual Register*, (1795), 'Chronicle', p.3.
59 John Thewall, *Speech*, 26 October 1795.
60 G A Williams, *Artisans and Sans-Culottes*, (London 1968), p.100; E P Thompson, op.cit., p.144; *Annual Register*, (1795), 'Chronicle', p.37.
61 S T Coleridge, *Reflections on Having Left a Place of Retirement*, lines 44-8.
62 *Annual Register*, (1795), 'Chronicle', p.43; John Thewall, *Speech*, 12 November 1795.
63 *Morning Chronicle*, 8 December 1795.
64 Quoted in L Patten and P Mann (eds), *The Collected Works of Samuel Taylor Coleridge; Lectures, 1795 on Politics and Religion*, (London, 1971), p.li.
65 *To the Parliament and People of Great Britain. An explicit Declaration of the Principles and Views of the LCS*, Place Collection, XXXVII, p.111.
66 ibid., p.139; C Cestre, op.cit., p.124; Mrs Thewall, op.cit., p.410.
67 *Annual Register*, (1795), 'Chronicle', p.47.
68 Add.MSS.25,143,f.16.
69 A Cobban (ed.), *Debate on the French Revolution*, (London, 1950), pp.289-90.

Chapter 5 Mutiny and Rebellion, 1796–9

1   11 March 1796, P.C.1.23.A.38; Add.MSS.27,815,f.140; 1 December 1796, PC.1.23.A.36.
2   E P Thompson, *The Making of the English Working Class*, pp.163–5.
3   J Cornwall, *Coleridge*, (London, 1973), pp.120–33.
4   Add.MSS.27,808,f.75.
5   See provincial letters in Add.MSS.27,815.
6   C Emsley, *British Society*, pp.56–64.
7   *Annual Register*, (1796), 'History of Europe', p.148.
8   Details in Add.MSS.27,815.
9   R Coupland, (ed.), *The War Speeches of William Pitt*, (Oxford, 1935), p.143.
10 John Binns, *Recollections*, (Philadelphia, 1854), p.54; John Gale Jones, *Sketch of a Political Tour*, (London, 1797), p.43.
11 Report from Graham, May 1797, PC.1. 38.A.117.
12 Spies' reports, P.C.1.40.A.132.
13 Quoted in G E Manwaring and B Dobrée, *The Floating Republic*, (London 1966), p.250.
14 *Report of the Committee of Secrecy*, 1799, p.18.
15 Manwaring and Dobrée, op.cit., pp.242–3.
16 Circular, 21 July 1797, PC.1.38.A.123; Add.MSS.27,808,f.81.
17 Narrative of the Proceedings, 31 July 1797, in P.C.1.40.A.132; *The Times*, 1 August 1797.
18 Quoted in G Costigan, *A History of Modern Ireland*, (New York, 1969), p.117.
19 Quoted in R Kee, *The Most Distressful Country*, (London, 1976),p.53.
20 G Costigan, op.cit., p.122; R Kee, op.cit., p.62.
21 ibid., p.67.
22 ibid., p.84.
23 Quoted in G Costigan, op.cit., p.127.
24 *Address of the LCS to the Irish Nation*, 10 January 1798, P.C.1.44.A.155.
25 F MacDermot, 'Arthur O'Connor', *Irish Historical Studies*, XV (1966), p.52.
26 Add.MSS.35,143,f.461; Add.MSS.27,808,f.90.
27 11 May 1798, P.C.1.3526.
28 Barlow's Reports, P.C. 1.38. A. 123.
29 R R Madden, *The United Irishmen*, 7 vols, (London, 1842–6), II; Reports of Robert Gray, P.C.1. 41.A.139, and A.136.
30 Add.MSS.27,808,f.92.
31 Letters dated 12, 15 February 1798, P.C.1.43.A.152.
32 Details in Bayley's letters, P.C.1.41.A.136; and examinations of witnesses, P.C.1.41.A.135; P.C.1.42.A.143.
33 'Secret Committee of England', T.S.11.956.3501.(2).
34 See R Kee, op.cit., ch.9.
35 Bayley, 16, 27, 31 March 1798, P.C.1.41.A.136.
36 Letters dated April 1798, P.C.1.41.A.139.

37 Portland to Bayley, 21 April 1798, P.C.1.41.A.139.
38 Reports of Tunbridge and Gent, 1798, P.C.1.42.A.144; P.C.1.3119; P.C.1.43.A.150; 'United Irishmen', P.C.1.43.152.
39 Letters from Crawford, P.C.1.43.A.150; P.C.1.3117.
40 *The Anti-Jacobin Review and Magazine*, July–December 1799, I, p.1.
41 ibid., III, pp.127–8.
42 ibid., I, p.107.
43 *Report of the Committee of Secrecy*, 1799; *Annual Register*, (1799), p.188.
44 39.Geo.III.c.79.

Chapter 6 The Tradition Preserved

1 S Maccoby, *English Radicalism, 1786-1832*, (London, 1955), pp.152–218; M W Patterson, *Sir Francis Burdett and his Times*, 2 vols, (London, 1931), I, pp.132–218; G Wallas, *The Life of Francis Place*, (London, 1898), pp.39–48.
2 W Reitzel (ed.), *The Autobiography of William Cobbett*, (London, 1967), pp.95–8; G Wallas, op.cit., p.42; M Thale (ed.), *The Autobiography of Francis Place*, (Cambridge, 1972), pp. xviii, 221; also *Biographical Dictionary*, I, for biographical details of Burdett, Cobbett and Place.
3 M Thale, op.cit., p.xi; M W Patterson, op.cit., pp.192–209, 212.
4 ibid., pp.240–94; J Stevenson, *Popular Disturbances in England, 1700-1870*, (London, 1979), pp.185–9.
5 For Whitbread, see *Biographical Dictionary*, I.
6 W Thomas, *The Philosophic Radicals*, (Oxford, 1979), pp.15–45 paints an engaging picture of Place, Romilly and Mill at Bentham's country home in 1817. Place first met Bentham through Mill in 1812.
7 D Read, *The English Provinces*, pp. 22–34, 52–61.
8 ibid., p.55.
9 J R Dinwiddy, *Christopher Wyvill and Reform*, (York, 1971), pp.9–10.
10 D Read, *Press and People, 1790-1850*, (London, 1961), pp.109–10.
11 J R Dinwiddy, op.cit., pp. 21–2.
12 G D H Cole and R Postgate, *The Common People*, (London, 1938; reprinted 1966), p.167; M Thomis and P Holt, *Threats of Revolution in Britain, 1789-1848*, (London, 1977), p. 36.
13 A W Smith, 'Irish Rebels and English Radicals, 1798–1820', *Past and Present*, 7 (April 1955), pp.81–3; M Elliott, 'The "Despard Conspiracy" reconsidered', *Past and Present*, 75 (May 1977), pp.46–61. The most recent account, A Goodwin, *The Friends of Liberty*, follows Dr Elliott's argument. E P Thompson, in *The Making of the English Working Class*, takes both points of view, but places his emphasis on the latter.
14 M Elliott, op.cit., E P Thompson, op.cit., p.484.
15 D Read, *The English Provinces*, p. 63.
16 J Foster, *Class Struggle and the Industrial Revolution*, p.38.

17 E P Thompson, op.cit., pp.472–8; J R Dinwiddy, J L Baxter and F K Donnelly, debate in *Past and Present*, 64 (August 1794), pp.113–35; J L Baxter and F K Donnelly, 'Sheffield and the English Revolutionary Tradition', *International Review of Social History*, XXV (1975), pp.398–423. For economic background, see R A E Wells, *Dearth and Distress in Yorkshire, 1793-1802*, (York, 1977).

18 M Thomis *The Luddites*; F O Darvall, *Popular Disturbances and Public Order in Regency England*, (London, 1934); E P Thompson, op.cit., pp. 484–602.

19 R A Church and S D Chapman, 'Gravener Henson and the Making of the English Working Class', in E L Jones and G E Mingay (eds.), *Land, Labour and Population in the Industrial Revolution*, (London, 1967), pp. 131–61; E P Thompson, op.cit., pp.496–7.

20 D Bythell, *The Handloom Weavers*, (Cambridge, 1969), pp.205–10; J R Dinwiddy, 'Luddism and Politics in the Northern Counties', *Social History*, IV (1979), pp. 33–51.

21 ibid., pp.51–63; W B Crump and G Ghorbal, *History of the Huddersfield Woollen Industry*, (Huddersfield, 1935), pp.98–100.

22 E P Thompson provides this in *The Making . . .*, ch.xiv, but see also his introduction to F Peel, *The Risings of the Luddites, Chartists and Plug-Drawers* (1880; new edition, London, 1968). The evidence is thoroughly re-examined by J R Dinwiddy, op.cit.

23 A Prentice, *Historial Sketches and Personal Recollections of Manchester*, (1851; new edition, London, 1970), pp.51–2.

24 J R Dinwiddy, op.cit., pp.48–51.

25 ibid., pp.54–5, 59–60; E P Thompson, op.cit., p.602

26 J Cannon, *Parliamentary Reform, 1640-1832*, pp. 146–64.

27 J W Osborne, *John Cartwright*, (Cambridge, 1972), pp. 55–69.

28 ibid., pp. 76,82,87–98.

29 ibid., pp.100–2; Dinwiddy, op.cit., p.60.

Chapter 7 Post-war Discontents, 1815–20

1 A Prentice, *Historical Sketches and Personal Recollections of Manchester*, p.63.

2 S Bamford, *Passages in the Life of a Radical* (1839; H Dunkley (ed.), London, 1893), p.11.

3 J Stevenson, *Popular Disturbances in England, 1700-1870*, pp.190–3; F O Darvall, *Popular Disturbances and Public Order in Regency England*, pp. 155–6; R J White, *Waterloo to Peterloo*, (London 1957; republished 1963), p.177; A J Peacock, *Bread or Blood*, (London, 1965).

4 Quoted in L M Munby (ed.), *The Luddites and Other Essays*, (London, 1971), p.42.

5 J Stevenson, 'Food Riots in England, 1792-1818', p.67, in R Quinault

and J Stevenson, (eds.), *Popular Protest and Public Order*, (London, 1974), pp. 33–74.

6   D Read, *Press and People, 1790-1850*, p.82.
7   ibid., pp.112, 116–18.
8   *Cobbett's Weekly Political Register*, 26 October, 16 November 1816. The Stamp Duty had been increased to 4d gross in 1815.
9   S Bamford, op.cit., pp.11–12.
10 James Watson, autobiographical speech reported in *Reasoner* supplement, 5 February 1854, reprinted in E Royle (ed.). *The Infidel Tradition from Paine to Bradlaugh*, (London, 1976), pp. 99–106, esp. p.100.
11 *Cobbett's W P R*, 7 December, 21 December 1816. The hawking of such papers was declared illegal in 1817.
12 ibid., 16 November 1816.
13 S Bamford, op.cit., pp.13–14.
14 ibid., pp.18–22; J W Osborne, *John Cartwright*, pp. 114–16.
15 S Bamford, op.cit., pp.21-3; E P Thompson, *The Making of the English Working Class*, pp. 616–20.
16 S Bamford, op. cit., p.32.
17 T M Parssinen, 'The Revolutionary Party in London, 1816–20', *Bulletin of the Institute of Historical Research*, XLV (1972), pp. 266–82; I Prothero, *Artisans and Politics in Early Nineteenth-Century London*, (London 1979; republished 1981), pp.88–91; E P Thompson, op.cit., pp.633–5. For Davenport, Evans, Thistlewood and Watson, see *Biographical Dictionary*, I.
18 S Bamford, op.cit., pp.21,23–6, 33; R J White, op.cit., pp.150–1.
19 S Bamford, op.cit., pp.31–5; R J White, op.cit., pp.155–7.
20 S Bamford, op.cit., p.37; R J White, op.cit., pp.157–8.
21 S Bamford, op.cit., pp.70-3; R J White, op.cit., p.158; E P. Thompson, op.cit., pp.651–2.
22 S Bamford, op.cit., p.42.
23 ibid., p.44.
24 ibid.
25 E P Thompson, op.cit., pp.653–5.
26 S Bamford, op.cit., pp.135-7; M Thomis and P Holt, *Threats of Revolution in Britain, 1789-1848*, p.45.
27 E P Thompson, op.cit., pp.661–2. For Weightman, see F Peel, *The Risings of the Luddites, Chartists and Plug-drawers*, p.285.
28 M Thomis and P Holt, op.cit., pp.46–52; E P Thompson, op.cit., pp.658–61. Both these very different books are agreed that Oliver exploited, but did not create the rising.
29 F Peel, op.cit., pp.294–300.
30 D Read, op.cit., p.113.
31 E P Thompson, op.cit., p.670.
32 S Bamford, op.cit., p.135.
33 S Maccoby, *English Radicalism, 1786-1832*, pp. 340–4.
34 W Thomas, *The Philosophic Radicals*, pp. 41-94; see also J M Main, 'Radical Westminster, 1807-20', *Historical Studies*, XII, (1966), pp.186-204.
35 R F Wearmouth, *Some Working-class Movements of the Nineteenth*

Century, (London, 1948), p.32.

36   D Read, *Peterloo*, (Manchester, 1958), pp. 47-9.
37   R F Wearmouth, op.cit., p.36; D Read, op.cit., pp.49-51.
38   I Prothero, op.cit., pp. 91-2.
39   ibid., pp. 110-12.
40   ibid., pp. 112-14; T M Parssinen, op.cit., p.277.
41   S Bamford, op.cit., pp. 149-55; A Prentice, op.cit., pp.167-8.
42   S Bamford, op.cit., pp.155-69; A Prentice, op.cit., pp. 168-9.
43   D Read, op.cit., pp.57-73; A Prentice, op.cit., pp. 164-6.
44   D Read, op.cit., p.73.
45   ibid., p.71.
46   *Biographical Dictionary*, I, entry on W T Sherwin.
47   I Prothero, op.cit., pp.96, 105, 108; T M Parssinen, op.cit., p.277.
48   E P Thompson, op.cit., pp.675-6. For Wooler, Hone, Sherwin, Davison, Wade and Leigh Hunt, see *Biographical Dictionary*, I.
49   W H Wickwar, *The Struggle for the Freedom of the Press*, (London, 1928), pp. 57-9; A Calder Marshall, *Lewd, Blasphemous and Obscene*, (London, 1972), pp. 17-68.
50   For Eaton, Thelwall, Jones and Carlile, see *Biographical Dictionary*, I.
51   *Sherwin's W P R*, 21 August 1819.
52   W H Wickwar, op.cit., pp.67-75, 82-96; E Royle, *Victorian Infidels*, (Manchester, 1974), pp.31-3. For Carlile's own account of his early life and development, see *Republican*, 3 March 1820, 28 January 1825, 14 July 1826.
53   D Read, op.cit., p. 157.
54   I Prothero, op.cit., pp.116-31; E P Thompson, op.cit., pp. 700-5.
55   W H Wickwar, op.cit., pp. 136-41.
56   M Thomis and P Holt, op.cit., pp.62-84.
57   E P Thompson, op.cit., pp. 706-7; J R Dinwiddy, 'Luddism and Politics in the Northern Counties', op.cit., p. 55.
58   R J White, op.cit., p.191.

Chapter 8 The Formative Decade

1   E P Thompson, *The Making of the English Working Class*, p.711.
2   J Stevenson, 'The Queen Caroline Affair', p.117, in J Stevenson (ed.), *London in the Age of Reform*, pp. 117-48.
3   ibid., p.128.
4   ibid., *passim*; the popular movement it dealt with in more detail in I Prothero, *Artisans and Politics in Early Nineteenth-Century London*, pp. 132-55.
5   J Cannon, *Parliamentary Reform, 1640-1832*, pp. 177-80.
6   R J White, *Waterloo to Peterloo*, pp. 180-1; D Read, *Peterloo*, p.134.
7   D Read, *The English Provinces*, p.80; J Cannon, op.cit., pp.184, 188.

8   I Prothero, op.cit., pp. 132-3.
9   R F Wearmouth, *Some Working-Class Movements of the Nineteenth Century*, pp.44-8.
10 J Belchem, 'Republicanism, popular constitutionalism and the radical platform in early nineteenth-century England', *Social History*, VI (1981), pp. 1-32, esp. pp. 17-22; see also above, p.123.
11 *Republican*, 21 June 1822.
12 I Prothero, op.cit., pp. 110, 115, 121.
13 E Royle, *Victorian Infidels*, p.38.
14 J F C Harrison, *Robert Owen and the Owenites in Britain and America*, (London, 1969), pp. 108-21; and *The Second Coming. Popular Millenarianism, 1780-1850*, (London, 1979), pp. 152-60; W H Oliver, *Prophets and Millennialists. The Uses of Biblical Prophecy in England from the 1790s to the 1840s*, Auckland and Oxford, 1978), pp. 150-216. See also *Biographical Dictionary*, I, q.v.
15 W R Ward, 'Swedenborgianism: heresy, schism or religious protest?', in D Baker (ed.), *Schism, Heresy and Religious Protest*, (Cambridge, 1972), pp. 303-9.
16 G A Williams, *Rowland Detrosier. A Working-Class Infidel, 1800-34*, (York, 1965), pp. 11-12.
17 W H Oliver, op.cit., pp.197-207; J F C Harrison, *The Second Coming*, pp. 142-52, 156-7.
18 E Royle, op.cit., pp.33-7.
19 W H Wickwar, *The Struggle for the Freedom of the Press, 1819-32*, pp.102-14, 120-4.
20 *Reasoner* supplement, 5 February 1854, reprinted in E Royle (ed.), *The Infidel Tradition from Paine to Bradlaugh*, pp.99-106.
21 *Republican*, 27 October 1820, reprinted ibid., pp.23-4. 'The Society for the Suppression of Vice' was founded in 1802. 'The Constitutional Association for opposing the progress of disloyal and seditious principles' was founded in 1820 following the Queen Caroline agitation.
22 W H Wickwar, op.cit., pp. 217-20; see also the recollections of B B Jones, printed in *Reasoner*, 5 June 1859, reprinted in E Royle, op.cit., pp.25-31.
23 W H Wickwar, op.cit., pp.228-38.
24 ibid. pp. 201-4; A Prentice, *Historical Sketches and Personal Recollections of Manchester*, pp. 237-8.
25 *Republican*, 18 January 1822, reprinted in E Royle, op.cit., pp.31-2; see also *Republican*, 22 February, 5 April, 6 December 1822; and House of Commons, 16 April 1823, *Hansard*, 2nd series VIII, cols 1014-19.
26 D Read, *Peterloo*, p.162; *Republican*, 22 February 1822, reprinted in E Royle, op.cit., pp.115-17.
27 *Republican*, 6 December 1822.
28 ibid., 6 December 1822, 25 April 1823, 17, 24 September, 1 October 1824; *Hansard*, op.cit.
29 *Republican*, 4 January 1822.
30 ibid., 14 January 1825.
31 ibid., 20 September 1822.

32   *Lion*, 18 January, 9, 23 May 1828.
33   E Royle, *Victorian Infidels*, pp. 38–40; *Prompter*, 15 January 1831.
34   *Republican*, 1 November 1822. Bentham used the pseudonym of 'Philip Beauchamp'.
35   A McLaren, *Birth Control in Nineteenth-Century England*, (London, 1978), pp.51–8; *Republican*, 6 May 1825.
36   *Lion*, 22, 29 February, 16 May 1828, 1 May 1829.
37   I Prothero, op.cit., pp.68–70.
38   R G Kirby and A E Musson, *The Voice of the People*, (Manchester, 1975), pp. 14–27.
39   S and B Webb, *The History of Trade Unionism*, pp. 93–108; I Prothero, op.cit., pp.72–82.
40   R G Kirby and A E Musson, op.cit., p.29.
41   ibid., pp. 346–64; John Brown, *A Memoir of Robert Blinco*, (reprint of Doherty's 1832 edition, Firle, 1977).
42   I Prothero, op.cit., pp.190–1.
43   ibid., pp. 191–209; for Hodgskin and Thompson, see *Biographical Dictionary*, I.
44   G D H Cole, *A History of Socialist Thought, vol.1: The Forerunners, 1789-1850*, (London, 1953; reprinted 1965), pp. 110–17.
45   A Briggs, 'The Language of "Class" in early Nineteenth–Century England', p.52, in A Briggs and J Saville (eds), *Essays in Labour History*, (London, 1960; revised ed. 1967), pp. 43–73.
46   F Podmore, *Robert Owen*, (London, 1906; reprinted New York, 1968), pp. 238–41.
47   *Dictionary of Labour Biography*, I; *Republican*, 9 December 1825. For Orbiston, see R G Garnett, *Co-operation and the Owenite Socialist Communities in Britain, 1825-45*, (Manchester, 1972), pp. 65–99.
48   ibid., pp.41–51; I Prothero, op.cit., pp. 237–64.
49   T W Mercer (ed.), *Dr William King and the Co-operator, 1828-30*, (Manchester, 1922), pp. xvii–xxv.
50   See the lists in G J Holyoake *History of Co-operation*, 2 vols, (London, 1906), II, pp. 476–9.
51   I Prothero, op.cit., p.243; R G Garnett, op.cit., pp. 130–41.
52   For details, see J Walvin, 'The Public Campaign in England against Slavery, 1787–1834', in D Eltis and J Walvin (eds), *The Abolition of the Atlantic Slave Trade*, (Madison, Wisc., 1981), pp. 63–79.
53   E R Norman, *A History of Modern Ireland*, (London, 1971), p.56.
54   ibid., pp. 81–3.
55   E Royle, op.cit., p.39; M Brock, *The Great Reform Act*, (London, 1973), p.62; C Flick, *The Birmingham Political Union and the Movements for Reform in Britain, 1830-1839*, (Folkestone, 1979), p.43.

Chapter 9 The Great Betrayal 1830-7

1   J Cannon, *Parliamentary Reform, 1640-1832*, pp. 186-203.

2   C Flick, *The Birmingham Political Union*, pp. 17-26.

3   A Briggs, 'The background of the parliamentary reform movement in three English cities (1830-2)', *Cambridge Historical Journal*, X (1952), pp. 293-317; D Read, *Press and People, 1790-1850*, pp. 119-22, 152-5.

4   D Fraser, 'The Agitation for Parliamentary Reform', in J T Ward (ed.), *Popular Movements, c. 1830-1850*, (London, 1970), pp. 29-53; D C Moore, *The Politics of Deference*, (Hassocks, 1976), pp. 138-242, which incorporates earlier articles on the subject; J Cannon, op.cit., pp. 246-8; M Brock, *The Great Reform Act*, pp. 146-7.

5   E J Hobsbawm and G Rudé, *Captain Swing* (London, 1969; Harmondsworth, 1973); G Rudé, 'English Rural and Urban Disturbances on the eve of the First Reform Bill, 1830-1831', *Past and Present*, 37 (July 1967), pp. 87-102.

6   N McCord, 'Some Difficulties of Parliamentary Reform', *Historical Journal*, X (1967), pp. 376-90.

7   *Leeds Mercury*, 17, 24 July 1830.

8   ibid., 7 April, 12 May 1832.

9   D Read, op.cit., pp.119-22.

10 J Hamburger, *James Mill and the Art of Revolution*, (New Haven, 1963); C Flick, op.cit., pp.63-9.

11 For details of the Act, see N Gash, *Politics in the Age of Peel*, (London, 1953), pp. 3-101.

12 M Brock, op.cit., p.249; M Thomis, *Politics and Society in Nottingham, 1785-1835*, pp.223-6; A T Patterson, *Radical Leicester*, (Leicester, 1954), pp.187-8; D Read, op.cit., pp.141-2.

13 D J Rowe, 'London Radicalism in the Era of the Great Reform Bill', pp.150, 170, in J Stevenson (ed.), *London in the Age of Reform*, pp. 149-76.

14 D J V Jones, *Before Rebecca*, (London, 1973), p.158; G A Williams, *The Merthyr Rising*, (London, 1978), pp. 224-30; E P Thompson, *The Making of the English Working Class*, p.75.

15 J H Wiener, *The War of the Unstamped*, (Ithaca and London, 1969), pp.138-40, 152-5; A G Barker, *Henry Hetherington*, (London, 1938), p. 15; P Hollis, *The Pauper Press*, (Oxford, 1970), pp. 222-5.

16 ibid., pp.172-3; J Wiener, op.cit., pp.188-93; A R Schoyen, *The Chartist Challenge*, (London, 1958), pp.6, 9-10.

17 S Chadwick, *A Bold and Faithful Journalist*, (Huddersfield, 1976), pp. 8-24; *Poor Man's Guardian*, 17 September, 5 November, 10 December 1831; *Voice of the West Riding*, 3 August 1833.

18 J Wiener, op.cit., pp. 246-9.

19 I Prothero, *Artisans and Politics in Early Nineteenth-Century London*, pp. 281-99; P Hollis, op.cit., pp. 264-71.

20 J F C Harrison, *Robert Owen and the Owenites in Britain and America*, pp. 202-9; W H Oliver, 'The Labour Exchange Phase of the Co-operative

Movement', *Oxford Economic Papers*, n.s.X (1958), pp. 355–67.

21 G D H Cole, *Attempts at General Union*, (London, 1953); W H Fraser, 'Trade Unionism', in J T Ward, op.cit., pp.95–115; W H Oliver, 'The Consolidated Trades' Union of 1834', *Economic History Review* 2nd. series, XVII, (1964), pp. 77–95; for J E Smith, see J Saville, 'J E Smith and the Owenite Movement, 1833–4', in S Pollard and J Salt (eds), *Robert Owen. Prophet of the Poor*, (London, 1971), pp. 115–44.

22 R G Kirby and A E Musson, *The Voice of the People*, pp. 272–301.

23 D Read, op.cit., pp. 123–4; *Leeds Mercury*, 19 March 1831; *Leeds Intelligencer*, 24 March 1831. For the Ten Hours movement, see J T Ward, *The Factory Movement*, (London, 1962) and the same author's essay in his *Popular Movements*, pp. 54–77; also C Driver, *Tory Radical*, (New York, 1946; new impression 1970).

24 *Leeds Mercury*, 28 April, 5 May 1832; *Leeds Intelligencer*, 26 April, 3 May 1832.

25 D Fraser (ed.), *A History of Modern Leeds* (Manchester, 1980), p.278.

26 C Driver, op.cit., pp. 344–50, 358–60.

27 M Thomis, op.cit., p.249.

28 G D H Cole, *Chartist Portraits*, (London, 1941; new edition 1965), pp. 103–5.

29 U R Q Henriques, *The Early Factory Acts and their Enforcement*, (London, 1971), pp. 8–17.

30 See S G and E O A Checkland (eds), *The Poor Law Report of 1834*, (Harmondsworth, 1974), pp. 9–59.

31 N C Edsall, *The Anti-Poor Law Movement, 1834-44*, (Manchester, 1971); M E Rose, 'The Anti-Poor Law Agitation', in J T Ward (ed.), *Popular Movements*, pp. 78–94.

32 N C Edsall, op.cit., pp. 53–115; M E Rose, op.cit., pp. 86–92.

33 D Read, *Cobden and Bright*, (London, 1967), pp. 17–18.

34 D Fraser, *Urban Politics in Victorian England*, (London 1976; new impression 1979), pp. 100–1, 115–24.

35 The defeat of the reformers in the 1830s is the theme of N Gash, *Reaction and Reconstruction in English Politics, 1832-1852*, (Oxford, 1965); and W Thomas, *The Philosophic Radicals*.

36 P Hollis, op.cit., pp. 62–91.

Chapter 10 The Charter and No Surrender

1 C Flick, *The Birmingham Political Union*, pp. 114–22, esp. p.116.

2 J T Ward, *Chartism*, (London, 1973), pp. 70–8; I Prothero, *Artisans and Politics*, pp. 310–15. Ward's is the fullest recent study of Chartism, but see also D Jones, *Chartism and the Chartists*, (London, 1975); and E Royle, *Chartism*, (London, 1980).

3 D Jones, op.cit., pp.60–4.

4   *Northern Star*, 19 October 1839.
5   Thomas Carlyle, *Chartism*, (London, 1839, 2nd ed., 1842), pp. 2–3.
6   Minutes of the LWMA, 3 January 1837, 15 May 1838, Add. MSS. 37,773; J T Ward, op.cit., pp.82–5.
7   R G Gammage, *History of the Chartist Movement*, (London 1854; 2nd edition 1894), p.7.
8   D Read and E Glasgow, *Feargus O'Connor. Irishman and Chartist*, (London, 1961), pp. 56–9; J A Epstein, 'Feargus O'Connor and the Northern Star', *International Review of Social History*, XXI (1976), pp. 51–97.
9   For comparative circulation figures, see D Read, *Press and People*, pp. 209–18.
10   *Northern Star*, 29 September 1838.
11   ibid., 26 October 1839. In all, sixty-four localities were represented by fifty-three people.
12   The 'Bedchamber Crisis' in which Peel refused to form a government unless the Queen removed her Whig Ladies of the Bedchamber, lasted from Melbourne's resignation on 7 May until his resumption of office on 10 May. House of Commons, 12 July 1839, *Hansard*, XLIX, cols 220–74.
13   Letter from LDA to William Lovett, General Convention Letter Book, 1839, Add.MSS. 34,245.
14   D Williams, 'Chartism in Wales', pp. 227–32, in A Briggs (ed.), *Chartist Studies*, (London, 1959, revised ed. 1967), pp. 220–48.
15   H Jephson, *The Platform. Its Rise and Progress*, 2 vols (London, 1892), II, p.269.
16   *Annual Register* (1839), 'History of Europe', pp. 304–7.
17   *Northern Star*, 13 July 1839.
18   See W Napier, *The Life and Opinions of General Charles James Napier*, 4 vols (London, 1857), II, *passim*.
19   D Williams, op.cit., pp. 234–41; see also the same author's *John Frost: a Study in Chartism*, (University of Wales, 1939; London, 1969), pp. 195–239.
20   A J Peacock, *Bradford Chartism*, (York, 1969), pp. 23–46; J Baxter, 'The Life and Struggle of Samuel Holberry', pp. 11–16, in *Samuel Holberry – 1814–42. Sheffield's Revolutionary Democrat*, (Holberry Society Publication, Sheffield, 1978), pp. 7–19.
21   A Wilson, 'Chartism in Glasgow', pp. 249–59, in A Briggs (ed.), op.cit., pp. 249–87; H Hamilton, *The Economic Evolution of Scotland*, (Historical Association, London, 1933), pp. 17, 22, For further details of Scottish Chartism, see L C Wright, *Scottish Chartism*, (Edinburgh, 1953); and A Wilson, *The Chartist Movement in Scotland*, (Manchester, 1970).
22   See the map in D Jones, op.cit., p.9.
23   G Kitson Clark, 'Hunger and Politics in 1842', *Journal of Modern History*, XXV (1953), pp. 355–74.
24   For the strikes, see A G Rose, 'The Plug Riots of 1842 in Lancashire and Cheshire', *Transactions of the Lancashire and Cheshire Antiquarian Society*, LXVII (1957), pp. 75–112; and F C Mather, 'The General Strike of

1842', in J Stevenson and R Quinault (eds), *Popular Protest and Public Order*, pp. 115–40; also M Jenkins, *The General Strike of 1842*, (London, 1980).

25   E.g., F Peel, *The Rising of the Luddites, Chartists and Plug-Drawers*, p.333.

26   D Read and E Glasgow, op.cit., pp. 104–7.

27   G D H Cole, *Chartist Portraits*, p. 211. The same was true of Henry Vincent.

28   G J Harney to F Engels, 30 March 1846, in F G and R M Black (eds), *The Harney Papers*, (Assen, 1969), pp. 239–45.

29   D Read, *Press and People*, p.216; J A Epstein, op.cit., p.97.

30   B Wilson, *The Struggles of an Old Chartist*, (Halifax, 1887); B Brierley, *Home Memories and Recollections of a Life*, (Manchester, 1886); and *Failsworth, My Native Village*, (Oldham, 1895).

31   C Godfrey, 'The Chartist Prisoners, 1839–41', *International Review of Social History*, XXIV (1979), pp. 189–236.

32   ibid., p.228.

33   House of Commons, 12 July 1839, *Hansard* XLIX, col. 246.

34   J A Epstein, op.cit.

35   E.g., Place's *Historical Narrative*, Add.MSS.27.820. For Examples of the bad press, see E Royle, *Chartism*, pp. 112–14, 124–5, but for a counter-example, see ibid., pp.114–16.

36   Harney to Engels, 30 March 1846, op.cit.

37   E.g., see Lawrence Pitkethly, *New Moral World*, 21 December 1839.

28   E Yeo, 'Robert Owen and Radical Culture', pp. 89–91, in S Pollard and J Salt (eds), *Robert Owen, Prophet of the Poor*, pp.84–114; see also R G Garnett, *Co-operation and the Owenite Socialist Communities in Britain, 1825-45*, pp. 142–59.

39   E Royle, *Victorian Infidels*, pp.47–51, 59–67; J F C Harrison, *Robert Owen and the Owenites*, pp.216–32.

40   See annual Congress reports in *New Moral World*, esp. 25 May–8 June 1844, 24 May–7 June and 26 July, 9 August 1845; also *Herald of Progress*, 9 May 1846. For the community generally, see R G Garnett, op.cit., pp. 165–213.

41   *Northern Star*, 14 January 1843.

42   *Moral World*, 6 September 1845.

43   For details of the Land Plan, see A M Hadfield, *The Chartist Land Company*, (Newton Abbot, 1970); and J MacAskill, 'The Chartist Land Plan', in A Briggs (ed.), op.cit., pp. 304–41.

44   D J Rowe, 'Tyneside Chartism', pp.76–81, in N McCord (ed.), *Essays in Tyneside Labour History*, (Newcastle, 1977), pp. 62–87.

45   S and B Webb, *The History of Trade Unionism*, pp. 185–95.

46   *Northern Star*, 25 March 1848.

47   The best published account is D Large, 'London in the Year of Revolutions, 1848' pp. 187–94, in J Stevenson (ed.), *London in the Age of Reform*, pp. 177–211.

48   *Annual Register* (1848), 'History', pp. 125–8.

49   See John Saville's introduction to R G Gammage's *History* (Kelley, New York, 1969).

50 I J Prothero, 'Chartism in London', *Past and Present*, 44 (August 1969), pp. 76–105; D Large, op.cit., pp. 201–2.

51 ibid., pp. 195–201.

52 J Saville (ed.), *Ernest Jones: Chartist*, introduction, pp. 30–3.

53 At Ashton-under-Lyne a policeman was shot by Chartists on 14 August, and the troops were called — R G Gammage, op.cit., p.337.

54 R O'Higgins, 'The Irish Influence on the Chartist Movement', *Past and Present*, 20 (November 1961), pp.83–96.

55 J H Treble, 'O'Connor, O'Connell and the attitudes of Irish immigrants towards Chartism in the North of England, 1838–48', in J Butt and I F Clarke (eds), *The Victorians and Social Protest*, (Newton Abbot, 1973), pp. 33–70.

56 Quoted by J Morley, *The Life of Richard Cobden*, 2 vols, (London, 1896), I, p.249.

57 D Read, *Cobden and Bright*, pp.38–9.

58 ibid., pp.18, 75; N McCord, *The Anti-Corn Law League, 1838-46* (London, 1958; 2nd ed., 1968), pp. 19–20.

59 ibid., p.21.

60 L Brown, 'The Chartists and the Anti-Corn Law League', pp. 343–4, in A Briggs (ed.), op.cit., pp. 342–71.

61 *Charter*, 29 December 1839.

62 *Chartist Circular*, 28 September 1839.

63 N Gash, *Reaction and Reconstruction in English Politics, 1832-1852*, pp. 149–50. For Cobden and Bright after 1846, see D Read, op.cit.; and for radicalism see F E Gillespie, *Labor and Politics in England, 1850-1867* (Durham, N.C., 1927, reprinted London, 1966).

64 L Brown, op.cit., pp. 349–50.

65 ibid., pp. 350–1.

66 N McCord, op.cit., pp.99–103; *Northern Star*, 12 March 1842.

67 G Kitson Clark, op.cit., pp. 365–70; A G Rose, op.cit., pp.83–4; F C Mather, op.cit., pp.119–20.

68 N McCord, op.cit., p.71.

69 D Fraser (ed.), *A History of Modern Leeds*, (Manchester, 1980), p.285; *Bradford Observer*, 3 December 1840 (I owe this reference to Mr J Smith). Smiles was in fact becoming less radical after 1840 — J F C Harrison, 'Chartism in Leeds', pp. 83–4, in A Briggs (ed.), op.cit. pp. 65–98.

70 A T Patterson, *Radical Leicester*, pp.315, 341–2; J F C Harrison, 'Chartism in Leicester', pp.138–9. In A Briggs (ed.), op.cit., pp.99–146.

71 G D H Cole, *Chartist Portraits*, pp. 163–86; J Sturge, *Reconciliation between the Middle and Labouring Classes*, (Birmingham, 1842).

72 J F C Harrison, op.cit., pp.83–5.

73 D Read and E Glasgow, op.cit., p.95.

74 J T Ward, op.cit., pp. 165–6.

75 B Harrison, 'Henry Vincent', in J M Bellamy and J Saville (eds), *Dictionary of Labour Biography*, 6 vols to date (London, 1972–82), I.

76 D Read and E Glasgow, op.cit., pp.102–3; D Read, *Cobden and Bright*, pp. 37–8; *Northern Star*, 31 January 1846.

77 F E Gillespie, op.cit., pp.86–7.

78   *Northern Star*, 17 November 1849. This editorial may have been written
     by G A Fleming, the sub-editor, or by O'Connor himself. Harney was
     still hostile to middle-class reformers — see *Democratic Review*, Septem-
     ber 1849. Jones, the last major leader to reconcile himself to co-
     operation with moderate radicals, did not do so until 1858.
79   B Harrison and P Hollis, 'Chartism, liberalism and the life of Robert
     Lowery', *English Historical Review*, LXXXII (1967), pp. 503-35.

Conclusion

1   *Red Republican*, 9-30 November 1850.
2   G Rudé, *Paris and London in the Eighteenth Century*, (London, 1974), pp.
    247-67; H Mayhew, *London Labour and the London Poor*, 4 vols (London,
    1861-2; reprinted New York, 1968), I. p.20.
3   W R Ward, *Religion and Society in England, 1790-1850*, (London, 1972),
    pp.50-62; 89-90; E Halévy, *England in 1815*, (1913; new edition,
    London, 1961), pp. 430-2.
4   W R Ward, op.cit., pp. 135-76.
5   See R F Wearmouth, *Methodism and the Working Class Movements of
    England*, (London, 1937) for this approach.
6   E Halévy, 'La Naisance du Methodisme en Angleterre', *Revue de Paris*
    (1, 15 August 1906), pp. 519-39, 841-67, translated by B Semmel as *The
    Birth of Methodism*, (Chicago and London, 1971); and *England in 1815*,
    p.387. See also M Hill, *A Sociology of Religion*, (London, 1973), pp.
    183-204.
7   E P Thompson, *The Making of the English Working Class*, ch.11. p.388.
8   J L Baxter, 'The Great Yorkshire Revival, 1792-6', *Sociological Yearbook
    of Religion in Britain*, VII (1974), pp. 46-76; R Currie and R M Hartwell,
    'The Making of the English working class', *Economic History Review*,
    2nd series, XVIII (1965), pp. 640-1.
9   see above, p.127.
10 By Currie and Hartwell, op.cit., also J Kent, 'The Wesleyan Methodists
    to 1849', pp. 265-6, in R Davies, A R George and G Rupp (eds), *A
    History of the Methodist Church in Great Britain*, vol.2. (London, 1978),
    pp. 213-75.
11 J F C Harrison, *The Second Coming*, p.225.
12 E P Thompson, op.cit., pp.391-400; H Perkin, *The Origins of Modern
    English Society, 1780-1880*, (London, 1969), pp. 353-61.
13 E Halévy, *England in 1815*, pp. 425-6; also W R Ward, op.cit., pp.
    63-70.
14 H Perkin, op.cit, pp. 347-53; E J Evans, 'Some reasons for the growth
    of English rural anti-clericalism', *Past and Present*, 66 (May 1975), pp.
    84-109.
15 H Perkin, op.cit., pp. 196-208; E Royle, *Radical Politics, 1790-1900*:

Religion and Unbelief, (London, 1971).

16 E Halévy, op.cit., pp. 454-5.

17 M Craton, *Sinews of Empire,* (London, 1974), pp. 248-9, 259-60, 272-3;
    E F Hurwitz, *Politics and the Public Conscience,* (London, 1973), esp. pp.
    15-20.

18 E.g., on the importance of religion to Richard Cobden, and on John
    Morley's failure to appreciate it, see D Read, *Cobden and Bright,* p. 31.

19 R S Neale, *Class and Ideology in the Nineteenth Century,* (London, 1972),
    pp. 146-51.

20 J Walvin, 'The impact of slavery on British Radical Politics: 1787-1838',
    Annals of the New York Academy of Sciences, 292, (Summer 1977), p.351.

21 G D H Cole, *Chartist Portraits,* p.169.

22 See N McKendrick, 'Home Demand and Economic Growth: a new
    view of the role of women and children in the industrial revolution', in
    N McKendrick (ed.), *Historical Perspectives,* pp. 152-210.

23 G D H Cole, op.cit., p.169.

24 S Bamford, *Passages in the Life of a Radical,* pp. 141-2.

25 L Faucher, *Manchester in 1844,* (Manchester, 1844), pp. 121-2.

26 D Thompson (ed.), *The Early Chartists,* (London, 1971), pp. 128-30;
    F Peel, *The Risings of the Luddites, Chartists and Plug-drawers,* pp. 333-4;
    Annual Register (1848), 'History', p.127.

27 D Thompson, op.cit., pp. 115-27.

28 J Saville, 'Robert Owen on the Family and the Marriage System of the
    Old Immoral World', in M Cornforth (ed.), *Rebels and their Causes,*
    (London, 1978), pp. 107-21.

29 *NMW,* 29 November 1834; R Owen, *Lectures on the Marriages of the
    Priesthood of the Old Immoral World,* (Leeds, 1835).

30 E Yeo, 'Robert Owen and Radical Culture', pp. 96-7, in S Pollard and J
    Salt (eds), *Robert Owen, Prophet of the Poor,* pp. 84-114; *NMW,* 4 April
    1840, 3 February 1844.

31 See W R Waterman, *Frances Wright,* (New York, 1924); A H G Perkins
    and T Wolfson, *Frances Wright, Free Inquirer,* (New York, 1939); also M
    Lane, *Frances Wright and the 'Great Experiment'* (Manchester, 1972.

32 See R K P Pankhurst, 'Anna Wheeler: a pioneer socialist and
    feminist', *Political Quarterly,* XXV (1954), pp. 132-43; and the entry by
    M Galgano in *Biographical Dictionary.* I.

33 For Emma Martin, see *Dictionary of Labour Biography,* VI.

34 J F C Harrison, *Robert Owen and the Owenites,* p.209.

35 ibid., pp. 98-9, 109-11; and *The Second Coming,* pp. 28-38, 86-134.

36 ibid., pp. 96, 108-9.

37 *Isis,* 12 February 1832.

38 Elizabeth Sharples Carlile to Thomas Cooper, 23 April 1850; Letters
    and Papers of Charles Bradlaugh, no.19A, (Bishopsgate Institute,
    London).

39 *Isis,* 3 March 1832.

40 E P Thompson, 'Eighteenth-century English society: class struggle
    without class?' *Social History,* III (1978), pp. 146-50.

41 A Briggs, 'Middle-class consciousness in English politics, 1780-1846',

Past and Present, 9 (April 1956); and 'The Language of "Class" in early nineteenth-century England', in A Briggs and J Saville (eds), *Essays in Labour History*, pp.43-73.

42 For examples, see P Hollis (ed.), *Class and Conflict in Nineteenth-Century England, 1815-1850*, (London, 1973).

43 See the opening words of his *The Condition of the Working-Class in England* (1845).

44 W Thomas, *The Philosophic Radicals*, pp.449-52.

45 It is interesting to note that two of the most famous fictional accounts of capitalist manufacturers — Charlotte Brontë's Moore in *Shirley*, and Elizabeth Gaskell's Thornton in *North and South* — both emphasise this predicament.

46 J Brewer, 'English Radicalism in the age of George III', in J G A Pocock (ed.), *Three British Revolutions*, pp. 323-67.

47 J Foster, *Class Struggle and the Industrial Revolution*, pp. 203-50; P Joyce, *Work, Society and Politics*, (Brighton, 1980); N Kirk, 'Cotton Workers and Deference', Society for the Study of Labour History, *Bulletin* no.42, (Spring 1981), pp. 41-3.

48 This theme is taken further by E Royle, *Radicals, Secularists and Republicans*, (Manchester, 1980), pp. 218-45.

49 H Mayhew, op.cit., I, p.20.

50 ibid.

51 For examples of the strength of community radicalism, see B Brierley, *Failsworth My Native Village*; B Wilson, *The Struggles of an Old Chartist*; and F Peel, *The Risings of the Luddites, Chartists and Plug-drawers*. The sense also comes across in Samuel Bamford's *Passages in the Life of a Radical*.

52 This is not to claim that all manufacturers were Joseph Brothertons, John Fieldens and Robert Owens — or even John and Jacob Brights. But neither were they all like Dickens' gross caricature of a manufacturer, Josiah Bounderby in *Hard Times*. See H I Dutton and J E King, *Ten Per Cent and No Surrender*, (Cambridge, 1981), pp. 198-201 for a discussion of Dickens' and Mrs Gaskell's treatment of the Preston Strike of 1853 in the characters of Bounderby and Thornton respectively.

SELECT BIBLIOGRAPHY

A O Aldridge, *Man of Reason. The Life of Thomas Paine* (Cresset, London, 1960).

R Anstey, *The Atlantic Slave Trade and British Abolition, 1760-1810* (Macmillan, London, 1975).

A Aspinall, *Politics and the Press, c.1780-1850* (Home and Van Thal, London, 1949).

B Bailyn, *The Ideological Origins of the American Revolution* (Harvard University Press, Cambridge, Mass., 1967).

J L Baxter, 'The Great Yorkshire Revival, 1792-6', *Sociological Yearbook of Religion in Britain*, VII (1974), pp.46-76.

J L Baxter and F K Donnelly, 'The Revolutionary "Underground" in the West Riding: Myth or Reality?', *Past and Present*, 64 (August 1974), pp. 124-32.

J L Baxter and F K Donnelly, 'Sheffield and the English revolutionary tradition', *International Review of Social History*, XXV (1975), pp. 398-423.

J O Baylen and N J Gossman (eds), *Biographical Dictionary of Modern British Radicals*, 1 vol to date (Harvester, Hassocks/Humanities Press, Atlantic Highlands, N.J., 1979).

J Belchem, 'Republicanism, popular constitutionalism and the radical platform in early nineteenth-century England', *Social History*, VI (1981), pp. 1-32.

J M Bellamy and J Saville (eds), *Dictionary of Labour Biography*, 6 vols to date (Macmillan, London 1972-82).

E C Black, *The Association. British Extraparliamentary Political Organisations*, (Harvard University Press, Cambridge, Mass., 1963).

C Bonwick, *English Radicals and the American Revolution*, (University of North Carolina, Chapel Hill, N.C., 1977).

J Brewer, *Party Ideology and Popular Politics at the Accession of George III*, (Cambridge University Press, Cambridge, 1976),

J Brewer, English Radicalism in the age of George III', in J G A Pocock (ed.), *Three British Revolutions: 1641, 1688, 1776*, (Princeton University Press, Princeton, 1980.

A Briggs, 'The background of the parliamentary reform movement in three English cities (1830-2)', *Cambridge Historical Journal*, X (1952), pp. 293-317.

A Briggs, 'Middle-class consciousness in English Politics, 1780-1846', *Past and Present*, 9 (April 1956) pp. 65-74.

A Briggs (ed.), *Chartist Studies*, (Macmillan, London/St Martin's Press, New York, 1959; reprinted 1965).

A Briggs 'The Language of "Class" in Early Nineteenth-Century England', in A Briggs and J Saville (eds), *Essays in Labour History*, (Macmillan, London/St Martin's Press, New York, 1960; revised ed., 1967), pp. 43-73.

M Brock, *The Great Reform Act* (Hutchinson, London, 1973).

P A Brown, *The French Revolution in English History*, (Allen and Unwin, London 1918; reprinted Cass, London, 1965).

H Butterfield, *George III, Lord North and the People 1779-80*. (Bell, London, 1949).

J Cannon, *Parliamentary Reform, 1640-1832*, (Cambridge University Press, Cambridge, 1973).

I R Christie, *Wilkes, Wyvill and Reform*, (Macmillan, London 1962)

I R Christie, *Myth and Reality in late Eighteenth-Century British Politics*, (Macmillan, London, 1970).

R A Church and S D Chapman, 'Gravener Henson and the Making of the English Working Class', in E L Jones and G E Mingay (eds), *Land, Labour and Population in the Industrial Revolution*, (Arnold, London, 1967).

G Kitson Clark, 'Hunger and Politics in 1842', *Journal of Modern History*, XXV (1953), pp.355-74.

G D H Cole, *Chartist Portraits*, (Macmillan, London/St Martin's Press, New York, 1941; new ed. 1965).

G D H Cole, *Attempts at General Union*, (Macmillan, London/St Martin's Press, New York, 1953).

G D H Cole, *A History of Socialist Thought: vol.1, The Forerunners, 1789-1850*, (Macmillan, London/St Martin's Press, New York, 1953; reprinted 1965).

C B Cone, *The English Jacobins*, (Charles Scribner's Sons, New York, 1968).

M Craton, *Sinews of Empire*, (Temple Smith, London 1974).

R Currie and R M Hartwell, 'The Making of the English Working Class', *Economic History Review*, 2nd series, XVIII (1965), pp. 640-1.

F O Darvall, *Popular Disturbances and Public Order in Regency England*, (Oxford University Press, Oxford, 1934).

H T Dickinson, *Liberty and Property. Political Ideology in Eighteenth-Century Britain*, (Methuen, London, 1979).

J R Dinwiddy, *Christopher Wyvill and Reform, 1790-1820*, (University of York, Borthwick Papers No.39, York, 1971).

J R Dinwiddy, 'The "Black Lamp" in Yorkshire, 1801-1802', *Past and Present*, 64 (August 1974), pp. 113-23; and 'The Revolutionary "Underground" in the West Riding — a rejoinder', ibid., pp. 133-5.

J R Dinwiddy, 'Luddism and politics in the northern counties', *Social History*, IV (1979), pp.33-51.

F K Donnelly, 'Ideology and early English working-class history: Edward Thompson and his critics', *Social History* no.2. (May 1976), pp. 219-38.

N C Edsall, *The Anti-Poor Law Movement, 1834-44*, (Manchester University Press, Manchester/Rowman & Littlefield, Totowa, N.J., 1971).

M Elliott, 'The "Despard Conspiracy" reconsidered', *Past and Present*, 75 (May 1977), pp. 46-61.

C Emsley, *British Society and the French Wars, 1793-1815*, (Macmillan, London, 1979).

C Emsley, 'An aspect of Pitt's "Terror": prosecutions for sedition during the 1790s', *Social History*, VI (1981), pp. 155–84.

J A Epstein, 'Feargus O'Connor and the Northern Star', *International Review of Social History*, XXI (1976), pp.51-97.

E J Evans, 'Some reasons for the growth of English rural anti-clericalism', *Past and Present*, 66 (May 1975), pp.84–109.

C Flick, *The Birmingham Political Union and the Movements for Reform in Britain, 1830-1839*, (Dawson, Folkestone/Archon, Hamden, Conn., 1978).

J Foster, *Class Struggle and the Industrial Revolution. Early Industrial Capitalism in Three English Towns*, (Weidenfeld & Nicolson, London 1974).

R G Garnett, *Co-operation and the Owenite Socialist Communities in Britain, 1825-45*, (Manchester University Press, Manchester/Humanities Press, New York, 1972).

C Godfrey, 'The Chartist Prisoners, 1839–41', *International Review of Social History*, XXIV (1979), pp. 189-236.

A Goodwin, *The Friends of Liberty. The English Democratic Movement in the Age of the French Revolution*, (Hutchinson, London, 1979).

B Harrison and P Hollis, 'Chartism, liberalism and the life of Robert Lowery', *English Historical Review*, LXXXII (1967), pp. 503-35.

J F C Harrison, *Robert Owen and the Owenites in Britain and America. The Quest for the New Moral World*, (Routledge, London, 1969).

P Hollis, *The Pauper Press. A Study in Working-Class Radicalism of the 1830s*, (Oxford University Press, Oxford, 1970).

P Hollis (ed.), *Class and Conflict in Nineteenth-Century England, 1815-1850*, (Routledge, London and Boston, 1973).

E F Hurwitz, *Politics and the Public Conscience. Slave Emancipation and the Abolitionist Movement in Britain*, (Allen & Unwin, London/Barnes & Noble, New York, 1973).

D Jones, *Chartism and the Chartists*, (Allen Lane, London, 1975).

R G Kirby and A E Musson, *The Voice of the People. John Doherty, 1798-1854. Trade Unionist, Radical and Factory Reformer*, (Manchester University Press, Manchester, 1975).

S Maccoby, *English Radicalism, 1762-1785*, (Allen & Unwin, London, 1955).

S Maccoby, *English Radicalism, 1786-1832* (Allen & Unwin, London, 1955).

S Maccoby, *English Radicalism, 1832-1852* (Allen & Unwin, London, 1935).

N McCord, *The Anti-Corn Law League, 1838-1846*, (Allen & Unwin, 1958); 2nd ed., 1968).

N McCord, 'Some difficulties of parliamentary reform', *Historical Journal*, X (1967), pp. 376-90.

N McCord, 'Tyneside discontents and Peterloo', *Northern History*, II (1967), pp. 91-111.

J M Main, 'Radical Westminster, 1807-20', *Historical Studies*, XII (1966), pp. 186-204.

H W Meikle, *Scotland and the French Revolution*, (Glasgow, 1912; new ed. Cass, London, 1969).

J Money, *Experience and Identity. Birmingham and the West Midlands, 1760-1800* (Manchester University Press, Manchester, 1977).

L M Munby (ed.), *The Luddites and Other Essays*, (Katanka, London, 1971).

R S Neale, *Class and Ideology in the Nineteenth Century*, (Routledge, London and Boston, 1972).

F O'Gorman, *The Whig Party and the French Revolution*, (Macmillan, London, 1967).

R O'Higgins, 'The Irish influence on the Chartist movement', *Past and Present*, 20 (November 1961), pp. 83–96.

W H Oliver, 'The Labour Exchange phase of the Co-operative Movement', *Oxford Economic Papers* , n.s.X (1958), pp. 355–67.

W H Oliver, 'The Consolidated Trades' Union of 1834', *Economic History Review*, 2nd series XVII (1964), pp. 77–95.

J W Osborne, *John Cartwright*, (Cambridge University Press, Cambridge, 1972).

R R Palmer, *The Age of the Democratic Revolution*, 2 vols, (Princeton University Press, Princeton, 1959, reprinted 1969).

T M Parssinen, 'The Revolutionary Party in London, 1816–20', *Bulletin of the Institute of Historical Research*, XLV (1972), pp. 266–82.

T M Parssinen, 'Association, convention and anti-parliament in British radical politics, 1771-1848', *English Historical Review*, LXXXVIII (1973), pp. 504–33.

A T Patterson, *Radical Leicester. A History of Leicester, 1780-1850*, (Leicester University Press, Leicester, 1954).

H Perkin, *The Origins of Modern English Society, 1780-1880*, (Routledge, London/University of Toronto Press, Toronto, 1969).

J H Plumb, 'Political Man' in J Clifford (ed.), *Man Versus Society in Eighteenth-Century Britain* (Cambridge University Press, Cambridge, 1968).

S Pollard and J Salt (eds), *Robert Owen. Prophet of the Poor*, (Macmillan, London, 1971).

I Prothero, *Artisans and Politics in Early Nineteenth-Century London, John Gast and His Times* (Dawson, Folkestone, 1979; Methuen, London, 1981).

D Read, *Peterloo. The 'Massacre' and its Background*, (Manchester University Press, Manchester/Kelley, Clifton, N.J., 1958).

D Read, *Press and People, 1790-1850. Opinion in Three English Cities* (Arnold, London, 1961).

D Read, *The English Provinces, c.1760-1960. A Study in Influence* (Arnold, London, 1964).

D Read, *Cobden and Bright. A Victorian Political Partnership* (Arnold, London, 1967).

D Read and E Glasgow, *Fergus O'Connor. Irishman and Chartist*, (Arnold London, 1961).

C Robbins, *The Eighteenth-Century Commonwealthman* (Harvard University Press, Cambridge, Mass., 1959).

E Royle, *Radical Politics, 1790-1900. Religion and Unbelief,* (Longman, London, 1971).

E Royle, *Victorian Infidels. The Origins of the British Secularist Movement, 1791-1866* (Manchester University Press, Manchester/Rowman & Littlefield, Totowa, N.J., 1974).

E Royle, *Chartism*, (Longman, London, 1980).

E Royle, (ed.), *The Infidel Tradition from Paine to Bradlaugh*, (Macmillan, London, 1975).

G Rudé, *Wilkes and Liberty*, (Clarendon Press, Oxford, 1962).

G Rudé, 'English Rural and Urban Disturbances on the Eve of the First Reform Bill, 1830-1831', *Past and Present*, 37 (July 1967), pp.87-102.

G Rudé, *Paris and London in the Eighteenth-Century. Studies in Popular Protest*, (Fontana/Collins, London 1974).

J Saville, *Ernest Jones: Chartist*, (Lawrence & Wishart, London, 1952).

A R Schoyen, *The Chartist Challenge: A Portrait of George Julian Harney*, (Heinemann, London, 1958).

A W Smith, 'Irish Rebels and English Radicals, 1798-1820', *Past and Present*, 7 (April 1955), pp. 81-3.

J Stevenson, *Popular Disturbances in England, 1700-1870*, (Longman, London and New York, 1979).

J Stevenson, (ed.), *London in the Age of Reform*, (Blackwell, Oxford, 1977).

J Stevenson and R Quinault (eds), *Popular Protest and Public Order. Six Studies in British History, 1790-1920*, (Allen & Unwin, London, 1974).

W Thomas, *The Philosophic Radicals: Nine Studies in Theory and Practice, 1817-1841*, (Clarendon Press, Oxford, 1979).

M I Thomis, *Politics and Society in Nottingham, 1785-1835*, (Blackwell, Oxford, 1969).

M I Thomis, *The Luddites: Machine-Breaking in Regency England*, (David & Charles, Newton Abbott, 1970).

M I Thomis, and P Holt, *Threats of Revolution in Britain, 1789-1848*, (Macmillan, London, 1977).

D Thompson (ed.), *The Early Chartists*, (Macmillan, London, 1971).

E P Thompson, *The Making of the English Working Class*, (Gollancz, London, 1963; Penguin, London, 1968).

E P Thompson, 'Eighteenth-Century English society: class struggle without class?', *Social History*, III (1978), pp.133-65.

J H Treble, 'O'Connor, O'Connell and the attitudes of Irish immigrants towards Chartism in the North of England, 1838-48', in J Butt and I F Clarke (eds), *The Victorians and Social Protest*, (David & Charles, Newton Abbot/The Shoe String Press, Hamden, Conn., 1973).

G S Veitch, *The Genesis of Parliamentary Reform*, (Constable, London, 1913; reprinted 1965).

J Walvin, 'The impact of slavery on British radical politics: 1787-1838', *Annals of the New York Academy of Sciences*, 292 (Summer 1977), pp.343-55.

J Walvin, 'The public campaign in England against slavery, 1787-1834', in D Eltis and J Walvin (eds), *The Abolition of the Atlantic Slave Trade*, (University of Wisconsin Press, Madison, Wisc., 1981).

J Walvin (ed.), *Slavery and British Society, 1776-1848*, (Macmillan, London, 1982).

J T Ward, (ed.), *Popular Movements, c.1830-1850*, (Macmillan, London/St Martin's Press, New York, 1970).

J T Ward, *Chartism*, (Batsford, London, 1973).

W R Ward, *Religion and Society in England, 1790-1850*, (Batsford, London, 1972).

R F Wearmouth, *Some Working-Class Movements of the Nineteenth-Century*, (Epworth, London, 1948).

S and B Webb, *The History of Trade Unionism*, (Longmans, London, 1894; new impression 1956).

R J White, *Waterloo to Peterloo*, (Heinemann, London, 1957; Mercury Books, London, 1963).

W H Wickwar, *The Struggle for the Freedom of the Press, 1819-1832*, (Allen & Unwin, London, 1928).

J H Wiener, *The War of the Unstamped. The Movement to Repeal the British Newspaper Tax, 1830-1836*, (Cornell University Press, Ithaca and London, 1969).

G A Williams, *Rowland Detrosier. A Working-Class Infidel, 1800-34.* (University of York, Borthwick Papers No.28, York, 1965).

G A Williams, *Artisans and Sans-Culottes. Popular Movements in France and Britain during the French Revolution*, (Arnold, London, 1968).

A Wilson, *The Chartist Movement in Scotland*, (Manchester University Press, Manchester, 1970).

INDEX